December, 1979

THIS BOOK
BELONGS TO

Karen Goucher

We appreciated your
help with the Meth Choir-
Thank you -

Bill & Joan

Guidewords

ACKNOWLEDGMENTS

Grateful acknowledgment is made to the following authors and publishers for permission to use copyrighted material:

ABINGDON PRESS, "August" by Helen Maria Winslow from *The Year Around.* Compiled by Alice Isabel Hazeltine. Copyright © 1956 by Abingdon Press.

JOHN COOLIDGE. Extracts from "Autobiography of Calvin Coolidge." Copyright © 1929 by and permission of John Coolidge.

E. P. DUTTON & COMPANY, INC., "Christmas Pageant" and "American Plan" from *One to a Customer* by Margaret Fishback. Copyright © 1932 by E. P. Dutton & Company, Inc. Renewal copyright © 1963 by Margaret Fishback Antolini. Reprinted by permission of the publisher.

ELLIS, NORMA MILLAY. "Portrait by a Neighbor" from *Collected Poems,* copyrighted © 1922, 1950 by Edna St. Vincent Millay, published by Harper and Row. Permission of Norma Millay Ellis.

GOLDEN QUILL PRESS. "Heredity" from *Portrait of a Lady* by Alice Hunt Timmons. Permission of Robert T. Timmons.

HARCOURT BRACE JOVANOVICH, INC. "Caliban in the Coal Mines" by Louis Untermeyer. Copyright © 1914 by Harcourt Brace Jovanovich, Inc., renewed 1942 by Louis Untermeyer. Reprinted from his volume *Long Feud* by permission of the publishers.

HOLT, RINEHART and WINSTON, INC. Excerpt from *Out of My Life and Thought* by Dr. Albert Schweitzer. Translated by C. T. Campion. Copyright © 1933, 1949, and 1961 by Holt, Rinehart and Winston, Inc. Reprinted by permission of Holt, Rinehart and Winston, Inc.

HOUGHTON, MIFFLIN COMPANY. Extract from "The Promised Land" by Mary Antin. Permission of Houghton, Mifflin Company.

THE WOODCUT ART OF THOMAS BEWICK

Most of the illustrative art in GUIDEWORDS is reproduced from the Woodcuts of Thomas Bewick (1752-1828) and his school. It was under the influence of this talented craftsman that wood engraving flourished in England in the eighteenth and early nineteenth centuries.

These woodcuts display Bewick's skill both as an engraver and an artist. The pastoral charm of these illustrations reflects his profound love of the rural English countryside; they convey a nostalgic aura that is refreshingly different from slick modern illustrations and high-speed reproduction techniques.

PREFACE

Men and women from many lands, from many decades of the centuries, and of different races and cultures, have written this collection. Poets, businessmen, presidents, a Queen, generals, philosophers, religious leaders, educators - people of all walks of life - are represented. There are many whose names have been forgotten, and thus have been graduated to the vast ranks of the anonymous. They live on because through time their words have had meaning, beauty, inspiration and enchantment for their readers.

The selections are in prose and verse. Some of the verse is technically, intellectually and emotionally of the rare quality which makes it poetry, and so true magic. Some more closely approaches doggerel, but has aptness, pith, interest or humor which amply pays its way.

Many selections concern the deeply treasured values of life such as Truth, Justice and Beauty, and many are expressed in lines that have become immortal. Much of this writing voices the wonder and joy of life, its raptures and despairs, and man's capacity for courage and sacrifice, as well as for everyday living. In our own time of perplexity, turmoil and social upheaval, these can be a source of courage and enlightenment, material for quiet reflection.

Deletions, emphasis and omissions are the responsibility of the compiler. Deletions have been made usually because of space, but sometimes because of the feeling that length is often a deterrent to the reading of a long and serious work. Limitations of space explains the omission of many favorites, and faulty taste will have to cover other omissions. Horace expressed it so many years ago: "For a thousand heads, a thousand tastes." That must stand as a compiler's defense.

No attempt has been made to include a comprehensive selection of all the classic and beloved poems of English speaking people. That we leave to other anthologies. Instead we have brought together a one-volume treasury of wise, gay, inspired and common sense writing, old favorites and some surprises, to be read with delight.

Guidewords can also be used as a desk tool, a source of quotation in writing or conversation to express more clearly a thought and make conversation more colorful and lively. Cliches and stilted expressions come all too readily to mind. Here are some that are neither. To facilitate these uses, a subject index of the more pointed selections is included after the table of contents.

If, after browsing in the book, help is not always forthcoming for an expression of your own, one can agree with Emerson who said, "Next to the originator of a good sentence is the first quoter of it."

MIRIAM C. HUNTER
Breeze Hill Farm
January, 1971

Guidewords

AN ANTHOLOGY OF INSPIRATION AND HUMOR

Compiled by
MIRIAM C. HUNTER

SHAW-BARTON
COSHOCTON, OHIO
PUBLISHERS

ABOUT THE COMPILER

MIRIAM HUNTER is a joy to know. Interested in everything, gifted with a rare sense of humor, keenly observant, and a life-long omnivorous reader, she is uniquely qualified to put together a book such as GUIDEWORDS.

After attending school in the small Missouri River town where she was born, she studied at the University of Kansas. She received an A.B. from the University of Illinois and an LL.B. from the University of Minnesota. For some years she did economic research and financial library direction in a major New York City bank.

After marriage, she and her husband moved to St. Paul, and in 1940 came to Coshocton, Ohio. They have three children, now grown and active in their careers. She has long been a leader in community improvement activities, especially interested in the hospital, library and museum work of her community.

An avid researcher, she is the author and compiler of several books on specialized aspects of early regional history. Currently she is writing a book on one-room schools in east-central Ohio.

She and her husband, a retired advertising executive widely known for his work with the 4-H movement, live at Breeze Hill Farm, near Coshocton, where he raises Registered Polled Hereford cattle.

THE PUBLISHERS

APPROACH TO BREEZE HILL FARM
by Stanley S. Shaw
with apologies to Thomas Bewick

CONTENTS

Here we have brought together a year's reading - "As the Earth Turns" - in twelve parts, made up of the thought of all times, that hopefully will be enlightening, inspirational and nourishing to a people who have seen their world, the earth, as it looks from the moon, a view no earlier people in all of history have been privileged to see.

While some selections are more especially appropriate than others for the monthly sections in which they appear, all will bear reading on any day of any season.

INDEX BY CATEGORIES

(See also Author and Title Index on page 252.)

JANUARY

"On the wind of January
Down flits the snow . . ."

from A MORNING WISH

The sun is just rising on the morning of another day, the first day of the new year. What can I wish that this day, this year, may bring to me? Nothing that shall make the world of others poorer, nothing at the expense of other men; but just those few things which in their coming do not stop with me, but touch me rather, as they pass and gather strength:

A few friends who understand me, and yet remain my friends.

A work to do which has real value without which the world would feel the poorer.

A return for such work small enough not to tax unduly any one who pays.

A mind unafraid to travel, even though the trail be not blazed.

An understanding heart.

A sight of the eternal hills and unresting sea, and of something beautiful the hand of man has made.

A sense of humor and the power to laugh.

A little leisure with nothing to do.

A few moments of quiet, silent meditation. The sense of the presence of God.

And the patience to wait for the coming of these things, with the wisdom to know them when they come.

W. R. HUNT

A GUIDE FOR THE NEW YEAR

And I said to the man who
stood at the gate of the year:
Give me a light that I may
tread safely into the unknown!

And he replied:
Go out into the darkness
and put thine hand into
the Hand of God.

That shall be to thee better
than light and safer than
a known way.

from
ANACREONTIC* FOR THE NEW YEAR

And ye, who have met with Adversity's blast,
And been bow'd to the earth by its fury;
To whom the Twelve Months, that have
recently pass'd
Were as harsh as a prejudiced jury—
Still, fill to the Future! and join in our
chime,
The regrets of remembrance to cozen,
And having obtained a New Trial of Time,
Shout in hopes of a kindlier dozen.

THOMAS HOOD, 1799 - 1845

*Greek lyric Poet Anacreon

To help your brother along the road
To do his work, and lift his load;
To add your gift to the world's good cheer—
Is to have and to give a Glad New Year.

New Year's Day is every man's birthday.

CHARLES LAMB, 1775 - 1834

We are bound, by every rule of justice and equity, to give the New Year credit for being a good one until he proves himself unworthy of the confidence we repose in him.

CHARLES DICKENS, 1812 - 1870

I would not care to sit upon a throne,
Or build my house upon a mountain-top,
Where I must dwell in glory all alone
And never friend come in or poor man
stop.

God grant that I may live upon this earth
And face the tasks which every morning
brings
And never lose the glory and the worth
Of humble service and the simple things.

THE FOUR FREEDOMS

In the future days which we seek to make secure, we look forward to a world founded upon four essential freedoms.

The first is freedom of speech and expression—everywhere in the world.

The second is freedom of every person to worship God in his own way—everywhere in the world.

The third is freedom from want, which, translated into world terms, means economic understanding which will secure to every nation a healthy peacetime life for its inhabitants—everywhere in the world.

The fourth is freedom from fear, which, translated into world terms, means a world-wide reduction of armaments to such a point and in such a thorough fashion that no nation will be in a position to commit an act of physical aggression against any neighbor—anywhere in the world.

PRESIDENT FRANKLIN DELANO ROOSEVELT
1882 - 1945
from Address to Congress, January 6, 1941

❧

Friendship improves happiness, and abates misery, by doubling our joy, and dividing our grief.

JOSEPH ADDISON, 1672 - 1719

❧

WHAT'S THE RAILROAD?

What's the railroad to me?
I never go to see
Where it ends.
It fills a few hollows,
And makes banks for the swallows,
It sets the sand a-blowing,
And the blackberries a-growing.

HENRY DAVID THOREAU, 1817 - 1862

THE MESSAGE OF THE NEW YEAR

I asked the New Year for some message
sweet,
Some rule of life with which to guide my
feet;
I asked, and paused: he answered soft and
low, "God's will to know."

"Will knowledge then suffice, New Year?"
I cried;
And, ere the question into silence died,
The answer came, "Nay, but remember, too,
God's will to do."

Once more I asked, "Is there no more to
tell?"
And once again the answer sweetly fell,
"Yes! this thing, all other things above:
God's will to love."

❧

OLD JANUARY

Then came old January, wrapped well
In many weeds to keep the cold away;
Yet did he quake and quiver, like to quell,
And blow his nails to warm them if he may.

EDMUND SPENSER, 1552 - 1599

❧

The fatality of good resolutions is that they are always too late.

OSCAR WILDE, 1856 - 1900

❧

Most of us have never lived in normal times.

❧

He who has begun, has the work half done.

HORACE, 65 - 8 B.C.

14

TELL HIM SO

If you hear a kind word spoken
*   Of some worthy soul you know,*
It may fill his heart with sunshine
*   If you only tell him so.*

If a deed, however humble,
*   Helps you on your way to go,*
Seek the one whose hand has helped you,
*   Seek him out and tell him so!*

If your heart is touched and tender
*   Toward a sinner, lost and low,*
It might help him to do better
*   If you'd only tell him so!*

Oh, my sisters, oh, my brothers,
*   As o'er life's rough path you go,*
If God's love has saved and kept you,
*   Do not fail to tell men so!*

KIND WORDS

Kind words are the bright flowers of earthly existence; use them, and especially around the fireside circle. They are jewels beyond price, and powerful to heal the wounded heart and make the weighed-down spirit glad.

A genuine word of kindness is often the best lever to raise a depressed spirit to its natural level.

The art of saying appropriate words in a kindly way is one that never goes out of fashion, never ceases to please, and is within the reach of the humblest.

WEATHER LORE:

The chill is on from near and far
In all the months that have an R.

KINDNESS GARDEN

Kind hearts are the gardens.
*   Kind thoughts are the roots.*
Kind words are the blossoms.
*   Kind deeds are the fruits.*

Love is sweet sunshine
*   That warms into life,*
For only in darkness
*   Grow hatred and strife.*

There was a naughty Boy
*   And a naughty Boy was he*
He ran away to Scotland
*   The people for to see—*
*   There he found*
*   That the ground*
*   Was as hard*
*   That a yard*
*   Was as long,*
*   That a song*
*   Was as merry,*
*   That a cherry*
*   Was as red—*
*   That lead*
*   Was as weighty*
*   That fourscore*
*   Was as eighty*
*   That a door*
*   Was as wooden*
*   As in England—*
*   So he stood in*
*   His shoes*
*   And he wondered*
*   He wondered*
*   He stood in his*
*   Shoes and he wonder'd.*
                          JOHN KEATS, 1795 - 1821

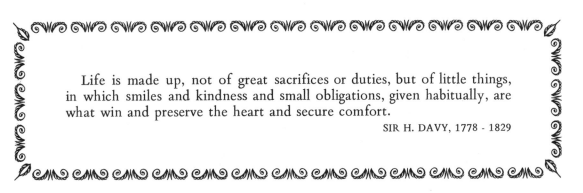

Life is made up, not of great sacrifices or duties, but of little things, in which smiles and kindness and small obligations, given habitually, are what win and preserve the heart and secure comfort.

SIR H. DAVY, 1778 - 1829

from the INAUGURAL ADDRESS
JOHN FITZGERALD KENNEDY 1917 - 1963
January 20, 1961

The world is very different now. For man holds in his mortal hands the power to abolish all forms of human poverty and all forms of human life. And yet the same revolutionary beliefs for which our fore-bears fought are still at issue around the globe—the belief that the rights of man come not from the generosity of the state but from the hand of God.

We dare not forget today that we are the heirs of that first revolution. Let the word go forth from this time and place, to friend and foe alike, that the torch has been passed to a new generation of Americans—born in this century, tempered by war, disciplined by a hard and bitter peace, proud of our ancient heritage—and unwilling to witness or permit the slow undoing of those human rights to which this nation has always been committed, and to which we are committed today at home and around the world.

Let every nation know, whether it wishes us well or ill, that we shall pay any price, bear any burden, meet any hard-ship, support any friend, oppose any foe to assure the survival and the success of liberty. This much we pledge—and more.

* * *

"And so, my fellow Americans: ask not what your country can do for you—ask what you can do for your country.

"My fellow citizens of the world: ask not what America will do for you, but what together we can do for the freedom of man."

I pray to Heaven to bestow the best of blessings on this House and all that shall hereafter inhabit it. May none but honest and wise men ever rule under this roof.

JOHN ADAMS (1st president to live in White House)

⟨W⟩

The finest prison in the world.

HARRY S. TRUMAN,
speaking of the White House

⟨W⟩

Politician: An animal who can sit on a fence and yet keep both ears to the ground.

⟨W⟩

Bad officials are elected by good citizens who do not vote.

U.S. POLITICAL SLOGANS:

Tippecanoe and Tyler too.	1840
Free Soil, Free Men, Free Speech, Fremont.	1856
Turn the Rascals Out	1872
The Solid South -	1878
A Public Office is a Public Trust.	1884
Mugwump -	1872 and 1884
The Full Dinner Pail.	1900
He kept us out of War.	1916
Keep Cool with Coolidge	1924
Let's look at the record.	1928
A chicken in every pot, a car in every garage.	1928

16

Greatness comes in simple trappings.

The simple things are the ones most needed today if we are to surmount what divides us and cement what unites us. To lower our voices would be a simple thing.

In these difficult years, America has suffered from a fever of words, from inflated rhetoric that promises more than it can deliver; from angry rhetoric that fans discontents into hatreds; from bombastic rhetoric that postures instead of persuading.

We cannot learn from one another until we stop shouting at one another—until we speak quietly enough so that our words can be heard as well as our voices.

For its part government will listen. We will strive to listen in new ways—to the voices of quiet anguish, the voices that speak without words the voices of the heart—to the injured voices, the anxious voices, the voices that have despaired of being heard.

Those who have been left out we will try to bring in. Those left behind, we will help to catch up.

For all our people, we will set as our goal the decent order that makes progress possible and our lives secure.

The American dream does not come to those who fall asleep.

But we are approaching the limits of what government alone can do.

Our greatest need now is to reach beyond government, to enlist the legions of the concerned and the committed. What has to be done has to be done by government and people together or it will not be done at all. The lesson of past agony is that without the people we can do nothing; with the people we can do everything.

To match the magnitude of our talks, we need the energies of our people—enlisted not only in grand enterprises, but more importantly in those small splendid efforts that make headlines in the neighborhood newspaper instead of the national journal.

* * *

With these, we can build a great cathedral of the spirit—each of us raising it one stone at a time, as he reaches out to his neighbor, helping, caring, doing.

I do not offer a life of uninspiring ease. I do not call for a life of grim sacrifice. I ask you to join in a high adventure—one as rich as humanity itself, and exciting as the times we live in.

THE VAGABOND

Give to me the life I love,
  Let the lave go by me,
Give the jolly heaven above
  And the byway nigh me.
Bed in the bush with stars to see,
  Bread I dip in the river—
There's the life for a man like me,
  There's the life for ever.

Let the blow fall soon or late,
  Let what will be o'er me;
Give the face of earth around
  And the road before me.
Wealth I seek not, hope nor love,
  Nor a friend to know me;
All I seek, the heaven above
  And the road below me.

Or let autumn fall on me
  Where afield I linger,
Silencing the bird on tree,
  Biting the blue finger.
White as meal the frosty field—
  Warm the fireside haven—
Not to autumn will I yield,
  Not to winter even!

Let the blow fall soon or late,
  Let what will be o'er me;
Give the face of earth around
  And the road before me.
Wealth I ask not, hope nor love,
  Nor a friend| to know me;
All I ask, the heaven above
  And the road below me.

ROBERT LOUIS STEVENSON

LIBERTY AND UNION

From the Second *Reply to Hayne*, Jan. 26, 1830

I profess, sir, in my career hitherto to have kept steadily in view the prosperity and honor of the whole country and the preservation of our Federal Union. It is to that Union we owe our safety at home, and our consideration and dignity abroad. It is to that Union that we are chiefly indebted for whatever makes us most proud of our country. That Union we reached only by the discipline of our virtues in the severe school of adversity. It had its origin in the necessities of disordered finance, prostrate commerce, and ruined credit. Under its benign influences these great interests immediately awoke, as from the dead, and sprang forth with newness of life. Every year of its duration has teemed with fresh proofs of its utility and its blessings; and although our territory has stretched out wider and wider, and our population spread farther and farther, they have not outrun its protection or its benefits. It has been to us all a copious fountain of national, social, and personal happiness.

* * *

While the Union lasts we have high, exciting, gratifying prospects spread out before us, for us and our children. Beyond that I seek not to penetrate the veil. God grant that, in my day, at least, that curtain may not rise! God grant that on my vision never may be opened what lies behind! When my eyes shall be turned to behold for the last time the sun in heaven, may I not see him shining on the broken and dishonored fragments of a once glorious Union; on States dissevered, discordant, belligerent; on a land rent with civil feuds, or drenched, it may be, in fraternal blood! Let their last feeble and lingering glance rather behold the gorgeous ensign of the Republic, now known and honored throughout the earth, still full high advanced, its arms and trophies streaming in their original luster, not a stripe erased or polluted, nor a single star obscured, bearing for its motto no such miserable interrogatory as, "What is all this worth?" nor those other words of delusion and folly, "Liberty first and Union afterward"; but everywhere, spread all over in characters of living light, blazing on all its ample folds, as they float over the sea and over the land, and in every wind under the whole heavens, that other sentiment dear to every American heart—Liberty *and* Union, now and forever, one and inseparable!

DANIEL WEBSTER, 1782 - 1852

THE WIND OF JANUARY

On the wind of January
Down flits the snow,
Traveling from the frozen North
As cold as it can blow.
Poor robin redbreast,
Look where he comes;
Let him in to feel your fire,
And toss him of your crumbs.

CHRISTINA ROSSETTI, 1830 - 1894

It hain't no use to grumble and complain,
It's jest as easy to rejoice;
When God sorts out the weather and sends
rain,
Why rain's my choice.

JAMES WHITCOMB RILEY, 1849 - 1916

THE POET'S CALENDAR: JANUARY

Janus am I; oldest of potentates;
Forward I look, and backward, and below
I count, as god of avenues and gates, the
years that through my portals come and go.
I block the roads, and drift the fields with
snow;
I chase the wild-fowl from the frozen fen;
My frosts congeal the rivers in their flow,
My fires light up the hearths and hearts of
men.

HENRY W. LONGFELLOW, 1807 - 1882

SNOW FLAKES

Out of the bosom of the air,
*   Out of the cloud-folds of her garments*
*   shaken,*
*   Over the woodlands brown and bare,*
Over the harvest-fields forsaken,
*   Silent and soft and slow*
*   Descends the snow.*

Even as our cloudy fancies take
*   Suddenly shape in some divine expression,*
Even as the troubled heart doth make
*   In the white countenance confession.*
*   The troubled sky reveals*
*   The grief it feels.*

This is the poem of the air,
*   Slowly in silent syllables recorded;*
This is the secret of despair,
*   Long in its cloudy bosom hoarded,*
*   Now whispered and revealed*
*   To wood and field.*

HENRY WADSWORTH LONGFELLOW, 1807 - 1882

❧✧❧

I frequently tramped eight or ten miles through the deepest snow to keep an appointment with a beech tree, or a yellow birch, or an old acquaintance among the pines.

HENRY DAVID THOREAU, 1817 - 1862

YOU ARE WELCOME HERE

Be at your ease
Get up when you're ready
Go to bed when you please.
Happy to share with you such as we've got
The leaks in the roof and the soup in the pot
You don't have to thank us or laugh at our
*   jokes,*
Sit deep and come often, you're one of the
*   folks.*

from COME DINE WITH ME

From whom he means to make an often guest, One dish shall serve; and welcome make the rest.

JOSEPH HALL, 1574 - 1656

❧✧❧

'Tis equal wrong if a man speed on a guest who is loath to go, and if he keep back one that is eager to be gone. One should make welcome the present guest, and send forth him that would go.

HOMER

❧✧❧

Replying to Homer—
For I, who hold sage Homer's rule the best, Welcome the coming, speed the going guest.

ALEXANDER POPE, 1688 - 1774

❧✧❧

Fish and guests in three days are stale.

JOHN LYLY, 1554 - 1606

❧✧❧

from his JOURNAL

Hospitality consists in a little fire, a little food, and an immense quiet.

RALPH WALDO EMERSON, 1803 - 1882

❧✧❧

There was a young man so benighted
He didn't know when he was slighted,
*   But went to the party*
*   And ate just as hearty*
As if he'd been duly invited!

❧✧❧

Tact: To make your guests feel at home even though you wish they were.

❧✧❧

Some people can stay longer in an hour than others can in a week

WILLIAM DEAN HOWELLS, 1837 - 1920

❧✧❧

Go often to the house of thy friend, for weeds choke up the unused path.

WILLIAM SHAKESPEARE

Open the old cigar-box, get me a Cuba
    stout,
For things are running crossways, and
    Maggie and I are out.

We quarreled about Havanas—we fought
    o'er a good cheroot—
And I know she is exacting, and she says
    I am a brute.

Open the old cigar-box—let me consider a
    space,
In the soft blue veil of the vapor, musing
    on Maggie's face.

Maggie is pretty to look at—Maggie's a
    loving lass,
But the prettiest cheeks must wrinkle, the
    truest of loves must pass.

There's peace in a Laranaga, there's calm
    in a Henry Clay,
But the best cigar in an hour is finished
    and thrown away—

Thrown away for another as perfect and
    ripe and brown—
But I never could throw away Maggie for
    fear o' the talk o' the town!

Maggie, my wife at fifty—gray and dour
    and old—
With never another Maggie to purchase
    for love or gold.

And the light of Days that have Been, the
    dark of the Days that Are,
And Love's torch stinking and stale, like
    the butt of a dead cigar—

The butt of a dead cigar you are bound
    to keep in your pocket—
With never a new one to light, though it's
    charred and black to the socket.

Open the old cigar-box—let me consider
    awhile;
Here is a mild Manilla—there is a wifely
    smile.

Which is the better portion—bondage
    bought with a ring,
Or a harem of dusky beauties, fifty tied
    in a string?

Counselors cunning and silent—comforters
    true and tried,

And never a one of the fifty to sneer at a
    rival bride.

Thought in the early morning, solace in
    time of woes,
Peace in the hush of the twilight, balm
    ere my eyelids close.

This will the fifty give me, asking naught
    in return,
With only a Suttee's passion—to do their
    duty and burn.

This will the fifty give me. When they are
    spent and dead.
Five times other fifties shall be my
    servants instead.

For Maggie has written a letter to give me
    my choice between
The wee little whimpering Love and the
    great god Nick o' Teen.

And I have been servant of Love for
    barely a twelvemonth clear,
But I have been Priest of Partagas a matter
    of seven year;

And the gloom of my bachelor days is
    flecked with the cheery light
Of stumps that I burned to Friendship,
    and Pleasure, and Work, and Fight.

And I turn my eyes to the future that
    Maggie and I must prove,
But the only light on the marshes is the
    Will-o-the-Wisp of Love.

Will it see me safe through my journey, or
    leave me bogged in the mire?
Since a puff of tobacco can cloud it, shall
    I follow the fitful fire?

Open the old cigar-box—let me consider
    anew—
Old friends, and who is Maggie, that I
    should abandon you?

A million surplus Maggies are willing to
    bear the yoke;
And a woman is only a woman, but a
    good cigar is a Smoke.

Light me another Cuba—I hold to my
    first-sworn vows,
If Maggie will have no rival, I'll have no
    Maggie for spouse!

RUDYARD KIPLING, 1865 - 1936

from THE FIRST SNOW-FALL

The snow had begun in the gloaming,
And busily all the night
Had been heaping field and highway
With a silence deep and white.

Every pine and fir and hemlock
Wore ermine too dear for an earl,
And the poorest twig on the elm-tree
Was ridged inch deep with pearl.

From sheds new-roofed with Carrara
Came Chanticleer's muffled crow,
The stiff rails softened to swan's-down
And still fluttered down the snow.

I stood and watched by the window
The noiseless work of the sky,
And the sudden flurries of snow-birds,
Like brown leaves whirling by.

JAMES RUSSELL LOWELL, 1819 - 1891

SNOWFLAKES

Whenever a snow-flake leaves the sky,
It turns and turns to say "Goodby!
Good-bye, dear cloud, so cool and gray!"
Then lightly travels on its way.

And when a snow-flake finds a tree,
"Good-day" it says—"Good-day to thee,
Thou art so bare and lonely, dear,
I'll rest and call my comrades here."

But when a snow-flake, brave and meek,
Lights on a rosy maiden's cheek,
It starts—"How warm and soft the day
'Tis summer"—and it melts away.

MARY MAPES DODGE, 1831 - 1905

IT'S THE BRAIN THAT COUNTS

You can get along with a wooden leg, but you can't get along with a wooden head. It is the brain that counts, but in order that your brain may be kept clear you must keep your body fit and well. That cannot be done if one drinks liquor, which breaks down the command of the individual over his own life and his own destiny.

CHARLES MAYO, 1865 - 1939

from SLEEP

Come Sleep! O Sleep, the certain knot of
*   peace,*
The baiting-place of wit, the balm of woe,
The poor man's wealth, the prisoner's
*   release,*
The indifferent judge between the high
*   and low!*
With shield of proof, shield me from out
*   the press*
Of those fierce darts Despair at me doth
*   throw:*
O make in me those civil wars to cease!
I will good tribute pay if thou do so.
Take thou of me, smooth pillows, sweetest
*   bed,*
A chamber deaf to noise and blind to light,
A rosy garland, and a weary head:
And if these things, as being thine in right,
*   Move not thy heavy grace, thou shalt in*
*   me,*
Livelier than elsewhere, Stella's image see.

SIR PHILIP SIDNEY, 1554 - 1586

from
"LETTERS TO HIS SON" - Letter 30

Lord Chesterfield suggesting modesty in comportment—
. . . would avoid the accusation of pedantry on one hand, or the suspicion of ignorance on the other, abstain from learned ostentation. Speak the language of the company that you are in, speak it purely, and unlarded with any other. Never seem wiser, nor more learned, than the people you are with. Wear your learning, like your watch, in a private pocket: and do not pull it out and strike it; merely to show that you have one. If you are asked what o'clock it is, tell it; but do not proclaim it hourly and unasked, like the watchman.

LORD CHESTERFIELD, 1694 - 1773

from BEAUTIFUL SNOW

Oh! the snow, the beautiful snow,
Filling the sky and the earth below;
Over the house tops, over the street,
Over the heads of the people you meet;
   Dancing,
      Flirting,
         Skimming along,
Beautiful snow! it can do nothing wrong.
Flying to kiss a fair lady's cheek,
Clinging to lips in a frolicsome freak;
Beautiful snow, from the heavens above,
Pure as an angel and fickle as love!

Oh! the snow, the beautiful snow!
How the flakes gather and laugh as they
   go!
Whirling about in its maddening fun,
It plays in its glee with everyone.
   Chasing,
      Laughing,
         Hurrying by,
It lights up the face and it sparkles the
   eye;
And even the dogs, with a bark and a
   bound,
Snap at the crystals that eddy around.
The town is alive, and its heart in a glow,
To welcome the coming of beautiful snow.

How the wild crowd go swaying along,
Hailing each other with humor and song!
How the gay sledges like meteors flash by—
Bright for a moment, then lost to the eye!
   Ringing,
      Swinging,
         Dashing they go
Over the crest of the beautiful snow;
Snow so pure when it falls from the sky,
To be trampled in mud by the crowd
   rushing by;
To be trampled and tracked by the
   thousands of feet
Till it blends with the horrible filth in the
   street.

JAMES W. WATSON, 1824 - 1890

COURAGE

Courage! What if the snows are deep,
And what if the hills are long and steep
And the days are short and the nights are
   long
And the good are weak and the bad are
   strong
Courage! The now is a field of play,
And the longest hill has a well-worn way,
There are songs that shorten the longest
   night,
There's a day when wrong shall be ruled
   by right,
So Courage! Courage! 'Tis never so far
from a plodded path to a shining star.

❦

Success is speaking words of praise
In cheering other people's ways,
In doing just the best you can
With every task and every plan.
It's silence when your speech would hurt.
Politeness when your neighbor's curt.
It's deafness when the scandal flows,
And sympathy with others' woes.
It's loyalty when duty calls,
It's courage when disaster falls,
It's patience when the hours are long;
It's found in laughter and in song;
It's in the silent time of prayer,
In happiness and in despair
In all of life and nothing less
We find the thing we call success.

❦

Ideals are like stars. You will not succeed in touching them with your hands;
but, like the seafaring man, you choose
them as your guides, and following them,
you will reach your destiny.

CARL SCHURZ, 1829 - 1906

EULOGY OF THE DOG

Gentlemen of the Jury: The best friend a man has in the world may turn against him and become his enemy. His son or daughter whom he has reared with loving care may prove ungrateful. Those who are nearest and dearest to us, those whom we trust with our happiness and our good name, may become traitors to their faith. The money that a man has he may lose. It flies away from him, perhaps when he needs it most. A man's reputation may be sacrificed in a moment of ill-considered action. The people who are prone to fall on their knees to do us honor when success is with us may be the first to throw the stone of malice when failure settles its clouds upon our heads.

The one absolutely unselfish friend that man can have in this selfish world, the one that never deserts him, the one that never proves ungrateful or treacherous, is his dog. A man's dog stands by him in prosperity and in poverty, in health and in sickness. He will sleep on the cold ground, where the wintry winds blow and the snow drives fiercely, if only he can be near his master's side. He will kiss the hand that has no food to offer, he will lick the wounds and sores that come in encounter with the roughness of the world. He guards the sleep of his pauper master as if he were a prince. When all other friends desert, he remains. When riches take wings and reputation falls to pieces, he is as constant in his love as the sun in its journey through the heavens.

If fortune drives the master forth an outcast in the world, friendless and homeless, the faithful dog asks no higher privilege than that of accompanying him, to guard against danger, to fight against his enemies. And when the last scene of all comes, and death takes his master in its embrace, and his body is laid away in the cold ground, no matter if all other friends pursue their way, there by the graveside will the noble dog be found, his head between his paws, his eyes sad but open in alert watchfulness, faithful and true even to death.

GEORGE G. VEST, 1830 - 1904

23

JENNY KISS'D ME

Jenny kiss'd me when we met,
Jumping from the chair she sat in;
Time, you thief, who love to get
Sweets into your list, put that in!
Say I'm weary, say I'm sad,
Say that health and wealth have miss'd
me,
Say I'm growing old, but add,
Jenny kiss'd me.

LEIGH HUNT, 1784 - 1859

Paul Dehn changed the last two lines to:

"Say I've had a filthy cold
Since Jenny kiss'd me."

❧

I trust a good deal to common fame, as we all must. If a man has good corn, or woods, or boards, or pigs to sell, or can make better chairs or knives, crucibles or church organs than anybody else, you will find a broad, hardbeaten road to his house, though it be in the woods.

RALPH WALDO EMERSON, Journal, 1855.

The phrase "build a better mousetrap than your neighbor" as often quoted, does not appear in any of Emerson's writings.

❧

I owe all my success in life to having been always a quarter of an hour beforehand.

LORD NELSON, 1758 - 1865

from THE DEVIL'S DICTIONARY

Absolute monarchy, n. One in which the monarch does as he pleases as long as he pleases the assassins.

Acquaintance, n. A person whom we know well enough to borrow from, but not well enough to lend to.

Bore, n. A person who talks when you want him to listen.

Coward, n. One who in a perilous emergency thinks with his legs.

Faith, n. Belief without evidence in what is told by one who speaks without knowledge, of things without parallel.

Hospitality, n. The virtue which induces us to feed and lodge certain persons who are not in need of food and lodging.

Me, pro. The objectional case of I. The personal pronoun in English has three cases, the dominative, the objectional and the oppressive. Each is all three.

Once, adv. Enough

To be positive. To be mistaken at the top of one's voice.

AMBROSE BIERCE, 1842 - 1914

❧

from THE LIE

Tell zeal it wants devotion;
Tell love it is but lust;
Tell time it meets but motion;
Tell flesh it is but dust:
*   And wish them not reply,*
*   For thou must give the lie.*

Tell age it daily wasteth;
Tell honour how it alters;
Tell beauty how she blasteth;
Tell favour how it falters:
*   And as they shall reply,*
*   Give every one the lie.*

SIR WALTER RALEIGH, 1552 - 1618

❧

There is a lot more to life than just living as long as possible. "And all the days of Methuselah were nine hundred sixty and 9 yrs: and he died." This is the longest life in history and the shortest biography. Nothing bad about Methuselah, but also nothing good. A life is more than just length of years.

CHARLES L. ALLEN

24

TO A CAT

There is no reason I can find
That you should make me feel so small;
I have a fair to middling mind
While you have almost none at all.
No proud position do you fill;
Your features are extremely plain
And yet I wilt beneath your chill
Disdain.

At night I lie back in my chair
From all my work and worry free
And then I see that sneering stare
Which, from the hearth, you fix on me.
I know I should not strive to please
A dull, unprepossessing cat
But I'm distrait and ill at ease
At that.

Some day when in those half closed eyes
I see that sinister regard,
To your annoyance and surprise
You'll land out yonder in the yard.
For praise or place I little care,
From hope of fame I'm quite exempt,
But listen, cat! I cannot bear
Contempt.

ᎧᎳᎤ

WORDS

The five most important words:
I am proud of you.
The four most important words:
What is your opinion?
The three most important words:
If you please.
The two most important words:
Thank you.
The least important word:
"I."

ᎧᎳᎤ

I cannot agree that it should be the declared public policy of Illinois that a cat visiting a neighbor's yard or crossing the highway is a public nuisance. It is in the nature of cats to do a certain amount of unescorted roaming.... Also consider the owner's dilemma: To escort a cat abroad on a leash is against the nature of the cat, and to permit it to venture forth for exercise unattended into a night of new dangers is against the nature of the owner. Moreover, cats perform useful service, particularly in rural areas, in combatting rodents—work they necessarily perform alone and without regard for property lines.... The problem of cat versus bird is old as time. If we attempt to resolve it by legislation, who knows but what we may be called upon to take sides as well in the age-old problem of dog versus cat, bird versus bird, or even bird versus worm. In my opinion, the State of Illinois and its local governing bodies already have enough to do without trying to control feline delinquency.

For these reasons, and not because I love birds less or cats the more, I veto and withhold my approval of Senate Bill No. 93.

ADLAI STEVENSON,
veto of "Cat Bill," April 23, 1949

ᎧᎳᎤ

THE KILKENNY CATS

There wanst was two cats of Kilkenny,
Each thought there was one cat too many,
So they quarrell'd and fit,
They scratch'd and they bit,
Till, barrin' their nails,
And tips of their tails,
Instead of two cats, there warnt any.

HYACINTHS TO FEED THY SOUL

If of thy mortal goods thou are bereft,
And from thy slender store two loaves alone
to thee are left,
Sell one, and with the dole
Buy hyacinths to feed thy soul.

MOSLEH EDDIN SAADI, 1184 - 1291

Gulistan: Garden of Roses (A Mohammedan sheik)

TO F. C.

Fast falls the snow, O lady mine,
Sprinkling the lawn with crystals fine,
But by the gods we won't repine
  While we're together,
We'll chat and rhyme, and kiss and dine,
  Defying weather.

So stir the fire and pour the wine,
And let those sea-green eyes divine
Pour their love-madness into mine:
  I don't care whether
'Tis snow or sun or rain or shine
  If we're together.

MORTIMER COLLINS, 1827 - 1876

⚜

He that loves a rosy cheek,
  Or a coral lip admires,
Or from star-like eyes doth seek
  Fuel to maintain his fires,
As Old Time makes these decay,
So his flames must waste away.

THOMAS CAREW, 1595 - 1639

⚜

O MISTRESS MINE,
WHERE ARE YOU ROAMING?

O Mistress mine, where are you roaming?
Oh, stay and hear; your true love's coming,
  That can sing both high and low.
Trip no further, pretty sweeting,
Journeys end in lovers meeting.
  Every wise man's son doth know.

What is love? 'tis not hereafter;
Present mirth hath present laughter;
  What's to come is still unsure.
In delay there lies no plenty;
Then come kiss me, sweet and twenty;
  Youth's a stuff will not endure.

WILLIAM SHAKESPEARE

TO A LADY ASKING HIM HOW LONG
HE WOULD LOVE HER

It is not, Celia, in our power
  To say how long our love will last;
It may be we within this hour
  May lose those joys we now do taste:
The Blessed, that immortal be,
From change in love are only free.

Then since we mortal lovers are,
  Ask not how long our love will last;
But while it does, let us take care
  Each minute be with pleasure passed:
Were it not madness to deny
To live because we're sure to die?

GEORGE ETHEREGE, 1635 - 1691

⚜

LOVE NOT ME FOR COMELY GRACE

Love not me for comely grace
For my pleasing eye or face;
Nor for any outward part,
No, nor for a constant heart:
  For these may fail or turn to ill,
  So thou and I shall sever.
Keep, therefore, a true woman's eye,
And love me still, but know not why;
  So hast thou the same reason still
  To dote upon me ever.

⚜

A mighty pain to love it is,
And 'tis a pain that pain to miss;
But of all pains, the greatest pain,
It is to love, and love in vain.

ABRAHAM COWLEY, 1618 - 1667

⚜

Two things only a man cannot hide: that
he is drunk and that he is in love.

ANTIPHANES

⚜

If all our misfortunes were laid in one
common heap, whence every one must
take an equal portion, most people would
be contented to take their own and depart.

SOLON (Athenian legislator) 638 - 559 B.C.

26

A man without mirth is like a wagon without springs, in which one is caused disagreeably to jolt by every pebble over which it runs.

HENRY WARD BEECHER, 1813 - 1887

❦

An ounce of mirth is worth a pound of sorrow.

RICHARD BAXTER, 1615 - 1691

❦

A little kingdom I possess,
  Where thoughts and feelings dwell;
And very hard the task I find
  Of governing it well.

I do not ask for any crown
  But that which all may win;
Nor try to conquer any world
  Except the one within.

LOUISA MAY ALCOTT, 1832 - 1888

❦

No vice is as bad as advice.

MARIE DRESSLER, 1869 - 1934

❦

WHEN ICICLES HANG BY THE WALL

When icicles hang by the wall,
  And Dick the shepherd blows his nail,
And Tom bears logs into the hall,
  And milk comes frozen home in pail,
When blood is nipp'd and ways be foul,
Then nightly sings the staring owl—
  To-who;
Tu-whit, to-who, a merry note,
While greasy Joan doth keel the pot.

When all aloud the wind doth blow,
  And coughing drowns the parson's saw,
And birds sit brooding in the snow,
  And Marion's nose looks red and raw,
When roasted crabs hiss in the bowl,
Then nightly sings the staring owl—
  To-who;
Tu-whit, to-who, a merry note,
While greasy Joan doth keel the pot.

WILLIAM SHAKESPEARE

(from *Love's Labour's Lost*, Act V, Scene II)

WINTER

On all thy trees, on every bough,
Thousands of crystals sparkle now,
  Where'er our eyes alight;
Firm on the spotless robes we tread,
Which o'er thy beauteous form is spread,
  With glittering hoar-frost bright.

Our Father kind, who dwells above,
For thee this garment pure hath wove;
  He watches over thee.
Therefore in peace thy slumber take,
Our Father will the weary wake,
  New strength, new light to see.

Soon to the breath of spring's soft sighs,
Delighted thou again wilt rise,
  In wondrous life so fair.
I feel those sighs breathe o'er the plain,
Dear nature, then rise up again
  With flower-wreaths in thy hair.

FRIEDRICH KRUMMACHER, 1768 - 1845

❦

from MARCH 10, 1666 DIARY

The truth is, I do indulge myself a little the more in pleasure, knowing that this is the proper age of my life etc.

SAMUEL PEPYS, 1633 - 1703

❦

from JINGLE BELLS

Dashing thro' the snow in a one-horse open
  sleigh,
O'er the fields we go, laughing all the way;
Bells on bob-tail ring, making spirits bright;
What fun it is to ride and sing a sleighing
  song tonight!

Jingle Bells! Jingle Bells! Jingle all the way!
Oh! what fun it is to ride in a one-horse
  open-sleigh!

J. PIERPONT, 1785 - 1866

ABOU BEN ADHEM

Abou Ben Adhem (may his tribe increase!)
Awoke one night from a deep dream of
    peace,
And saw, within the moonlight in his room,
Making it rich, and like a lily in bloom,
An angel writing in a book of gold:—
Exceeding peace had made Ben Adhem
    bold,
And to the presence in the room he said,
    "What writest thou?" The vision
        raised its head,
And with a look made of all sweet accord,
Answered, "The names of those who love
    the Lord"
        "And is mine one?" said Abou. "Nay,
            not so,"
Replied the angel. Abou spoke more low,
But cheerly still; and said, "I pray thee,
    then,
Write me as one that loves his fellow men."
    The angel wrote, and vanish'd. The
        next night
It came again with a great waking light,
And show'd the names whom love of God
    had blest,
And lo! Ben Adhem's name led all the rest.
                    LEIGH HUNT, 1784 - 1859

HOLY ORDER

Abou Ben Adhem's name led all the rest . . .
    Prompting a thesis wildly theoretical—
That even recording angels find it best
    To keep us alphabetical.
                    J. B. BOOTHROYD

RICHES

The countless gold of a merry heart,
    The rubies and pearls of a loving eye,
The indolent never can bring to the mart,
    Nor the secret hoard up in his treasury.
                    WM. BLAKE, 1757 - 1827

MY MIND TO ME A KINGDOM IS

My mind to me a kingdom is,
    Such present joys therein I find,
That it excels all other bliss
    That earth affords or grows by kind:
Tho much I want which most would have,
Yet still my mind forbids to crave.

Content to live, this is my stay;
    I seek no more than may suffice;
I press to bear no haughty sway;
    Look, what I lack my mind supplies:
Lo, thus I triumph like a king,
Content with that my mind doth bring.

Some have too much, yet still do crave;
    I little have, and seek no more.
They are but poor, tho much they have,
    And I am rich with little store:
They poor, I rich; they beg, I give;
They lack, I leave; they pine, I live.

My wealth is health and perfect ease;
    My conscience clear my chief defense;
I neither seek by bribes to please,
    Nor by deceit to breed offense:
Thus do I live; thus will I die;
Would all did so as well as I!
                    EDWARD DYER, d. 1607

Every now and then a man's mind is
stretched by a new idea and never shrinks
back to its original proportions.
        OLIVER WENDELL HOLMES, 1809 - 1894

BE STRONG

    Be Strong!
We are not here to play, to dream, to drift;
We have hard work to do, and loads to lift;
Shun not the struggle—face it; 'tis God's gift.
    Be Strong!

Say not, "The days are evil. Who's to blame?"
And fold the hands and acquiesce—oh shame!
Stand up, speak out, and bravely, in God's
        name.
    Be Strong!

It matters not how deep intrenched the
        wrong,
How hard the battle goes, the day how long;
Faint not—fight on! Tomorrow comes the
        song.
        MALTBIE DAVENPORT BABCOCK, 1858 - 1901

TO THE TERRESTRIAL GLOBE.

Roll on, thou ball, roll on!
Through pathless realms of space
   Roll on!
What though I'm in a sorry case?
What though I cannot meet my bills?
What though I suffer toothache's ills?
What though I swallow countless pills?
  Never you mind!
    Roll on!

Roll on, thou ball, roll on!
Through seas of inky air
   Roll on!
It's true I've got no shirts to wear,
It's true my butcher's bill is due,
It's true my prospects all look blue,—
But don't let that unsettle you
  Never you mind!
    Roll on!

          W. S. GILBERT, 1836 - 1911

TODAY

So here hath been dawning
  Another blue day;
Think, wilt thou let it
  Slip useless away?

Out of Eternity
  This new day is born;
Into Eternity,
  At night, will return.

Behold it aforetime
  No eye ever did;
So soon it forever
  From all eyes is hid.

Here hath been dawning
  Another blue day;
Think, wilt thou let it
  Slip useless away?

          THOMAS CARLYLE, 1795 - 1881

Here lies my wife: here let her lie!
Now she's at rest, and so am I.

          JOHN DRYDEN, 1631 - 1700

Wherever in the world I roam
Where'er you are, for me is home

          THEODORE STORM, 1817 - 1888

To the Spanish Ambassador [1580]

The use of the sea and air is common to all; neither can a title to the ocean belong to any people or private persons, forasmuch as neither nature nor public use and custom permit any possession thereof.

          ELIZABETH I, 1533 - 1603

The time will come when men
Will be as free and equal as the waves,
That seem to jostle, but that never jar.

          ALFRED J. AUSTIN, 1835 - 1918

from TO NIGHT

Swiftly walk over the western wave,
  Spirit of Night!
Out of the misty eastern cave,
Where all the long and lone daylight,
Thou weavest dreams of joy and fear,
Which make thee terrible and dear,—
  Swift be thy flight!

When I arose and saw the dawn,
  I sighed for thee!
When light rode high, and the dew was gone,
And noon lay heavy on floor and tree,
And the weary Day turned to his rest,
Lingering, like an unloved guest,
  I sigh for thee!

Death will come when thou art dead,
  Soon, too soon,—
Sleep will come when thou art fled;
Of neither would I ask the boon
I ask of thee, beloved Night—
Swift be thine approaching flight,
  Come soon, soon!

          PERCY BYSSHE SHELLEY, 1792 - 1822

THE SYCOPHANTIC FOX AND THE GULLIBLE RAVEN

A raven sat upon a tree,
  And not a word he spoke, for
His beak contained a piece of Brie,
  Or, maybe, it was Roquefort?
    We'll make it any kind you please—
    At all events, it was a cheese.

Beneath the tree's umbrageous limb
  A hungry fox sat smiling;
He saw the raven watching him,
  And spoke in words beguiling:
    "J'admire," said he, "ton beau plumage,"
    (The which was simply persiflage).

Two things there are, no doubt you know,
  To which a fox is used,—
A rooster that is bound to crow,
  A crow that's bound to roost,
    And whichsoever he espies
    He tells the most unblushing lies.

"Sweet fowl," he said, "I understand
  You're more than merely natty;
I hear you sing to beat the band
  And Adelina Patti.
    Pray render with your liquid tongue
    A bit from 'Gotterdammerung.' "

This subtle speech was aimed to please
  The crow, and it succeeded:
He thought no bird in all the trees
  Could sing as well as he did.
    In flattery completely doused,
    He gave the "Jewel Song" from "Faust."

But gravitation's law, of course,
  As Isaac Newton showed it,
Exerted on the cheese its force,
  And elsewhere soon bestowed it.
    In fact, there is no need to tell
    What happened when to earth it fell.

I blush to add that when the bird
  Took in the situation,
He said one brief, emphatic word,
  Unfit for publication.
    The fox was greatly startled, but
    He only sighed and answered "Tut!"

The moral is: A fox is bound
  To be a shameless sinner.
And also: When the cheese comes round
  You know it's after dinner.
    But (what is only known to few)
    The fox is after dinner, too

GUY WETMORE CARRYL, 1873 - 1904

FEBRUARY

"Pale is the February sky
And brief the mid-day's sunny hours . . ."

HASTE NOT! REST NOT!

Without haste! without rest!
Bind the motto to thy breast;
Bear it with thee as a spell;
Storm or sunshine, guard it well!
Haste not! Let no thoughtless deed
Mar for aye the spirit's speed!
Ponder well, and know the right,
Onward then, with all thy might!
Haste not! years can ne'er atone
For one reckless action done.
Rest not! Life is sweeping by,
Go and dare, before you die;
Something mighty and sublime
Leave behind to conquer time!
Haste not! rest not! calmly wait;
Meekly bear the storms of fate!
Duty be thy polar guide—
Do the right whate'er betide!

J. W. VON GOETHE, 1749 - 1832

While the word is yet unspoken, you are master of it; when once it is spoken, it is master of you.

ARAB PROVERB

Men show their characters in nothing more clearly than in what they think laughable.

J. VON GOETHE, 1749 - 1832

When the gods are angry with a man they give him what he asks for.

GREEK PROVERB.

William Temple, Archbishop of Canterbury, used to say that his mother once remarked: "William, you know more than I do, but I know so much better."

"AMID THE RUSH AND ROAR"

We are hungry for the old simplicities;
For the friendliness on which our parents fed,
For the long unhurried hours of quiet peace,
For neighborliness that was their daily bread,
For sympathy welling up at some heart's
  brink,
And for wayside pools of love at which to
  drink.

Let us find amid the rush and roar,
  somewhere,
The old simplicities that should be there.

For certain is death for the born,
And certain is birth for the dead,
Therefore over the inevitable
Thou shouldst not grieve.

BHAGAVAD GITA

It is necessary to hope, though hope should always be deluded; for hope itself is happiness, and its frustrations, however frequent, are yet less dreadful than its extinction.

SAMUEL JOHNSON, 1709 - 1784

Nobody knows the age of the human race, but all agree that it is old enough to know better.

"LET NOTHING DISTURB THEE"

Nothing affright thee;
All things are passing;
God never changeth;
Patient endurance
Attaineth to all things.
Who God possesseth
In nothing is wanting:
Alone God sufficeth.

HENRY WADSWORTH LONGFELLOW, 1807 - 1882

WHAT MAKES A SAINT?

Why were the saints saints?
Because they were cheerful when it was difficult to be cheerful; patient
    when it was difficult to be patient;
And because they pushed on when they wanted to stand still; and kept
    silent when they wanted to talk; and were agreeable when they
    wanted to be disagreeable.
That was all.
It was quite simple, and always will be.

IDENTITY

Somewhere—in desolate windswept space—
In Twilight land—in No-man's land—
Two hurrying Shapes met face to face,
And bade each other stand.

"And who are you?" cried one agape,
Shuddering in the gloaming light.
"I know not," said the second Shape,
"I only died last night!"

THOMAS BAILEY ALDRICH, 1836 - 1907

⚜

O youth foregone, foregoing!
O dreams unseen, unsought!
God give you joy of knowing
What life your death has bought.

BRIAN HOOKER 1919

Inscribed on tablet at Yale University commemorating over
200 Yale men who lost their lives in the World War.

⚜

TO AGE

Welcome, old friend! These many years
  Have we lived door by door;
The Fates have laid aside their shears
  Perhaps for some few more.

Rather what lies before my feet
  My notice shall engage:
He who hath braved Youth's dizzy heat
  Dreads not the frost of age.

WALTER SAVAGE LANDOR, 1775 - 1864

from the
RUBÁIYÁT OF OMAR KHAYYÁM

The Moving Finger writes; and, having writ,
Moves on: nor all your Piety nor Wit
  Shall lure it back to cancel half a Line,
Nor all your Tears wash out a Word of it.

Translated by EDWARD FITZGERALD

⚜

HIS EPITAPH
(made by author for himself)

Even such is Time, which takes in trust
Our youth, our joys, and all we have,
And pays us but with age and dust,
Who, in the dark and silent grave,
When we have wandered all our ways,
Shuts up the story of our days.
  Yet from this earth, and grave, and dust,
  The Lord shall raise me up I trust.

SIR WALTER RALEIGH, 1552 - 1618

Said to have been written the night
before he was beheaded.

THE MAN AND HIS GOOSE

A certain man had a Goose, which laid him a golden egg every day. But, not contented with this, which rather increased than abated his avarice, he was resolved to kill the Goose; and cut up her belly, so that he might come to the inexhaustible treasure which he fancied she had within her. He did so, and, to his great sorrow and disappointment, found nothing.

from AESOP'S FABLES

BUILDING THE BRIDGE

An old man, going a lone highway,
Came, at evening, cold and gray,
To a chasm, vast, and deep, and wide,
Thru which was flowing a sullen tide.
The old man crossed in the twilight dim:
The sullen stream had no fears to him;
But he turned, when safe on the other side,
And built a bridge to span the tide.
"Old man," said a fellow pilgrim, near,
"You are wasting strength with building
* here;*
Your journey will end with the ending day;
You never again must pass this way;
You have crossed the chasm, deep and
* wide—*
Why build you the bridge at the eventide?"
The builder lifted his old gray head:
"Good friend, in the path I have come," he
* said,*
"There followeth after me today
A youth, whose feet must pass this way.
This chasm, that has been naught to me,
To that fair-haired youth may a pitfall be.
He, too, must cross in the twilight dim;
Good friend, I am building the bridge for
* him."*

WILL ALLEN DROMGOOLE

GIVING

Blessed are those who can give without remembering, and take without forgetting.
ELIZABETH BIBESCO

As it is more blessed to give than receive, so it must be more blessed to receive than to give back.

ROBERT FROST, 1875 - 1963

Quoting an old Jewish proverb:
What you give for cause of charity in health is gold; what you give in sickness is silver; what you give after death is lead.
NATHAN STRAUS, 1848 - 1931

from Lines composed a few miles
above Tintern Abbey . . .

On that best portion of a good man's life, His little, nameless, unremembered acts of kindness and of love.
WILLIAM WORDSWORTH, 1770 - 1850

Some folks give their mite,
Others give with their mite,
And some don't give who might.

We hear a great deal about the Lord loving cheerful givers; we wonder where He finds them.

ED HOWE, 1875 - 1937

35

PERFECT WOMAN

She was a phantom of delight
When first she gleamed upon my sight;
A lovely apparition, sent
To be a moment's ornament;
Her eyes as stars of twilight fair;
Like twilight's, too, her dusky hair;
But all things else about her drawn
From May-time and the cheerful dawn;
A dancing shape, an image gay,
To haunt, to startle, and waylay.

I saw her upon nearer view,
A Spirit, yet a Woman too!
Her household motions light and free,
And steps of virgin liberty;
A countenance in which did meet
Sweet records, promises as sweet;
A creature not too bright or good
For human nature's daily food;
For transient sorrows, simple wiles,
Praise, blame, love, kisses, tears, and smiles.

And now I see with eye serene
The very pulse of the machine;
A being breathing thoughtful breath,
A traveller between life and death;
The reason firm, the temperate will,
Endurance, foresight, strength, and skill;
A perfect Woman, nobly planned,
To warn, to comfort, and command;
And yet a Spirit still, and bright
With something of angelic light.
                    WILLIAM WORDSWORTH, 1770 - 1850

❧

"SHE WALKS IN BEAUTY"

She walks in beauty, like the night
Of cloudless climes and starry skies;
And all that's best of dark and bright
Meet in her aspect and her eyes:
Thus mellowed to that tender light
Which heaven to gaudy day denies.

One shade the more, one ray the less,
Had half impaired the nameless grace
Which waves in every raven tress
Or softly lightens o'er her face;
Where thoughts serenely sweet express
How pure, how dear their dwelling-place.

And on that cheek, and o'er that brow
So soft, so calm, yet eloquent,
The smiles that win, the tints that glow,
But tell of days in goodness spent,
A mind at peace with all below,
A heart whose love is innocent!
                    GEORGE GORDON BYRON, 1788 - 1824

❧

WHAT ONE MAY AND MAY NOT CALL A WOMAN

You may call a woman a kitten, but you must not call her a cat.

You may call her a mouse, but you must not call her a rat.

You may call her a chicken, but you must not call her a hen,

You may call her a duck, but you must not call her a goose.

You may call her a vision, but you must not call her a sight.

❧

from a Letter to her husband,
John Adams, March 31, 1776:

In the new code of laws which I suppose it will be necessary for you to make I desire you would remember the ladies and be more generous and favorable to them than your ancestors.
                    ABIGAIL ADAMS, 1744 - 1818

❧

An intelligent woman is a woman with whom one can be as stupid as one wants.
                    PAUL VALERY, 1871 - 1945

Society would be delightful were all women married, and all men single.
                    EDGAR SALTUS, 1855 - 1921

MORNING

Will there really be a morning?
  Is there such a thing as day?
Could I see it from the mountains
  If I were as tall as they?

Has it feet like water lilies?
  Has it feathers like a bird?
Is it brought from famous countries
  Of which I have never heard?

Oh, some scholar! Oh, some sailor!
  Oh, some wise man from the skies!
Please to tell a little pilgrim
  Where the place called morning lies!
                              EMILY DICKINSON

ᏇᎳᎦ

It is better to light one candle than curse the darkness.
                    MOTTO OF THE CHRISTOPHER SOCIETY

ᏇᎳᎦ

Build a little fence of trust
  Around today;
Fill the space with loving work
  And therein stay;
Look not between the shelt'ring bars
  Upon tomorrow,
But take whatever comes to thee,
  Of joy or sorrow.
                       MARY E. BUTTS, 1836 - 1902

ᏇᎳᎦ

If you're looking for the secret of good health and long life, here's a bit of advice from the old Negro baseball pitcher, Satchel Paige:

"Avoid fried meats which angry up the blood.

"If your stomach disputes you, lie down and pacify it with cool thoughts.

"Keep the juices flowing by jangling around gently as you move.

"Go light, very light on the vices, such as carrying around in society. The social rumble ain't restful.

"Avoid running at all times.

"Don't look back. Something might be gaining on you."

EVENING SONG

Look off, dear Love, across the sallow sands,
  And mark yon meeting of the sun and sea,
How long they kiss in sight of all the lands,
  Ah! longer, longer, we.

Now in the sea's red vintage melts the sun,
  As Egypt's pearl dissolved in rosy wine,
And Cleopatra night drinks all. 'Tis done,
  Love, lay thine hand in mine.

Come forth, sweet stars, and comfort heaven's heart;
  Glimmer, ye waves, round else unlighted sands.
O night! divorce our sun and sky apart,
  Never our lips, our hands.
                        SIDNEY LANIER, 1842 - 1881

ᏇᎳᎦ

The most serious charge that can be brought against New England is not Puritanism but February.
                          JOSEPH WOOD KRUTCH

ᏇᎳᎦ

What I call a good patient is one who, having found a good physician, sticks to him 'till he dies.
                  OLIVER WENDELL HOLMES, 1809 - 1894

ᏇᎳᎦ

A CENTIPEDE

A centipede was happy quite,
Until a frog in fun
Said, "Pray, which leg comes after which?"
This raised her mind to such a pitch,
She lay distracted in the ditch,
Considering how to run.

* * *

The last and least of things
That soar on quivering wings,
Or crowd among the grass-blades out of sight,
Have just as clear a right
To their appointed portion of delight
As queens and kings.
                      CHRISTINA ROSSETTI, 1830 - 1894

from THE TRAILING ARBUTUS

I wandered lonely where the pine trees made
Against the bitter East their barricade,
  And, guided by its sweet
Perfume, I found, within a narrow dell,
The trailing spring flower tinted like a shell
  Amid dry leaves and mosses at my feet.

From under dead boughs, for whose loss the
    pines
Moaned ceaseless overhead, the blossoming
    vines
  Lifted their glad surprise,
While yet the bluebird smoothed in leafless
    trees
His feathers ruffled by the chill sea-breeze,
  And snow-drifts lingered under April skies.
          JOHN GREENLEAF WHITTIER, 1807 - 1892

❦

Some write for pleasure
Some write for fame,
But I write only
(to sign my name).

❦

Give to every other human being every
right that you claim for yourself.
          R. G. INGERSOLL, 1833 - 1899

❦

FABLE

The Mountain and the Squirrel
Had a quarrel,
And the former called the latter "Little
    Prig";
Bun replied,
"You are doubtless very big;
But all sorts of things and weather
Must be taken in together,
To make up a year
And a sphere.
And I think it no disgrace
To occupy my place.
If I'm not so large as you,
You are not so small as I,
And not half so spry.
I'll not deny you make
A very pretty squirrel track;
Talents differ; all is well and wisely put;
If I cannot carry forests on my back,
Neither can you crack a nut."
          RALPH WALDO EMERSON, 1803 - 1882

HEREDITY

When I look into a mirror,
Other eyes than mine
Pierce the image in the glass
With delicate design.

When I call my child at play,
(If I listen well)
I can hear another voice,
Haunting as a bell.

So the centuries unwind
With a ghostly art;
Other voices, other eyes,
Mesmerize my heart.
          ALICE HUNT TIMMONS, 1902 - 1959

❦

Heredity is transmitted by both parents;
many a girl is the picture of her father
and the sound track of her mother.

❦

"Where does she find them? —on being
told that a "lady" was "awfully kind to
her inferiors."

❦

The man who has nothing to boast of but
his illustrious ancestors is like a potato—
the only good belonging to him is under-
ground.
          SIR THOMAS OVERBURY, 1581 - 1613

❦

from DEMOCRACY IN AMERICA

Thus not only does democracy make
every man forget his ancestors, but it
hides his descendants and separates his
contemporaries from him; it throws him
back forever upon himself alone and
threatens in the end to confine him entirely within the solitude of his own
heart.
          ALEXIS DE TOCQUEVILLE, 1805 - 1859

❦

Democracy: Where everybody is somebody, then nobody is anybody.

❦

Democratic government can rise no
higher than the intelligence, purpose, and
conscience of the individual citizen.

A scoutmaster told his cub scouts to remember "that in the woods we are the guests of the animals and trees and plants." I like that!

A refined person is very careful of the house and furniture where he is being entertained. He handles objects with even more care than if they were his own. Likewise, as guests of God, we are courtesy-bound to conserve the resources of God's good earth, its forests, its soil, its oil, its water power, that we may leave to our posterity a land richer than we found. We . . . sometimes act as if our country's wealth was inexhaustible and also wholly our own. Not so! . . . "The earth is the Lord's and the fulness thereof." Let us not forget that basic truth.

RALPH W. SOCKMAN

❧

MY SYMPHONY

To live content with small means;
To seek elegance rather than luxury, and
*   refinement rather than fashion;*
To be worthy, not respectable, and wealthy,
*   not rich;*
To listen to stars and birds, babes and sages
*   with open heart;*
To study hard;
To think quietly, act frankly, talk gently,
*   await occasions, hurry never;*
In a word, to let the spiritual, unbidden and
*   unconscious, grow up thru the common—*
This is my symphony.

WILLIAM HENRY CHANNING, 1780 - 1842

I have from early age been strongly fortified by the philosophy taught me by my maternal grandmother . . . . Your color, she counseled, has nothing to do with your worth. You are potentially as good as anyone. How good you may prove to be will have no relation to your color, but with what is in your heart and your head. That is something which each individual by his own effort can control. The right to be treated as an equal by all other men, she said, is man's birthright. Set a goal for yourself and determine to reach it in spite of all obstacles.

RALPH J. BUNCHE
Under Secretary General for Special Political Affairs
United Nations

❧

SHE DWELT AMONG
THE UNTRODDEN WAYS

She dwelt among the untrodden ways
*   Beside the springs of Dove,*
A Maid whom there were none to praise
*   And very few to love:*

A violet by a mossy stone
*   Half hidden from the eye!*
—Fair as a star, when only one
*   Is shining in the sky.*

She lived unknown, and few could know
*   When Lucy ceased to be;*
But she is in her grave, and, oh,
*   The difference to me!*

WILLIAM WORDSWORTH, 1770 - 1850

from THE SANSCRIT

Look to this day, for it is life; the very life of life. In its brief course lie all the verities and realities of your existence; the bliss of growth, the glory of action, the splendor of beauty. For yesterday is but a dream, and tomorrow is only a vision; but today, well lived, makes every yesterday a dream of happiness and every tomorrow a vision of hope. Look well, therefore, to this day, such is the salutation of the dawn.

GOLDEN KEYS

A bunch of golden keys is mine
To make each day with gladness shine.

"Good morning" is the golden key
That unlocks every day for me.

When at the table, "If you please"
I take from off my bunch of keys.

When friends give anything to me
I use my little "Thank you" key.

"Excuse me"—"Beg your pardon" too
If by some mistake some harm I do.

When evening comes, "Goodnight," I say
And close the door of each glad day.

With a golden ring these keys I bind
This motto—"Be ye kind."

I'll often use each golden key
And then a child polite I'll be.

I'd Rather have Fingers than Toes;
I'd Rather have Ears than a Nose;
And As for my Hair,
I'm Glad it's All There;
I'll be Awfully Sad, when it Goes!

I am only one,
But still I am one.
I cannot do everything.
But still I can do something:
And because I cannot do everything
I will not refuse to do the something that
*   I can do.*

EDWARD EVERETT HALE, 1822 - 1909

The American people have a right to bitter complaint over . . . disclosures of dishonor in high places. . . . Dishonor in public life has a double poison. When people are dishonorable in private business, they injure only those with whom they deal or their own chances in the next world. But when there is a lack of honor in government, the morals of the whole people are poisoned.

The drip of such poisons may have nothing to do with dishonor in some college athletics or the occasional policeman on the beat. But the rules of the game have been loosened somewhere. . . . No public man can be just a little crooked. There is no such thing as a no-man's-land between honesty and dishonesty. Our strength is not in politics, prices or production . . . . Our strength lies in spiritual concepts. It lies in public sensitiveness to evil . . . .

Our greatest danger is not from invasion by foreign armies. Our dangers are that we may commit suicide from within by complaisance with evil. Or by public tolerance of scandalous behavior. Or by cynical acceptance of dishonor. These evils have defeated nations many times in human history. The redemption of mankind by America will depend upon our ability to cope with these evils right here at home.

HERBERT HOOVER, 1874 - 1964

I would rather that the people should wonder why I wasn't president than why I am.

SALMON P. CHASE, 1803 - 1873

No race can prosper until it learns that there is as much dignity in tilling a field as in writing a poem.

BOOKER T. WASHINGTON, 1858 - 1915

The world is a looking-glass, and gives back to every man the reflection of his own face. Frown at it, and it in turn will look sourly upon you; laugh at it and with it, and it is a jolly, kind companion.

WILLIAM MAKEPEACE THACKERAY, 1811 - 1863

TO ANNE

How many kisses do I ask?
Now you set me to my task.
First, sweet Anne, will you tell me
How many waves are in the sea?
How many stars are in the sky?
How many lovers you make sigh?
How many sands are on the shore?
I shall want just one kiss more.

WILLIAM STIRLING MAXWELL, 1818 - 1878

Before "hard roads" in the United States and when mud was a constant problem of transportation, they tell of a traveller who saw a hat in the middle of the road. He plodded out to get it, and found a man beneath. When he offered his help, the man under the hat replied, "Don't bother Mister, I have a good horse under me, and has just found bottom."

From Saint Brigid's Day, February 2nd; to St. Patrick's Day, every alternate day is grand and fine; from then on, every day is fine.

IRISH PROVERB

from A HEALTH

I fill this cup to one made up of loveliness alone, A woman, of her gentle sex the seeming paragon; To whom the better elements and kindly stars have given a form so fair, that, like the air, 'tis less of earth than heaven. Her health! and would on earth there stood some more of such a frame, That life might be all poetry, and weariness a name.

EDWARD COOTE PINKNEY, 1802 - 1828

FEBRUARY

Yet February suns uncertain shine,
For rain and frost alternately combine
To stop the plow, with sudden wintry
*   storms—*
And often fearful violence the month
*   deforms.*

EDMUND SPENSER, 1552? - 1599

FOUR-LEAF CLOVERS

I know a place where the sun is like gold,
*   And the cherry blooms burst with snow;*
And down underneath is the loveliest nook,
*   Where the four-leaf clovers grow.*

One leaf is for hope, and one is for faith,
*   And one is for love, you know,*
But God put another in for luck—
*   If you search, you will find where they*
*   grow.*

But you must have hope, and you must have
*   faith,*
*   You must love and be strong, and so,*
If you work, if you wait, you will find the
*   place*
*   Where the four-leaf clovers grow.*

ELLA HIGGINSON

GROUNDHOG DAY LEGEND

American legend tells that if the groundhog comes out of his winter's hole and sees his shadow on February 2, (Groundhog Day), he will go back and sleep for six more cold weeks. But if the day is cloudy and shadowless, the groundhog will stay out, anticipating an early spring. This stems from an old European belief that a sunshiny Candlemas Day (Feb. 2) means six more weeks of winter weather.

As far as the sun shines out on Candlemas
*   Day,*
So far will the snow blow in before May;
As far as the snow blows in on
*   Candlemas Day,*
So far will the sun shine out before May.

41

THE ETERNAL STRUGGLE

...It is the eternal struggle between these two principles—right and wrong—throughout the world. They are the two principles that have stood face to face from the beginning of time and will ever continue to struggle. The one is the common right of humanity, and the other the divine right of kings. It is the same principle in whatever shape it develops itself. It is the same spirit that says, "You toil and work and earn bread, and I will eat it." No matter in what shape it comes, whether from the mouth of a king who seeks to bestride the people of his own nation and live from the fruit of their labor, or from one race of men as an apology for enslaving another race, it is the same tyrannical principle.

ABRAHAM LINCOLN
From The Lincoln-Douglas Debates (1858)

GENERAL COMMENTS ON GRANT

If I knew what brand of whiskey he drinks I would send a barrel or so to some other generals... I can't spare this man; he fights. ..When Grant gets possession of a place, he holds on to it as if he had inherited it.

ABRAHAM LINCOLN

O CAPTAIN! MY CAPTAIN!
(In memory of Abraham Lincoln)

O Captain! my Captain! our fearful trip is
  done,
The ship has weather'd every rack, the prize
  we sought is won,
The port is near, the bells I hear, the people
  all exulting,
While follow eyes the steady keel, the vessel
  grim and daring;
    But O heart! heart! heart!
      O the bleeding drops of red,
    Where on the deck my Captain lies,
      Fallen cold and dead.

O Captain! my Captain! rise up and hear the
  bells;
Rise up—for you the flag is flung—for you
  the bugle trills,
    For you bouquets and ribbon'd wreaths
      —for you the shores acrowding,
    For you they call, the swaying mass,
      their eager faces turning;
      Here Captain! dear father!
        This arm beneath your head!
        It is some dream that on the deck,
          You've fallen cold and dead.

My Captain does not answer, his lips are pale
  and still
My father does not feel my arm, he has no
  pulse nor will
The ship is anchor'd safe and sound, its
  voyage closed and done,
From fearful trip the victor ship comes in
  with object won;
      Exult O shores, and ring O bells!
        But I with mournful tread,
      Walk the deck my Captain lies,
        Fallen cold and dead.

WALT WHITMAN, 1819 - 1892

REVERENCE FOR LAWS

Let reverence for the laws be breathed by every American mother to the lisping babe that prattles on her lap; let it be taught in schools, in seminaries, and in colleges; let it be written in primers, spelling-books, and in almanacs; let it be preached from the pulpit, proclaimed in legislative halls, and enforced in courts of justice. And, in short, let it become the political religion of the nation; and let the old and the young, the rich and the poor, the grave and the gay of all sexes and tongues and colors and conditions, sacrifice unceasingly upon its altars.

ABRAHAM LINCOLN

When I see the elaborate study and in-
genuity displayed by women in the pursuit of trifles, I feel no doubt of their
capacity for the most herculean undertak-
ings.

JULIA WARD HOWE, 1819 - 1910

The wheel that squeaks the loudest is the
one that gets the grease.
HENRY WHEELER SHAW, (Josh Billings), 1818 - 1885

Of all human powers operating on the
affairs of mankind, none is greater than
that of competition.

HENRY CLAY, 1777 - 1852
American lawyer and statesman

LIFE OF A COUNTER MAN

*I work behind the counter
In an automotive store.
Sometimes I'm called a "genius"
Sometimes I'm called much more*

*I claim I'm no mechanic
Yet when the job goes sick
The mechanic comes and asks me
What makes the damn thing tick.*

*I'm supposed to know the numbers
Of bolts and nuts and gears
For every car that was ever made
For more than forty years.*

*I'm an engineer and machinist
And what not, Ah my Lord,
I'm supposed to be an Edison
Combined with Henry Ford.*

*But life would be a pleasure
And I'd grin from ear to ear
If the customer would tell me
The MODEL, MAKE and YEAR.*

Pasted over the counter in an auto parts store!
Coshocton, Ohio

THE COUNTRY STORE

*It filled the corner where the crossroads
  meet
A hitching rail once stood beside the door,
An old pot bellied stove to warm the feet
A black coal hod to keep the trash from the
  floor
Here neighbors used to gather every night
They sat on sturdy chairs with tilted legs;
Here every man could feed his appetite
For news and wait for sorting of his eggs
This was the meeting place of country men
They waded mud or plowed through winter
  snow
To purchase from the stock they offered
  then
Of flour, nails and bright sprigged calico
The store is gone but I recall the time
When I could buy all Heaven for a dime.*

A man needed a gardener and received a
letter concerning a man named Jones. The
writer said that Jones had an excellent
knowledge of gardening. He can make
either vegetable or flower gardens bloom!
And he told other admirable attributes of
Jones. "That's just the man I need,"
thought the man who needed a gardener.
He reached the end of the page, and
turned to the next one. On it was written
just three words — "But he won't!"

PLAN FOR REGULATING
MY FUTURE CONDUCT

Those who write of the art of poetry teach us that if we would write what may be worth the reading, we ought always, before we begin, to form a regular plan and design of our piece: otherwise, we shall be in danger of incongruity. I am apt to think it is the same as to life. I have never fixed a regular design in life; by which means it has been a confused variety of different scenes. I am now entering upon a new one: let me, therefore, make some resolutions, and form some scheme of action, that, henceforth, I may live in all respects like a rational creature.

1. It is necessary for me to be extremely frugal for some time, till I have paid what I owe.

2. To endeavour to speak truth in every instance; to give nobody expectations that are not likely to be answered, but aim at sincerity in every word and action—the most amiable excellence in a rational being.

3. To apply myself industriously to whatever business I take in hand, and not divert my mind from my business by any foolish project of growing suddenly rich; for industry and patience are the surest means of plenty.

4. I resolve to speak ill of no man whatever, not even in a matter of truth; but rather by some means excuse the faults I hear charged upon others, and upon proper occasions speak all the good I know of everybody.

BENJAMIN FRANKLIN, 1706 - 1790

BENJAMIN FRANKLIN'S TOMBSTONE
IN PHILADELPHIA CHURCHYARD

The Body of
B. Franklin,
Printer;
Like the Cover of an old Book,
Its Contents torn out,
And stript of its Lettering and Gilding,
Lies here, Food for Worms.
But the Work shall not be wholly lost:
For it will, as he believ'd, appear once more,
In a new & more perfect Edition,
Corrected and amended
By the Author.
He was born Jan. 6. 1706.
Died 17.....

Written by Franklin as his epitaph 62 years before his death. He died at age 84, April 17, 1790

THE SAYINGS OF POOR RICHARD

"Early to bed and early to rise,
Makes a man healthy, wealthy, and wise."
"Eat to live, and not live to eat."
"He that spills the Rum loses that only;
He that drinks it, often loses both that and himself"

ON FINANCES

Beware of little expenses, a small leak will sink a ship.

He that buys upon credit pays interest upon what he buys.

Consider then when you are tempted to buy unnecessary household stuff, or any superfluous thing, whether you w'l be willing to pay interest, and interest upon interest for it as long as you live; and more if it grows worse by using.

ON MARRIAGE

Keep your eyes wide open before marriage, half shut afterwards.

He that takes a wife takes care.

ON EDUCATION

I am persuaded we are fully able to furnish our colleges amply with every means of public instruction, and I cannot but wonder that our legislatures have generally paid so little attention to a business of so great importance.

Letter from Benjamin Franklin to John Witherspoon

THE MEN THAT DON'T FIT IN

There's a race of men that don't fit in,
A race that can't stay still;
So they break the hearts of kith and kin,
And they roam the world at will.
They range the field and they rove the flood,
And they climb the mountain's crest;
Theirs is the curse of the gypsy blood,
And they don't know how to rest.

If they just went straight they might go far;
They are strong and brave and true;
But they're always tired of the things that
are,
And they want the strange and new.
They say: "Could I find my proper groove,
What a deep mark I would make!"
So they chop and change, and each fresh
move
Is only a fresh mistake.

And each forgets, as he strips and runs
With a brilliant, fitful pace,
It's the steady, quiet, plodding ones
Who win in the lifelong race.
And each forgets that his youth has fled,
Forgets that his prime is past,
Till he stands one day, with a hope that's
dead,
In the glare of the truth at last.

He has failed, he has failed; he has missed
his chance;
He has just done things by half.
Life's been a jolly good joke on him,
and now is the time to laugh.
Ha, ha! He is one of the Legion Lost;
He was never meant to win;
He's a rolling stone, and it's bred in the bone;
He's a man who won't fit in.

ROBERT W. SERVICE, 1874 - 1958

THE POET'S SIMPLE FAITH

You say, "Where goest Thou?" I cannot tell,
And still go on. But if the way be straight
I cannot go amiss: before me lies
Dawn and-the day: the night behind me: that
Suffices me: I break the bounds: I see,
And nothing more; believe and nothing less.
My future is not one of my concerns.

VICTOR HUGO, 1802 - 1885

THE UNIVERSAL LANGUAGE

The wise men ask, "What language did Christ
speak?"
They cavil, argue, search, and little prove,
O Sages, leave your Syriac and your Greek!
Christ spoke the universal language—love.

ELLA WHEELER WILCOX, 1855 - 1919

Prejudices, it is well known, are most difficult to eradicate from the heart whose soil has never been loosened or fertilized by education; they grow there, firm as weeds among stones.

CHARLOTTE BRONTE, 1816 - 1855

There are two ways of being happy: We may either diminish our wants or augment our means—either will do—the result is the same; and it is for each man to decide for himself, and do that which happens to be the easiest.

If you are idle or sick or poor, however hard it may be to diminish your wants, it will be harder to augment your means.

If you are active and prosperous or young or in good health, it may be easier for you to augment your means than to diminish your wants.

But if you are wise, you will do both at the same time, young or old, rich or poor, sick or well; and if you are very wise you will do both in such a way as to augment the general happiness of society.

BENJAMIN FRANKLIN, 1706 - 1790

TOO CANDID BY HALF

As Tom and his wife were discoursing one
*   day*
Of their several faults in a bantering way,
*   Said she, "Though my wit you disparage,*
I'm sure, my dear husband, our friends will
*   attest*
This much, at the least, that my judgment is
*   best."*
*   Quoth Tom, "So they said at our marriage."*

JOHN GODFREY SAXE, 1816 - 1887

TO LUCASTA, ON GOING TO THE WARS

Tell me not, Sweet, I am unkind
*   That from the nunnery*
Of thy chaste breast and quiet mind,
*   To war and arms I fly.*

True, a new mistress now I chase,
*   The first foe in the field;*
And with a stronger faith embrace
*   A sword, a horse, a shield.*

*   Yet this inconstancy is such*
*   As you too shall adore;*
*   I could not love thee, dear, so much,*
*   Loved I not honor more.*

RICHARD LOVELACE 1618 - 1658

KISSIN'

Some say kissin's ae sin,
*   But I say, not at a';*
For it's been in the warld
*   Ever sin' there were twa.*
If it werena lawfu',
*   Lawyers wadna' low it;*
If it werena haly,
*   Meenisters wadna' dae it;*
If it werena modest,
*   Maidens wadna' taste it;*
If it werena plenty,
*   Puir folk couldna' hae it.*

First it rained, and then it snew,
Then it friz, and then it thew,
And then it friz again.

TO MY VALENTINE

The rose is red, the violet's blue,
*   The honey's sweet, and so are you.*
Thou art my love and I am thine;
*   I drew thee to my Valentine.*
The lot was cast and then I drew,
*   And fortune said it should be you.*

A love song is just a caress set to music.

SIGMUND ROMBERG, 1887 - 1951

Many a man has fallen in love with a
girl in a light so dim he would not have
chosen a suit by it.

MAURICE CHEVALIER

I LOVED THEE

I loved thee, beautiful and kind,
*   And plighted an eternal vow;*
So alter'd are they face and mind,
*   'Twere perjury to love thee now.*

ROBERT EARL NUGENT, 1709 - 1788

To write a love letter, we must begin
without knowing what we intend to say,
and end without knowing what we have
written.

JEAN JACQUES ROUSSEAU, 1712 - 1788

WASHINGTON TO LAFAYETTE

From one of the first letters written by George Washington on his return to Mount Vernon to take up his old life of a Virginia planter, to his good friend, the Marquis de la Lafayette after Christmas 1788.

* * *

"At length, my dear Marquis, I am become a private citizen on the banks of the Potomac, and under the shadow of my own vine and my own fig tree. Free from the bustle of a camp and the busy scenes of public life, I am solacing myself with those tranquil enjoyments of which the soldier who is ever in pursuit of fame; the statesman whose watchful days and sleepless nights are spent in devising schemes to promote the welfare of his own, perhaps the ruin of other countries (as if this globe was insufficient for us all); and the courtier who is always watching the countenance of his prince, in hopes of catching a gracious smile, can have very little conception. I am not only retired from all public employments, but I am retiring within myself, and shall be able to view the solitary walk and tread the paths of private life with heartfelt satisfaction. Envious of none, I am determined to be pleased with all, and this, my dear friend, being the order for my march, I will move gently down the stream of life until I sleep with my fathers."

from MORAL MAXIMS

Few men have virtue to withstand the highest bidder.

To persevere in one's duty and be silent is the best answer to calumny.

Truth will ultimately prevail where there is pains taken to bring it to light.

GEORGE WASHINGTON, 1732 - 1799

Liberty is always dangerous, but it is the safest thing we have.

HARRY EMERSON FOSDICK, 1878 - 1969

Men hate each other because they fear each other; they fear each other because they don't know each other; they don't know each other because they are separated from each other.

MARTIN LUTHER KING, JR., 1929 - 1968

AFFURISMS

A sekret ceases tew be a sekret if it iz once confided—it is like a dollar bill, once broken, it iz never a dollar agin.

JOSH BILLINGS [HENRY WHEELER SHAW], 1818 - 1885

from
THE TWENTY-SECOND OF FEBRUARY

Pale is the February sky,
  And brief the mid-day's sunny hours;
The wind-swept forest seems to sigh
  For the sweet time of leaves and flowers.

Yet has no month a prouder day,
  Not even when the summer broods
O'er meadows in their fresh array,
  Or autumn tints the glowing woods.

For this chill season now again
  Brings, in its annual round, the morn
When, greatest of the sons of men,
  Our glorious Washington was born.

WILLIAM CULLEN BRYANT, 1794 - 1878

from TABLE TALK

There are three classes into which all elderly women that I ever knew were to be divided; first, that dear old soul; second, that old woman; third that old witch.

SAMUEL T. COLERIDGE, 1772 - 1834

TREASURE

They call thee rich; I deem thee poor;
Since, if thou darest not use thy store,
But savest only for thine heirs,
The treasure is not thine, but theirs.

LUCILLIUS, 180 - 103 B.C.
Translated by William Cowper, 1731 - 1800

❧

from SONG ON WEDLOCK

Phyllis, 'tis true thy glass does run,
    But since mine too keeps equal pace,
My silver hair may trouble thee,
    As much as me thy ruined face.

THOMAS FLATMAN, 1637 - 1688

❧

WISE OLD OWL

There was an old owl who lived in an oak,
    The more he saw, the less he spoke,
The less he spoke, the more he heard,
    Why can't we be like that wise old bird?

Motto over Calvin Coolidge's fireplace, often quoted by
John D. Rockefeller, Jr.

TO A SNOW-FLAKE

What heart could have thought you?—
Past our devisal
(O filigree petal!)
Fashioned so purely,
Fragilely, surely,
From what Paradisal
Imagineless metal,
Too costly for cost?
Who hammered you, wrought you,
From argentine vapor?—
"God was my shaper.
Passing surmisal,
He hammered, He wrought me,
From curled silver vapor,
To lust of His mind:—
Thou couldst not have thought me!
So purely, so palely,
Tinily, surely,
Mightily, frailly,
Insculped and embossed,
With His hammer of wind,
And His graver of frost."

FRANCIS THOMPSON, 1859? - 1907

❧

ON AN OLD WOMAN

Mycilla dyes her locks, 'tis said,
    But 'tis a foul aspersion;
She buys them black, they therefore need
    No subsequent immersion.

LUCILLIUS, 180 - 103 B.C.
Translated by William Cowper, 1731 - 1800

❧

Neither snow, nor rain, nor heat, nor
gloom of night stays these couriers from
the swift completion of their appointed
rounds.

Inscription on the Main Post Office, New York City,
adapted from Herodotus.

Sunshine is delicious, rain is refreshing,
wind braces us up, snow is exhilarating;
there is really no such thing as bad
weather, only different kinds of good
weather.

JOHN RUSKIN, 1814 - 1900

THE CALF-PATH

One day, thru the primeval wood,
A calf walked home, as good calves should;
But made a trail all bent askew,
A crooked trail as all calves do.

Since then two hundred years have fled,
And, I infer, the calf is dead.
But still he left behind his trail,
And thereby hangs my moral tale.

The trail was taken up next day
By a lone dog that passed that way;
And then a wise bellwether sheep
Pursued the trail o'er vale and steep,
And drew the flock behind him, too,
As good bellwethers always do.

And from that day, o'er hill and glade,
Thru those old woods a path was made;
And many men wound in and out,
And dodged, and turned, and bent about
And uttered words of righteous wrath
Because 'twas such a crooked path.

But still they followed—do not laugh—
The first migrations of that calf,
And thru this winding wood-way stalked,
Because he wobbled when he walked.

This forest path became a lane,
That bent, and turned, and turned again
This crooked lane became a road,
Where many a poor horse with his load
Toiled on beneath the burning sun,
And traveled some three miles in one.
And thus a century and a half
They trod the footsteps of that calf.

The years passed on in swiftness fleet,
The road became a village street;
And this, before men were aware,
A city's crowded thorofare;
And soon the central street was this
Of a renowned metropolis;
And men two centuries and a half
Trod in the footsteps of that calf.

Each day a hundred thousand rout
Followed the zigzag calf about;
And o'er his crooked journey went
The traffic of a continent.
A hundred thousand men were led
By one calf near three centuries dead:
They followed still his crooked way,
And lost one hundred years a day;
For thus such reverence is lent
To well-established precedent.

A moral lesson this might teach,
Were I ordained and called to preach;
For men are prone to go it blind
Along the calf-paths of the mind,
And work away from sun to sun
To do what other men have done.

They follow in the beaten track,
And out and in, and forth and back,
And still their devious course pursue,
To keep the path that others do.

But how the wise old woods-gods laugh,
Who saw the first primeval calf!
Ah! many things this tale might teach,—
But I am not ordained to preach.

                    SAM WALTER FOSS, 1858 - 1911

THE SECRET

We have a secret, just we three,
The robin, and I, and the sweet cherry tree;
The bird told the tree, and the tree told me,
And nobody knows it but just us three.

But of course the robin knows it best,
Because he built the—I shan't tell the rest;
And laid the four little—somethings—in it—
I'm afraid I shall tell it every minute.

But if the tree and the robin don't peep,
I'll try my best the secret to keep;
Tho I know when the little birds fly about
Then the whole secret will be out.

HOW TO BE HAPPY

Are you almost disgusted with life, little
    man?
    I'll tell you a wonderful trick
That will bring you contentment, if anything
    can,
    Do something for somebody, quick!

Are you awfully tired with play, little girl?
    Wearied discouraged, and sick—
I'll tell you the loveliest game in the world,
    Do something for somebody, quick!

Though, it rains, like the rain of the flood,
    little man,
    And the clouds are forbidding and thick,
You can make the sun shine in your soul,
    little man,
    Do something for somebody, quick!

Though the stars are like brass overhead,
    little girl,
    And the walks like a well-heated brick,
And our earthly affairs in a terrible whirl,
    Do something for somebody, quick!

What can't be cured
Must be endured.

HORSE SENSE

A horse can't pull while kicking.
    This fact I merely mention.
And he can't kick while pulling,
    Which is my chief contention.

Let's imitate the good old horse
    And lead a life that's fitting;
Just pull an honest load, and then
    There'll be no time for kicking.

GET A TRANSFER

If you are on the Gloomy Line,
    Get a transfer.
If you're inclined to fret and pine,
    Get a transfer.
Get off the track of doubt and gloom,
Get on the Sunshine Track—there's room—
    Get a transfer.

If you're on the Grouchy Track,
    Get a transfer.
Just take a Happy Special back,
    Get a transfer.
Jump on the train and pull the rope,
That lands you at the station Hope—
    Get a transfer.

UP-HILL

Does the road wind up-hill all the way?
    Yes, to the very end.
Will the day's journey take the whole long
    day?
    From morn to night, my friend.

But is there for the night a resting-place?
    A roof for when the slow dark hours
    begin.
May not the darkness hide it from my face?
    You cannot miss that inn.

Shall I meet other way-farers at night?
    Those who have gone before.
Then must I knock, or call when just in
    sight?
    They will not keep you standing at that
    door.

Shall I find comfort, travel-sore and weak?
    Of labour you shall find the sum.
Will there be beds for me and all who seek?
    Yea, beds for all who come.

CHRISTINA GEORGINA ROSSETTI, 1830 - 1894

50

MARCH

"Now are the winds about us in their glee,
March cometh from afar . ."

A KITE

I often sit and wish that I
Could be a kite up in the sky,
And ride upon the breeze and go
Whichever way I chanced to blow.

❧

Early Romans began their year with the spring, and their first month was named Martius after Mars, their God of War. The name we call this month now is March.

❧

Whosoever has a mind that is free, may go forth to the fields and to the woods, inhaling joyous renovation from the breath of Spring, or catching from the odours and sounds of Autumn some diviner mood of sweetest sadness, which improves the softened heart.

PERCY BYSSHE SHELLEY, 1792 - 1822

❧

"NO ONE CAN TAKE IT FROM YOU"

You wake up in the morning, and lo! your purse is magically filled with twenty-four hours of the magic tissue of the universe of your life. No one can take it from you. No one receives either more or less than you receive. Waste your infinitely precious commodity as much as you will, and the supply will never be withheld from you. Moreover, you cannot draw on the future. Impossible to get into debt. You can only waste the passing moment. You cannot waste ton.orrow; it is kept for you.

ARNOLD BENNETT, 1867 - 1931

When Clarence Darrow was a young attorney, an opponent referred to him as "A beardless youth." Darrow replied with a story. The King of Spain once dispatched a youthful nobleman to a court of a neighboring king who received the visitor with the objection "Does the King of Spain lack men, that he sends me a beardless boy?" The ambassador replied, "Sir, if my King had supposed you imputed wisdom to a beard he would have sent you a goat."

❧

PATRICK HENRY

The Second Virginia Convention met March 20, 1775 in Richmond in the plain white frame structure of St. John's Church, still standing. Patrick Henry offered three resolutions establishing a militia for defense. In defending them, Patrick Henry speaking softly and calmly rose to great heights: "Is life so dear, or peace so sweet as to be purchased at the price of chains and slavery? Forbid it, Almighty God! I know not what course others may take. But as for me—give me liberty, or give me death!" He finished by a blow to his left breast which seemed to drive a dagger into his patriotic heart.

❧

The best thing to give to your enemy is forgiveness; to an opponent, tolerance; to a friend, your heart; to your child, a good example, to a father, deference; to your mother, conduct that will make her proud of you; to yourself, respect; to all men, charity.

ARTHUR JAMES, LORD BALFOUR, 1848 - 1930

AMERICAN PLAN

Put the baby's bottle on
Two o'clock is here and gone!
Two and six and ten and two!
How so small a boy can do
Such a lot of eating, and
Live, I cannot understand.

Hurry, put the bottle on.
Six o'clock is here and gone!
Six and ten and two and six!
All that atom does is mix
Hours of milk with hours of deep,
Unimaginative sleep.

Time to put the bottle on,
Ten o'clock is here and gone!
Ten and two and six and ten!
Put the bottle on again.
Let another table d'hote
Trickle down his eager throat.

Why a greedy brat should be
So disarming puzzles me.
                    MARGARET FISHBACK

Of all the joys that lighten suffering earth, what joy is welcomed like a new-born child?

CAROLINE NORTON, 1808 - 1877

Every mother has the *most* beautiful baby.

Out of the mouth of babes—comes cereal.

CHARLEY'S OPINION OF THE BABY

Muzzer's bought a baby,
  Ittle bit's of zing;
Zink I mos could put him
  Froo my rubber ring.

Ain't he uwful ugly?
  Ain't he awful pink?
Jus come down from Heaven,
  Dat's a fib, I zink.

Doctor told anozzer
  Great big awful lie;
Nose ain't out of joyent,
  Dat ain't why I cry.

Zink I ought to love him!
  No, I won't! so zere;
Nassy, crying baby,
  Ain't got any hair.

Send me off wiz Biddy
  Every single day;
'Be a good boy, Charlie,
  Run away and play."

Dot all my nice kisses,
  Dot my place in bed;
Mean to take my drumstick
  And beat him on ze head.

NO BABY IN THE HOUSE

No baby in the house, I know,
  'Tis far too nice and clean.
No toys, by careless fingers strewn,
  Upon the floors are seen.
No finger-marks are on the panes,
  No scratches on the chairs;
No wooden men set up in rows,
  Or marshaled off in pairs;
No little stockings to be darned,
  All ragged at the toes;
No pile of mending to be done,
  Made up of baby-clothes;
No little troubles to be soothed;
  No little hands to fold;
No grimy fingers to be washed;
  No stories to be told;
No tender kisses to be given,
  No nicknames, "Dove" and "Mouse"
No merry frolics after ten,—
  No baby in the house!

CLARA DOLLIVER

GOING DOWN HILL ON A BICYCLE
A Boy's Song

With lifted feet, hands still,
I am poised, and down the hill
Dart, with heedful mind;
The air goes by in a wind.

Swifter and yet more swift,
Till the heart with a mighty lift
Makes the lungs laugh, the throat cry:—
"O bird, see; see, bird, I fly.

"Is this, is this your joy?
O bird, then I, though a boy,
For a golden moment share
Your feathery life in air!"

Say, heart, is there aught like this
In a world that is full of bliss?
'Tis more than skating, bound
Steel-shod to the level ground.

Speed slackens now, I float
Awhile in my airy boat;
Till, when the wheels scarce crawl,
My feet to the treadles fall.

Alas, that the longest hill
Must end in a vale; but still,
Who climbs with toil, wheresoe'er,
Shall find wings waiting there.

HENRY CHARLES BEECHING, 1859 - 1919

Cornelia, wife of Sempronius Gracchus, presented her sons to a lady who had been displaying her jewels and asking Cornelia about hers.

Pointing to such, well might Cornelia say,
When the rich casket shone in bright array, "These are my jewels!"

from Human Life   SAMUEL ROGERS, 1763 - 1855

THE LION AND THE MOUSE

A lion with the heat oppressed,
One day composed himself to rest:
But while he dozed as he intended,
A mouse, his royal back ascended;
Nor thought of harm, as Aesop tells,
Mistaking him for someone else;
And travelled over him, and round him,
And might have left him as she found him
Had she not—tremble when you hear—
Tried to explore the monarch's ear!
Who straightway woke, with wrath immense,
And shook his head to cast her thence.
"You rascal, what are you about?"
Said he, when he had turned her out,
"I'll teach you soon," the lion said,
"To make a mouse-hole in my head!"
So saying, he prepared his foot
To crush the trembling tiny brute;
But she (the mouse) with tearful eye,
Implored the lion's clemency,
Who thought it best at last to give
His little prisoner a reprieve.

'Twas nearly twelve months after this,
The lion chanced his way to miss;
When pressing forward, heedless yet,
He got entangled in a net.
With dreadful rage, he stamped and tore,
And straight commenced a lordly roar;
When the poor mouse, who heard the noise,
Attended, for she knew his voice.
Then what the lion's utmost strength
Could not effect, she did at length;
With patient labor she applied
Her teeth, the network to divide;
And so at last forth issued he,
A lion, by a mouse set free.

Few are so small or weak, I guess,
But may assist us in distress,
Nor shall we ever, if we're wise,
The meanest, or the least despise.

JEFFREYS TAYLOR, 1792 - 1853

PARABLE OF THE ISMS

Socialism:If you have two cows, you give one to your neighbor.

Communism:If you have two cows, you give them to the government and then the government gives you some milk.

Fascism:If you have two cows, you keep the cows and give the milk to the government; then the government sells you some milk.

New Dealism:If you have two cows, you shoot one and milk the other; then you pour the milk down the drain.

Nazism:If you have two cows, the government shoots you and keeps the cows.

Capitalism:If you have two cows, you sell one and buy a bull.

❦

American ends in "I can."

❦

If time be of all things most precious, wasting time must be the greatest prodigality, since lost time is never found again; and what we call time enough always proves little enough. Let us then be up and doing, and doing to a purpose; so by diligence shall we do more with less perplexity.

BENJAMIN FRANKLIN, 1706 - 1790

from MY SUMMER IN A GARDEN

What a man needs in gardening is a cast-iron back, with a hinge in it.

CHARLES DUDLEY WARNER, 1829 - 1900

❦

It is the lofty pine that by the storm
Is oftener tossed; towers fall with heavier
crash
Which higher soar.

HORACE, 65'- 8 B.C.

❦

For every neighbor who tries to keep up with the Joneses, there's another neighbor who thinks what the Joneses have is not good enough for her.

❦

The poor benighted Hinddo,
He does the best he kindo;
He sticks to caste
From the first to last;
For pants he makes his skindo.

❦

He who slings mud generally loses ground.

ADLAI STEVENSON, 1900 - 1965

from AESOP'S FABLES

A Lion used to prowl about a field in which Four Oxen used to dwell .. Whenever he came near they turned their tails to one another .. and he was met by the horns of one of them. At last, however, they fell quarrelling among themselves, and each went off to pasture alone .. Then the Lion attacked them one by one, and soon made an end of all four. UNITED WE STAND, DIVIDED WE FALL.

Aesop circa 6th century B.C.

LINCOLN'S SECOND INAUGURAL ADDRESS

Fellow-countrymen: At this second appearing to take the oath of the presidential office, there is less occasion for an extended address than there was at first. Then a statement, somewhat in detail, of a course to be pursued seemed very fitting and proper. Now, at the expiration of four years, during which public declarations have been constantly called forth on every point and phase of the great contest which still absorbs the attention and engrosses the energies of the nation, little that is new could be presented.

The progress of our arms, upon which all else chiefly depends, is as well known to the public as to myself, and it is, I trust, reasonably satisfactory and encouraging to all. With high hope for the future, no prediction in regard to it is ventured.

On the occasion corresponding to this four years ago, all thoughts were anxiously directed to an impending civil war. All dreaded it, all sought to avoid it. While the inaugural address was being delivered from this place, devoted altogether to saving the Union without war, insurgent agents were in the city seeking to destroy it with war—seeking to dissolve the Union and divide the effects by negotiation. Both parties deprecated war, but one of them would make war rather than let the nation survive, and the other would accept war rather than let it perish, and the war came. One-eighth of the whole population were colored slaves, not distributed generally over the Union, but localized in the Southern part of it. These slaves constituted a peculiar and powerful interest. All knew that this interest was somehow the cause of the war.

(continued on next page)

(Continued from previous page)

To strengthen, perpetuate, and extend this interest was the object for which the insurgents would rend the Union by war, while the government claimed no right to do more than to restrict the territorial enlargement of it.

Neither party expected for the war the magnitude or the duration which it has already attained. Neither anticipated that the cause of the conflict might cease when, or even before the conflict itself should cease. Each looked for an easier triumph, and a result less fundamental and astounding. Both read the same Bible and pray to the same God, and each invokes His aid against the other. It may seem strange that any men should dare to ask a just God's assistance in wringing their bread from the sweat of other men's faces, but let us judge not that we be not judged. The prayer of both could not be answered. That of neither has been answered fully. The Almighty has His own purposes. Woe unto the world because of offences, for it must needs be that offences come, but woe to that man by whom the offence cometh. If we shall suppose that American slavery is one of those offences which, in the providence of God, must needs come, but which having continued through His appointed time, He now wills to remove, and that He gives to both North and South this terrible war as the woe due to those by whom the offence came, shall we discern therein any departure from those divine attributes which the believers in a living God always ascribe to Him? Fondly do we hope, fervently do we pray, that this mighty scourge of war may speedily pass away. Yet if God wills that it continue until all the wealth piled by the bondsman's two hundred and fifty years of unrequited toil shall be sunk, and until every drop of blood drawn with the lash shall be paid by another drawn with the sword, as was said three thousand years ago, so still it must be said, that the judgments of the Lord are true and righteous altogether.

With malice toward none, with charity for all, with firmness in the right as God gives us to see the right, let us finish the work we are in, to bind up the nation's wounds, to care for him who shall have borne the battle, and for his widow and his orphans, to do all which may achieve and cherish a just and a lasting peace among ourselves and with all nations.

Delivered at Washington, March 4, 1865

What think you of the inaugural? That rail-splitting lawyer is one of the wonders of the day. Once at Gettysburg, and now again on a greater occasion he has shown a capacity for rising to the demands of the hour .. This inaugural strikes me in its grand simplicity and directness as being for all times the historical keynote of this war."

CHARLES FRANCIS ADAMS

In a letter to his father, Charles Francis Adams 1807 - 1886, shortly after Lincoln's Second Inaugural Address, March 4, 1865.

FOUND ON AN OLD SUN DIAL

Time flies,
Suns rise
And shadows fall.
Let time go by.
Love is forever over all.

'Tis a lesson you should heed;
Try, try, try again.
If at first you don't succeed,
Try, try, try again.

WILLIAM E. HICKSON, 1803 - 1870

A RECIPE TO PRESERVE CHILDREN

Take one large grassy field,
One-half dozen children,
Two or three small dogs,
A pinch of brook and some pebbles.

Mix the children and the dogs well together
  and put them in the field, constantly
  stirring.
Pour the brook over the pebbles;
Sprinkle the field with flowers;
Spread over all a deep blue sky and bake in
  the hot sun.
When brown, set away to cool—in a bathtub.

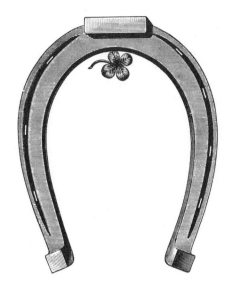

❧

God sends children for another purpose than merely to keep up the race - to enlarge our hearts; and to make us unselfish and full of kindly sympathies and affections; to give our souls higher aims; to call out all our faculties to extended enterprise and exertion; and to bring round our firesides bright faces, happy smiles and loving, tender hearts.

MARY HOWITT, 1799 - 1888

❧

from THERE WAS A CHILD WENT FORTH

There was a child went forth, every day,
And the first object he look'd on, that object
  he became,
And that object became part of him for the
  day or a certain part of a day,
Or for many years or stretching cycles of
  years.

WALT WHITMAN, 1819 - 1892

❧

PLUCK AND LUCK

One constant element of luck
Is genuine solid old Teutonic pluck.
Stick to your aim, the mongrel's hold will
  slip;
But only crowbars loose the bulldog's grip.
Small though he looks, the jaw that never
  yields
Drags down the bellowing monarch of the
  fields.

OLIVER WENDELL HOLMES, 1809 - 1894

A horseshoe is a symbol of good luck even though you cannot make both ends meet.

A little more drive, a little more pluck, a little more work—that's luck.

I believe in luck: how else can one explain the success of those you dislike?

JEAN COCTEAU, 1889 - 1963

❧

See a pin and pick it up,
All the day you'll have good luck;
See a pin, and let it lay,
Bad luck you'll have all the day!

❧

Luck means the hardships and privations which you have not hesitated to endure; the long nights you have devoted to work. Luck means the appointments you have never failed to keep; the trains you have never failed to catch.

MAX O'RELL

❧

Shallow men believe in luck .. Strong men believe in cause and effect.

RALPH WALDO EMERSON

59

IN CALM CONTENT

A little smoke lazed slowly up from my big
    cigar,
The club chair was both soft and warm, as
    club chairs sometimes are.
The bottle hobnobbed with the glass just
    where my arm was bent,
And there was naught for me to want—unless
    it were content.
For longingly I gazed away, all through a
    golden haze,
Back to the time that comes but once—back
    to my boyhood days;
I closed my eyes to better see that happy
    land of charm,
The long-lost days, when, free from care, I
    lived back on the farm.

I slowly stretched my weary frame—who
    knocked upon the door?
"Get up! Get up! you lazybones, it's nearly
    half-past four!"
The night before I'd sparking been and
    reached home rather late—

To-day I'd plough the old stump lot through
    hours more than eight.
The days went by and took their time, those
    "days of golden charm,"
And Satan found no mischief for me down
    there on the farm;
And some days it was piping hot and some
    days it would rain,
But always there was work to do—of jobs an
    endless chain.
I picked potatoes without stint—the sun
    bored through my back;
I swung the knife against the corn until my
    arm did rack;
I sweated at the old grindstone, I cleaned the
    stable floors,
And did some eight-and-forty things that
    lightly are called "chores."

One blessed night, 'most tired to death, I
    tumbled into bed—
And woke to see an angel's face on Sambo's
    sable head;
He brought another bottle in, relit my big
    cigar,
And back I leant in calm content that things
    are as they are.

SONG IN MARCH

Now are the winds about us in their glee,
Tossing the slender tree;
Whirling the sands about his furious car,
March cometh from afar;
Breaks the sealed magic of old Winter's
    dreams,
And rends his glassy streams;
Chafing with potent airs, he fiercely takes
Their fetters from the lakes,
And, with a power by queenly Spring
    supplied,
Wakens the slumbering tide.

With a wild love he seeks young Summer's
    charms
And clasps her to his arms;
Lifting his shield between, he drives away
Old Winter from his prey;—
The ancient tyrant whom he boldly braves,
Goes howling to his caves;
And, to his northern realm compelled to fly,
Yields up the victory;
Melted are all his bands, o'erthrown his
    towers,
And March comes bringing flowers.
    WILLIAM GILMORE SIMMS, 1806 - 1870

❧

MARCH

Blossom on the plum,
    Wild wind and merry;
    Leaves upon the cherry,
And one swallow come.

Red windy dawn,
    Swift rain and sunny;
    Wild bees seeking honey,
Crocus on the lawn;
    Blossom on the plum.

Grass begins to grow,
    Dandelions come;
Snowdrops haste to go
After last month's snow;
Rough winds beat and blow,
    Blossom on the plum.
    NORA HOPPER, 1871 - 1906

❧

It is not a small world to a man who
chases his hat on a windy March day.

March winds and April showers
Bring forth May flowers.

TO KEEP A TRUE LENT

Is this a fast, to keep
The larder lean,
And clean
From fat of veals and sheep?

Is it to quit the dish
Of flesh, yet still
To fill
The platter high with fish?

Is it to fast an hour,
Or ragged to go,
Or show
A downcast look, and sour?

No; 'tis a fast to dole
Thy sheaf of wheat
And meat
Unto the hungry soul.

It is to fast from strife,
From old debate
And hate;
To circumcise thy life.

To show a heart grief-rent;
To starve thy sin,
Not bin;
And that's to keep thy Lent.

ROBERT HERRICK, 1591 - 1674

My forefathers didn't come over on the
Mayflower, but they met the boat.

WILL ROGERS, of Indian descent.

WHO HAS SEEN THE WIND?

Who has seen the wind?
Neither I nor you:
But when the leaves hang trembling
The wind is passing through.

Who has seen the wind?
Neither you nor I:
But when the trees bow down their heads,
The wind is passing by.

CHRISTINA GEORGINA ROSSETTI, 1830 - 1894

SEEDS

In this brown husk a dale of hawthorn
dreams,
A cedar in this narrow cell is thrust
That will drink deeply of a century's
streams.
These lilies shall make summer on my dust.

Here in their safe and simple house of death,
Sealed in their shells, a million roses leap.
Here I can blow a garden with my breath,
And in my hand a forest lies asleep.

MURIEL STUART

A dry March and a dry May portend a
wholesome summer, if there be a shower-
ing April between.

FRANCIS BACON, 1561 - 1626

Man's business seemingly requireth haste. The average man eats in a
hurry and gets dyspepsia. He walks in a hurry and gets apoplexy. He
talks in a hurry and begins to stutter. He does business in a hurry and
becomes bankrupt. He votes in a hurry and produces corruption. He
marries in a hurry and gets a divorce. He trains his children in a hurry
and develops spendthrifts and delinquents. He makes his will in a hurry
and leaves a legal contest. He dies in a hurry and goes to the devil. And
his stride steadily increases! Slow down. Haste makes waste.

from TALES OF A TRAVELLER, TO THE READER, 1824

There is a certain relief in change, even though it be from bad to worse; as I have found in travelling in a stage-coach, that it is often a comfort to shift one's position and be bruised in a new place.

WASHINGTON IRVING, 1783 - 1859

᠅

A telegram to their father from Orville and Wilbur Wright, from Kitty Hawk, North Carolina, Dec. 17, 1903:

"Success four flights Thursday morning all against twenty-one mile wind started from level with engine power alone average speed through air thirty-one miles longest 59 seconds inform press home Christmas."

᠅

*I've been workin' on the railroad,
All the live-long day,
I've been workin' on the railroad,
Just to pass the time away.*

᠅

*Conductor, when you receive a fare,
Punch in the presence of the passenjare!
A blue trip slip for an eight-cent fare,
A buff trip slip for a six-cent fare,
A pink trip slip for a three-cent fare,
Punch in the presence of the passenjare!*

*Punch, brothers! punch with care!
Punch in the presence of the passenjare!*

quoted by MARK TWAIN

᠅

"We (that's my ship and I) took off rather suddenly. We had a report somewhere around four o'clock in the afternoon before that the weather would be fine, so we thought we would try it.

N. Y. Times May 23, 1927 – Charles A. Lindbergh and the "Spirit of St. Louis" on its first overseas flight.

WHEN FRIENDS GATHER ROUND US

*Oh! let us be happy when friends gather
        round us,
    However the world may have shadowed
        our lot
When the rose-braided links of affection have
        bound us,
    Let the cold chains of earth be despised
        and forgot.
And say not that friendship is only ideal;
    That truth and devotion are blessings
        unknown;
For he who believes every heart is unreal,
    Has something unsound at the core of his
        own.
Oh! let us be happy when moments of
        pleasure
    Have brought to our presence the dearest
        and best;
For the pulse ever beats a most heavenly
        measure
    When love and good will sweep the strings
        of the breast.*

ELIZA COOK, 1818 - 1889

᠅

Even the utmost goodwill and harmony and practical kindness are not sufficient for Friendship, for Friends do not live in harmony merely, as some say, but in melody. We do not wish for Friends to feed and clothe our bodies—neighbors are kind enough for that—but to do the like office to our spirits.

HENRY DAVID THOREAU, 1817 - 1862

᠅

Friendship is the highest degree of perfection in society.

M. DE MONTAIGNE, 1533 - 1592

᠅

A FRIEND

*There is no friend like an old friend
Who has shared our morning days,
No greeting like his welcome,
    No homage like his praise.
Fame is the scentless sunflower,
    With gaudy crown of gold;
But friendship is the breathing rose,
    With sweets in every fold.*

OLIVER WENDELL HOLMES, 1809 - 1894

INDIAN NAMES

Ye say, they all have passed away,
  That noble race and brave;
That their light canoes have vanished
  From off the crested wave;
That, 'mid the forests where they roamed,
  There rings no hunter's shout;
But their name is on your waters,—
  Ye may not wash it out.

'Tis where Ontario's billow
  Like Ocean's surge is curled;
Where strong Niagara's thunders wake
  The echo of the world;
Where red Missouri bringeth
  Rich tribute from the West,
And Rappahannock sweetly sleeps
  On green Virginia's breast.

Ye say, their cone-like cabins,
  That clustered o'er the vale,
Have fled away, like withered leaves
  Before the Autumn gale;
But their memory liveth on your hills,
  Their baptism on your shore,
Your everlasting rivers speak
  Their dialect of yore.

Old Massachusetts wears it
  Within her lordly crown,
And broad Ohio bears it
  Amid his young renown;
Connecticut hath wreathed it
  Where her quiet foliage waves,
And bold Kentucky breathes it hoarse
  Through all her ancient caves.

Wachuset hides its lingering voice
  Within its rocky heart.
And Alleghany graves its tone
  Throughout his lofty chart;
Monadnock, on his forehead hoar,
  Doth seal the sacred trust;
Your mountains build their monument,
  Though ye destroy their dust.
  LYDIA HUNTLY SIGOURNEY, 1791 - 1865

❦

To the Memory of the Locomotive Engineer, Whose Name as "Casey Jones" Became a Part of Folklore and the American
Language. "For I'm going to run her till
she leaves the rail—or make it on time
with the southbound mail."
  JOHN LUTHER JONES, 1864 - 1900

❦

from ESSAY ON MAN

Lo, the poor Indian! whose untutor'd
  mind

Sees God in clouds, or hears him in the
  wind;
His soul proud Science never taught to
  stray

Far as the solar walk or milky way;
Yet simple nature to his hope has giv'n,
Behind the Cloud-topt hill, an humbler
  Heav'n.

To be, contents his natural desire;
He asks no Angel's wing, no Seraph's fire;
But thinks, admitted to that equal sky,
His faithful dog shall bear him company.
  ALEXANDER POPE, 1688 - 1744

63

from THOMAS JEFFERSON'S
INAUGURAL ADDRESS—1801

Friends and Fellow Citizens:

Called upon to undertake the duties of the first executive office of the country, I will avail myself of that portion of my fellow citizens which is here assembled to express my grateful thanks for the favor with which they have been pleased to look toward me, to declare a sincere consciousness that the task is above my talents, and that I approach it with those anxious and awful presentiments which the greatness of the charge and the weakness of my powers so justly inspire. A rising nation, spread over a wide and fruitful land, traversing all the seas with the rich productions of their industry, engaged in commerce with nations who feel power and forget right, advancing rapidly to destinies beyond the reach of mortal eye—when I contemplate these transcendent objects, and see the honor, the happiness, and the hopes of this beloved country committed to the issue and the auspices of this day, I shrink from the contemplation, and humble myself before the magnitude of the undertaking . . .

During the contest of opinion through which we have passed the animation of discussions and of exertions has sometimes worn an aspect which might impose on strangers unused to think freely and to speak and to write what they think; but this being now decided by the voice of the nation, announced according to the rules of the Constitution, all will, of course, arrange themselves under the will of the law, and unite in common efforts for the common good. All, too, will bear in mind the sacred principle, that though the will of the majority is in all cases to prevail, that will to be rightful must be reasonable; that the minority possess their equal rights, which equal law must protect, and to violate would be oppression. Let us, then, fellow citizens, unite with one heart and one mind. Let us restore to social intercourse that harmony and affection without which liberty and even life itself are but dreary things. And let us reflect that, having banished from our land that religious intolerance under which mankind so long bled and suffered, we have yet gained little if we counte-

nance a political intolerance as despotic, as wicked, and capable of as bitter and bloody presecutions. During the throes and convulsions of the ancient world, during the agonized spasms of infuriated man, seeking through blood and slaughter his long-lost liberty, it was not wonderful that the agitation of the billows should reach even this distant and peaceful shore; that this should be more felt and feared by some and less by others, and should divide opinions as to measures of safety. But every difference of opinion is not a difference of principle. We have called by different names brethren of the same principle. We are all Republicans, we are all Federalists. If there be any among us who would wish to dissolve this Union or to change its republican form, let them stand undisturbed as monuments of the safety with which error of opinion may be tolerated where reason is left free to combat it. I know, indeed, that some honest men fear that a republican government cannot be strong, that this government is not strong enough; but would the honest patriot, in the full tide of successful experiment, abandon a government which has so far kept us free and firm on the theoretic and visionary fear that this government, the world's best hope, may by possibility want energy to preserve itself? I trust not. I believe this, on the contrary, the strongest government on earth. I believe it is the only one where every man, at the call of the law, would fly to the standard of the law, and would meet invasions of the public order as his own personal concern. Sometimes it is said that man cannot be trusted with the government of himself. Can he, then, be trusted with the government of others? Or have we found angels in the form of kings to govern him? Let history answer this question.

Let us, then, with courage and confidence pursue our own Federal and Republican principles, our attachment to union and representative government. Kindly separated by nature and a wide ocean from the exterminating havoc of one quarter of the globe; too high-minded to endure the degradations of the others;

possessing a chosen country, with room enough for our descendants to the thousandth and thousandth generation; entertaining a due sense of our equal right to the use of our faculties, to the acquisitions of our own industry, to honor and confidence from our fellow citizens, resulting not from birth, but from our actions and their sense of them; enlightened by a benign religion, professed, indeed, and practiced in various forms, yet all of them inculcating honesty, truth, temperance, gratitude, and the love of man; acknowledging and adoring an over-ruling Providence, which by all its dispensations proves that it delights in the happiness of man here and his greater happiness hereafter—with all these blessings, what more is necessary to make us a happy and a prosperous people? Still one thing more, fellow citizens—a wise and frugal government, which shall restrain men from injuring one another, shall leave them otherwise free to regulate their own pursuits of industry and improvement, and shall not take from the mouth of labor the bread it has earned. This is the sum of good government, and this is necessary to close the circle of our felicities . . .

THOMAS JEFFERSON, 1743 - 1826

TAKE TIME

Take time to work—
  It is the price of success.
Take time to think—
  It is the source of power.
Take time to play—
  It is the secret of perpetual youth.
Take time to read—
  It is the fountain of wisdom.
Take time to be friendly—
  It is the road to happiness.
Take time to dream—
  It is hitching your wagon to a star.
Take time to love and to be loved—
  It is the privilege of the gods.
Take time to look around—
  It is too short a day to be selfish.
Take time to laugh—
  It is the music of the soul.

from
THOMAS JEFFERSON'S WRITINGS:

I have sometimes asked myself whether my country is the better for my having lived at all.

The principle of spending money to be paid by posterity, under the name of funding, is but swindling futurity on a large scale.

Directions for his tomb found after his death in his own handwriting: "Author of the Declaration of American Independence—of the Statute of Virginia for religious freedom And Father of the University of Virginia.

If spring came but once in a century instead of once a year, or burst forth with the sound of an earthquake and not in silence, what wonder and expectation there would be in all hearts, to behold the miraculous change.

HENRY WADSWORTH LONGFELLOW

from THE PASSIONATE SHEPHERD
TO HIS LOVE

Come live with me and be my Love,
And we will all the pleasures prive
That hills and valleys, dales and fields,
Or woods or steepy mountain yields.

And we will sit upon the rocks,
And see the shepherds feed their flocks
By shallow rivers to whose falls
Melodious birds sing madrigals.

And I will make thee beds of roses
And a thousand fragrant posies;
A cap of flowers, and a kirtle
Embroidered all with leaves of myrtle.

CHRISTOPHER MARLOWE, 1564 - 1593

❧

from THE NYMPH'S REPLY TO
THE PASSIONATE SHEPHERD

If all the world and love were young,
And truth in every shepherd's tongue,
These pretty pleasures might me move
To live with thee, and by thy Love.

But Time drives flocks from field to fold;
When rivers rage and rocks grow cold;
And Philomel becometh dumb;
The rest complains of cares to come.

The flowers do fade, and wanton fields
To wayward Winter reckoning yields:
A honey tongue, a heart of gall,
Is fancy's spring, but sorrow's fall.

. . .

But could youth last, and love still breed,
Had joys no date, nor age no need,
Then these delights my mind might move
To live with thee and be thy Love.

WALTER RALEIGH, 1552 - 1618

❧

from IN EARLIEST SPRING

Tossing his mane of snows in wildest
*   eddies and tangles,*
Lion-like, March cometh in, hoarse, with
*   tempestuous breath,*
Through all the moaning chimneys, and
*   thwart all the hollows and angles*
Round the shuddering house, threating of
*   winter and death.*

WILLIAM DEAN HOWELLS, 1837 - 1920

THE LION
AND HIS THREE COUNCILLORS

The Lion called the sheep to ask her if his breath smelt: she said Ay; he bit off her head for a fool. He called the Wolf, and asked him: he said No; he tore him in pieces for a flatterer. At last he called the Fox, and asked him. Truly he had got a cold, and could not smell.

Wise men say nothing in dangerous times.

AESOP

❧

Many men wish a wife at forty could be exchanged like a bank note for two twenties.

❧

JOSH BILLINGS said—

Man without woman would be as stupid a game as playing checkers alone.

1818 - 1885

TRADITIONAL WEXFORD CURSE

May the grass grow at your door and the fox build his nest on your hearthstone. May the light fade from your eyes, so you never see what you love. May your own blood rise against you, and the sweetest drink you take be the bitterest cup of sorrow. May you die without benefit of clergy; may there be none to shed a tear at your grave, and may the hearthstone of hell be your best bed forever.

A COUNTRY HOME

I visited a country home: a modest, quiet house sheltered by great trees and set in a circle of field and meadow, gracious with the promise of harvest. Barns and cribs were filled, and the old smokehouse odorous with treasure; the fragrance of pink and hollyhock mingling with the aroma of garden and orchard, and resonant with the hum of bees and the poultry's busy clucking; inside the house, thrift, comfort, and that cleanliness that is next to godliness; the restful beds, the open fireplace, the books and papers, and the old clock that had held its steadfast pace amid the frolic of weddings, that had welcomed in steady measure the new-born babes of the family, and kept company with the watchers of the sickbed, and had ticked the solemn requiem of the dead; and the well-worn Bible that, thumbed by fingers long since stilled, and blurred with tears of eyes long since closed, held the simple annals of the family, and the heart and conscience of the home.

HENRY W. GRADY, 1850 - 1889

If you plant potatoes on St. Patrick's Day, they will be large and the crop big.

from PLANT A TREE

He who plants a tree, He plants love.
Tents of coolness spreading out above
Wayfarers he may not live to see.
  Gifts that grow are best;
  Hands that bless are blest;
  Plant: Life does the rest!
Heaven and earth help him who plants a
  tree,
And his work its own reward shall be.

LUCY LARCOM, 1824 - 1893

THE WEARING OF THE GREEN

"O Paddy dear, and did ye hear the news
  that's goin' round?
The shamrock is by law forbid to grow on
  Irish ground!
No more Saint Patrick's Day we'll keep,
  his color can't be seen,
For there's a cruel law ag'in the Wearin' o'
  the Green.
I met with Napper Tandy, and he took me
  by the hand,
And he said, 'How's poor ould Ireland,
  and how does she stand?'
'She's the most distressful country that
  ever yet was seen,
For they're hanging men and women there
  for the Wearin' o' the Green.'
So if the color we must wear be England's
  cruel red,
Let it remind us of the blood that Irishmen
  have shed;
And pull the shamrock from your hat, and
  throw it on the sod,
But never fear, 'twill take root there,
  though underfoot 'tis trod.
When laws can stop the blades of grass
  from growin' as they grow,
And when the leaves in summer-time their
  color dare not show,
Then I will change the color too I wear in
  my caubeen;
But till that day, please God, I'll stick to
  the Wearin' o' the Green.

Give me health and a day, and I will make the pomp of emperors ridiculous.

RALPH WALDO EMERSON, 1803 - 1882

from WHAT THIS WORLD NEEDS

If tombstones told the truth, everybody would wish to be buried at sea.

JOHN W. RAPER

from "THE FIGHTING RACE"

Well, here's thank God for the race and
  the sod!
Said Kelly and Burke and Shea.

J.I.C. CLARKE, 1846 - 1925

67

"SLEEP VERSES TO A GUEST"

Sleep sweetly in this quiet room,
O thou, whoe'r thou art,
And let no mournful yesterdays
Disturb thy peaceful heart;
Nor let to-morrow scare thy rest
With dreams of coming ill;
Thy maker is thy changeless friend,
His love surrounds thee still.
Forget thyself and all the world;
Put out each glaring light;
The stars are watching over thee;
Sleep sweetly, then—Good Night.

Even if a farmer intends to loaf, he gets up in time to get an early start.

E. W. HOWE, 1853 - 1937

from ARTEMUS WARD: HIS BOOK

Let us all be happy, and live within our means, even if we have to borrow money to do it.

CHARLES FARRAR BROWNE, 1834 - 1867

from MARCH

Ah, March! we know thou art
King-hearted, 'spite of ugly looks and
threats,
And, out of sight, art nursing April's
violets!

HELEN HUNT JACKSON, 1831 - 1885

Broad acres are a patent of nobility; and no man but feels more of a man in the world if he have a bit of ground that he can call his own. However small it is on the surface, it is four thousand miles deep; and that is a very handsome property.

CHARLES DUDLEY WARNER, 1829 - 1900

Let us not be too particular; it is better to have old second-hand diamonds than none at all.

MARK TWAIN

Money is a handmaiden if thou knowest how to use it; a mistress if thou knowest not.

HORACE, 65-8 B.C.

from KING LEAR, Act 1 Scene 4

Have more than thou showest,
Speak less than thou knowest,
Lend less than thou owest

. . . .

And thou shalt have more
Than two tens to a score.

WILLIAM SHAKESPEARE

I have told you of the man who always put on his spectacles when about to eat cherries, in order that the fruit might look larger and more tempting. In like manner I always make the most of my enjoyments, and, though I do not cast my eyes away from troubles, I pack them into as small a compass as I can for myself, and never let them annoy others.

ROBERT SOUTHEY, 1774 - 1843

My friends, money is not all . . . .

attributed to JUDGE KELLY

LIVING WITHIN YOUR MEANS

It is difficult to conceive a person finding himself in a situation which calls on him to maintain a position he cannot pay for. Any other course for me would have been cut short by the barnyard philosophy of my father, who would have contemptuously referred to such action as the senseless imitation of a fowl which was attempting to light higher than it could roost. There is no dignity quite so impressive, and no independence quite so important, as living within your means. In our country a small income is usually less embarrassing than the possession of a large one.

CALVIN COOLIDGE, 1872 - 1933
[Autobiography, chapter 4]

To his soldiers, First Battle of the Marne:

Soldiers, we are attacking. Advance as long as you can. When you can no longer advance, hold your position. When you can no longer hold it, die!

GENERAL JOSEPH JOFFRE, 1852 - 1931

☙❦❧

YOU DECIDE

You are the fellow that has to decide
Whether you'll do it or toss it aside
You are the fellow who makes up your
mind
Whether you'll lead or linger behind—
Whether you'll try for the goal that's afar
Or be contented to stay where you are.
Take it or leave it. Here's something to do,
Just think it over. It's all up to you!
What do you wish? To be known as a
shirk
Known as a good man who's willing to
work,
Scorned for a loafer or praised by your
chief
Rich man or poor man or beggar or thief?
Eager or earnest or dull through the day,
Honest or crooked? It's you who must
say!
You must decide in the face of the test
Whether you'll shirk it or give it your best.

☙❦❧

Drudgery is as necessary to call out the treasures of the mind as harrowing and planting those of the earth.

MARGARET FULLER

☙❦❧

Honor to Pioneers that Broke Sod that Men to Come Might Live.

Inscription, State Capitol, Lincoln, Nebraska.

☙❦❧

There is an idea abroad among moral people that they should make their neighbors good. One person I have to make good: myself. But my duty to my neighbor is much more nearly expressed by saying that I have to make him happy if I may.

R. L. STEVENSON, 1850 - 1894

☙❦❧

Illinois is heaven for men and horses, but hell for women and oxen.

Popular 19th century saying in Illinois.

"I WISH THEE . . ."

What shall I wish thee for the coming
year?
Twelve months of dream-like ease? no
care? no pain?
Bright spring, calm summer, autumn
without rain
Of bitter tears? Wouldst have it thus, my
friend?
What lesson, then, were learnt at the
year's end?

What shall I wish thee, then? God
knoweth well
If I could have my way no shade of woe
Should ever dim thy sunshine; but I know
Strong courage is not learnt in happy
sleep,
Nor patience sweet by eyes that never
weep.

Ah, would my wishes were of more avail
To keep from thee the many jars of life!
Still let me wish thee courage for the
strife,—
The happiness that comes of work well
done,—
And, afterwards, the peace of victory
won!

☙❦❧

The Spartans do not enquire how many the enemy are, but where they are.

AGIS II, 427 B.C.

WRITTEN IN MARCH

The Cock is crowing,
The stream is flowing,
The small birds twitter,
The lake doth glitter,
The green field sleeps in the sun;
The oldest and youngest
Are at work with the strongest;
The cattle are grazing,
Their heads never raising;
There are forty feeding like one!

Like an army defeated
The snow hath retreated,
And now doth fare ill
On the top of the bare hill;
The ploughboy is whooping—anon—anon
There's joy in the mountains;
There's life in the fountains;
Small clouds are sailing,
Blue sky prevailing;
The rain is over and gone!

WILLIAM WORDSWORTH, 1770 - 1810

THE PASSING OF MARCH

The braggart March stood in the season's
*   door*
*   With his broad-shoulders blocking up*
*   the way,*
Shaking the snow-flakes from the cloak he
*   wore,*
*   And from the fringes of his kirtle gray.*
Near by him April stood with tearful face,
*   With violets in her hands, and in her*
*   hair*
Pale, wild anemones; the fragrant lace
*   Half-parted from her breast, which*
*   seemed like fair,*
Dawn-tinted mountain snow, smooth-
*   drifted there.*

She on the blusterer's arm laid one white
*   hand,*
*   But he would none of her soft*
*   blandishment,*
Yet did she plead with tears none might
*   withstand,*
*   For even the fiercest hearts at last relent.*

And he, at last, in ruffian tenderness,
*   With one swift, crushing kiss her lips did*
*   greet.*
Ah, poor starved heart!—for that one rude
*   caress,*
*   She cast her violets underneath his feet.*
        ROBERT BURNS WILSON, 1850 - 1916

❧

THE NOBLE NATURE

It is not growing like a tree
*   In bulk, doth make man better be;*
Or standing long an oak, three hundred
*   year,*
To fall a log at last, dry, bald, and sear:
*   A lily of a day*
*   Is fairer far in May,*
*   Although it fall and die that night,—*
*   It was the plant and flower of Light.*
In small proportions we just beauties see,
And in short measures life may perfect be.
        BEN JONSON, 1573? - 1637

To every thing there is a season, and a
time to every purpose under the heaven:

A time to be born,
*   and a time to die;*
a time to plant,
*   and a time to pluck up*
*   that which is planted;*

A time to kill,
*   and a time to heal;*
a time to break down,
*   and a time to build up;*

A time to weep,
*   and a time to laugh;*
a time to mourn,
*   and a time to dance;*

A time to cast away stones,
*   and a time to gather*
*   stones together;*
a time to embrace,
*   and a time to refrain*
*   from embracing;*

A time to get,
*   and a time to lose;*
a time to keep,
*   and a time to cast away;*

A time to rend,
*   and a time to sew;*
a time to keep silence,
*   and a time to speak;*

A time to love,
*   and a time to hate;*
a time of war,
*   and a time of peace.*
        ECCLESIASTES 3:1—8

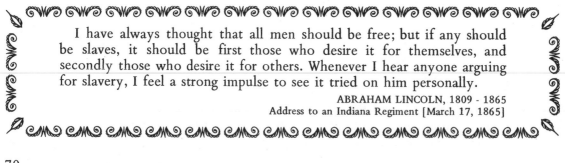

    I have always thought that all men should be free; but if any should
be slaves, it should be first those who desire it for themselves, and
secondly those who desire it for others. Whenever I hear anyone arguing
for slavery, I feel a strong impulse to see it tried on him personally.
        ABRAHAM LINCOLN, 1809 - 1865
        Address to an Indiana Regiment [March 17, 1865]

APRIL

"Oh sweet wild April
Came over the hills . . ."

THE RAINY DAY.

The day is cold, and dark, and dreary;
It rains, and the wind is never weary;
The vine still clings to the moldering wall,
But at every gust the dead leaves fall,
  And the day is dark and dreary.

My life is cold, and dark, and dreary;
It rains, and the wind is never weary;
My thoughts still cling to the moldering
  Past,
But the hopes of youth fall thick in the
  blast,
  And the days are dark and dreary.

Be still, sad heart! and cease repining
Behind the clouds is the sun still shining;
Thy fate is the common fate of all,
Into each life some rain must fall,
  Some days must be dark and dreary.

HENRY WADSWORTH LONGFELLOW, 1807 - 1882

The lure of the distant is deceptive.
The great opportunity is where you are.
JOHN BURROUGHS

IMAGINATION

Imagination! Who can sing thy force?
Or who describe the swiftness of thy
  course?
Soaring through air to find the bright
  abode,
Th' empyreal palace of the thundering
  God,
We on thy pinions can surpass the wind,
And leave the rolling universe behind:
From star to star the mental optics rove,
Measure the skies, and range the realms
  above;
There is one view we grasp the mighty
  whole,
Or with new world amaze th' unbounded
  soul.

PHILLIS WHEATLEY

Phillis Wheatley born in Africa, came in 1761 in a ship-load of slaves to Boston and was bought by John Wheatley. His wife became interested in her and taught her. Miss Wheatley's first poems were published in London.

A GOOD PROVIDER:

A Master of a house (as I have read)
Must be the first man up, and last in bed:
With the Sun rising he must walk his
  grounds;
See this, View that, and all the other
  bounds:
Shut every gate; mend every hedge that's
  torne,
Either with old, or plant therein new
  thorne:
Tread o'er his glebe, but with such care,
  that where
He sets his foot, he leaves rich compost
  there.

ROBERT HERRICK, 1591 - 1674

THE WINTER IS PAST

For, lo, the winter is past,
The rain is over and gone;
The flowers appear on the earth;
The time of the singing of birds is come,
And the voice of the turtle is heard in our
  land.

THE SONG OF SOLOMON, 2:11-12

HE AND SHE

When I am dead you'll find it hard,
  Said he,
To ever find another man
  Like me.

What makes you think as I suppose
  You do,
I'd ever want another man
  Like you!

EUGENE FITCH WARE, 1841 - 1911

When I left camp that morning I had not expected so soon the result that was then taking place, and consequently was in rough garb. I was without a sword—as I usually was when on horseback on the field—and wore a soldier's blouse for a coat, with the shoulder-straps of my rank to indicate to the army who I was. When I went into the house I found General Lee. We greeted each other, and after shaking hands, took our seats. I had my staff with me, a good portion of whom were in the room during the whole of the interview . . . . . General Lee was dressed in a full uniform, which was entirely new, and was wearing a sword of considerable value—very likely the sword which had been presented by the State of Virginia; at all events, it was an entirely different sword from the one which would ordinarily be worn in the field. In my rough traveling suit—the uniform of a private, with the straps of a lieutenant-general—I must have contrasted very strangely with a man so handsomely dressed, six feet high, and of faultless form. But this was not a matter that I thought of until afterward.

We soon fell into a conversation about old army times. He remarked that he remembered me very well in the old army; and I told him that as a matter of course I remembered him perfectly; but from the difference between our ranks and years (there being about sixteen years' difference between our ages), I had thought it very likely that I had not attracted his attention sufficiently to be remembered by him after such a long interval. Our conversation grew so pleasant that I almost forgot the object of our meeting.

After the conversation had run on in this way for some time, General Lee called my attention to the object of our meeting, and said that he had asked for this interview for the purpose of getting from me the terms I proposed to give his army. I said that I merely meant that his army should lay down their arms, not to take them up again during the war unless duly and properly exchanged. He said that

he had so understood my letter. Then we gradually fell off into conversation about matters foreign to the subject which had brought us together. This continued for some time, when General Lee again interrupted the course of the conversation by suggesting that the terms I proposed to give his army ought to be written out. I called to General Parker, secretary on my staff, for writing materials, and commenced writing out the terms . . . . . When I put my pen to the paper I did not know the first word that I should make use of in writing the terms. I only knew what was in my mind, and I wished to express it clearly, so that there could be no mistaking it. As I wrote on, the thought occurred to me that the officers had their own private horses and effects, which were important to them, but of no value to us; also that it would be an unnecessary humiliation to call upon them to deliver their side-arms.

No conversation—not one word—passed between General Lee and myself either about private property, side-arms or kindred subjects. When he read over that part of the terms about side-arms, horses, and private property of the officers, he remarked, with some feeling, I thought, that this would have a happy effect upon his army . . . . The much-talked-of surrendering of Lee's sword and my handing it back—this and much more that has been said about it is the purest romance. The word sword or side-arms was not mentioned by either of us until I wrote it in the terms. There was no premeditation, and it did not occur to me until the moment I wrote it down. If I had happened to omit it, and General Lee had called my attention to it, I should have put it in the terms, precisely as I acceded to the provision about the soldiers retaining their horses . . . . Lee and I separated as cordially as we had met, he returning to his own line; and all went into bivouac for the night at Appomattox.

GENERAL U. S. GRANT, 1822 - 1888
(Meeting with General Robert E. Lee at Appomattox.)

I am sick and tired of war. Its glory is all moonshine. It is only those who have never fired a shot nor heard the shrieks and groans of the wounded who cry aloud for blood, more vengeance, more desolation. War is hell.

GENERAL WILLIAM TECUMSEH SHERMAN
1820 - 1891

ᏩᎣ

THE BLUE AND THE GRAY

By the flow of the inland river,
  Whence the fleets of iron have fled,
Where the blades of the grave-grass quiver,
  Asleep are the ranks of the dead:
Under the sod and the dew,
  Waiting the judgment-day;
Under the one, the Blue,
  Under the other, the Gray.

No more shall the war-cry sever,
  Or the winding rivers be red;
They banish our anger forever
  When they laurel the graves of our dead!
Under the sod and the dew,
  Waiting the judgment-day;
Love and tears for the Blue,
  Tears and love for the Gray.

From the poem by FRANCIS MILES FINCH, 1827 - 1907

SPRING

When the bounds of spring are on winter's
  traces,
  The mother of months in meadow or
  plain
Fills the shadows and windy places
With lisp of leaves and ripple of rain . .

For winter's rains and ruins are over,
  And all the season of snows and sins;
And time remember'd is grief forgotten,
And frosts are slain and flowers begotten,
And in green underwood and cover
  Blossom by blossom the spring begins.

ALGERNON CHARLES SWINBURNE, 1865

ᏩᎣ

on the CIVIL WAR

A few immortal sentences, breathing the omnipotence of divine justice, have been potent to creak despotic fetters and abolish the whipping-post and slave market; but oppression neither went down in blood nor did the breath of freedom come from the cannon's mouth. Love is the liberator.

MARY BAKER EDDY, 1821 - 1910

FAREWELL TO HIS ARMY
Headquarters Army of Northern Virginia
April 10, 1865

After four years of arduous service, marked by unsurpassed courage and fortitude, the Army of Northern Virginia has been compelled to yield to overwhelming numbers and resources.

I need not tell the survivors of so many hard-fought battles, who have remained steadfast to the last, that I have consented to this result from no distrust of them; but, feeling that valor and devotion could accomplish nothing that could compensate for the loss that would have attended the continuation of the contest, I have determined to avoid the useless sacrifice of those whose past services have endeared them to their countrymen.

By the terms of the agreement, officers and men can return to their homes and remain until exchanged.

You may take with you the satisfaction that proceeds from the consciousness of duty faithfully performed, and I earnestly pray that a merciful God will extend to you His blessing and protection.

With an unceasing admiration of your constancy and devotion to your country, and a grateful remembrance of your kind and generous consideration of myself, I bid you all an affectionate farewell.

GENERAL R. E. LEE, 1807 - 1870

75

from "AN ESSAY ON MAN"

*Know then thyself: presume not God to
scan;*
The proper study of mankind is man.

*Laugh where we must; be candid where
we can;*
But vindicate the ways of God to man.

A wit's a feather, and a chief a rod;
An honest man's the noblest work of God.

Hope springs eternal in the human breast;
Man never is, but always to be blest.

from "AN ESSAY ON CRITICISM"

A little learning is a dangerous thing.
Drink deep, or taste not the Pierian Spring.
*There shallow draughts intoxicate the
brain*
And drinking largely sobers us again.

Be not the first by whom the new is tried
Nor yet the last to lay the old aside.

Whoever thinks a faultless piece to see,
*Thinks what ne'er was, nor is, nor e'er
shall be.*

ALEXANDER POPE, 1688 - 1744

If you have knowledge, let others light
their candles at it.

MARGARET FULLER

Our life is an apprenticeship to the
truth that around every circle another can
be drawn; that there is no end in nature;
but every end is a beginning; that there is
always another dawn risen on mid-noon,
and under every deep a lower deep opens.
Nature's abundance is endless!

Your sole contribution to the sum of
things is yourself.

FRANK CRANE

from THE LETTER OF
PAUL TO THE PHILIPPIANS

Finally, brethren, whatever is true,
whatever is honorable, whatever is just,
whatever is pure, whatever is lovely, whatever is gracious, if there is any excellence,
if there is anything worthy of praise,
think about these things. What you have
learned and received and heard and seen
in me, do; and the God of peace will be
with you.

PHILIPPIANS 4:8 - 9

A drop of ink may make a million
think.

GEORGE GORDON BYRON, 1788 - 1824

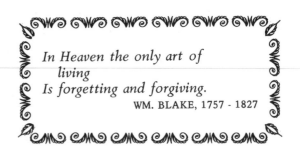

*In Heaven the only art of
living*
Is forgetting and forgiving.
WM. BLAKE, 1757 - 1827

HOME THOUGHTS, FROM ABROAD

Oh, to be in England
Now that April's there,
And whoever wakes in England
Sees, some morning, unaware,
That the lowest boughs and the brushwood
*   sheaf*
Round the elm-tree bole are in tiny leaf,
While the chaffinch sings on the orchard
*   bough*
In England—now!

And after April, when May follows
And the white-throat builds, and all the
*   swallows!*
Hark, where my blossomed pear-tree in
*   the hedge*
Leans to the field and scatters on the
*   clover*
Blossoms and dewdrops—at the bent
*   spray's edge—*
That's the wise thrush: he sings each song
*   twice over,*

Lest you should think he never could
*   recapture*
The first fine careless rapture!
And though the fields look rough with
*   hoary dew,*
All will be gay when noontide wakes anew
The buttercups, the little children's dower
—Far brighter than this gaudy melon-
*   flower!*

ROBERT BROWNING, 1812 - 1889

❦

A MAN OF WORDS

A man of words and not of deeds,
Is like a garden full of weeds;
And when the weeds begin to grow,
It's like a garden full of snow;
And when the snow begins to fall,
It's like a bird upon the wall;
And when the bird away does fly,
It's like an eagle in the sky;
And when the sky begins to roar,
It's like a lion at the door;
And when the door begins to crack,
It's like a stick across your back;
And when your back begins to smart,
It's like a penknife in your heart;
And when your heart begins to bleed,
You're dead, and dead, and dead indeed.

My message to you is simply "Look and Listen," that is, cultivate the habit of attention and try to gain opportunities to hear wise men and women talk. Indifference and inattention are the two most dangerous monsters that you will ever meet. Interest and attention will insure to you an education.

ROBERT A. MILLIKAN

❦

WHATEVER YOU DO

If thou art singing a hymn, thou art praising God.

Then the hymn comes to an end, and it is time for a meal. If thou keepest thyself from overeating, thou wilt be praising God.

Dost thou labor as a farmer? Be sure there are no weeds left in the ground thou art digging. This too will be an opportunity for praising God.

Thus by the innocency of thy labors thou canst praise God all day long.

ST. AUGUSTINE, 354—430

❦

SONNET TO A CLAM

Inglorious friend! most confident I am
*   Thy life is one of very little ease;*
*   Albeit men mock thee with thy similes*
And prate of being "happy as a clam!"
What though thy shell protects thy fragile
*   head*
*   From the sharp bailiffs of the briny sea?*
*   Thy valves are, sure, no safety-valves to*
*   thee.*
While rakes are free to desecrate thy bed,
And bear thee off—as foemen take their
*   spoil,*
*   Far from thy friends and family to*
*   roam:*
*   Forced, like a Hessian, from thy native*
*   home,*
To meet destruction in a foreign broil!
*   Though thou art tender, yet thy humble*
*   bard*
*   Declares, O clams, thy case is shocking*
*   hard!*

JOHN GODFREY SAXE, 1816 - 1887

THE AMERICAN CRISIS

These are the times that try men's souls. The summer soldier and the sunshine patriot will, in this crisis, shrink from the service of their country; but he that stands it now, deserves the love and thanks of man and woman. Tyranny, like hell, is not easily conquered; yet we have this consolation with us, that the harder the conflict, the more glorious the triumph . . . . Is is the object only of war that makes it honorable. And if there was ever a just war since the world began, it is this in which America is now engaged . . . . We fight not to enslave, but to set a country free, and to make room upon the earth for honest men to live in.

THOMAS PAINE, 1776
1737 - 1809

❖

"We must indeed all hang together, or most assuredly we will all hang separately.
BENJAMIN FRANKLIN

❖

CONCORD HYMN

By the rude bridge that arched the flood,
Their flag to April's breeze unfurled,
Here once the embattled farmers stood,
And fired the shot heard round the world.

The foe long since in silence slept;
Alike the conqueror silent sleeps;
And Time the ruined bridge has swept
Down the dark stream which seaward
    creeps.

On this green bank, by this soft stream,
We set to-day a votive stone;
That memory may their deed redeem,
When, like our sires, our sons are gone.

Spirit that made those heroes dare
To die, and leave their children free,
Bid Time and Nature gently spare
The shaft we raise to them and thee.

RALPH WALDO EMERSON, 1803 - 1882

❖

Doubt whom you will, but never yourself.
CHRISTIAN N. BOVEE, 1820 - 1904

One raw morning in Spring—it will be eighty years the nineteenth day of this month—Hancock and Adams, the Moses and Aaron of that Great Deliverance, were both at Lexington; they also had "obstructed an officer" with brave words. British soldiers, a thousand strong, came to seize them and carry them over sea for trial, and so nip the bud of Freedom auspiciously opening in that early Spring. The town militia came together before daylight, "for training." A great, tall man, with a large head and a high, wide brow, their captain—one who had "seen service"—marshaled them into line, numbering but seventy, and bade "every man load his piece with powder and ball. I will order the first man shot that runs away," said he, when some faltered "Don't fire unless fired upon, but if they want to have a war, let it begin here."

Gentlemen, you know what followed; those farmers and mechanics "fired the shot heard around the world." A little monument covers the bones of such as before had pledged their fortune and their sacred honor to the Freedom of America, and that day gave it also their lives. I was born in that little town, and bred up amid the memories of that day. When a boy I read the first monumental line I ever saw—"Sacred to Liberty and the Rights of Mankind." Since then I have studied the memorial marbles of Greece and Rome, in many an ancient town; nay, on Egyptian obelisks have read what was written before the Eternal roused up Moses to lead Israel out of Egypt; but no chiseled stone has ever stirred me to such emotions as those rustic names of men who fell "In the Sacred Cause of God and their Country."

THEODORE PARKER

❖

He jests at scars that never felt a wound.
SHAKESPEARE

❖

When they signed the Declaration of Independence, 1776 -

"There, I guess King George will be able to read that."

JOHN HANCOCK, 1737 - 1793

A man moved into Oklahoma City recently, too late for the refuse pick-up that week. Boxes began piling up. One morning he decided it was time for action, and sent the following telegram to the City Manager:

> "Roses are red,
> Violets are blue,
> Garbage pick-up
> Ten days overdue!"

When he returned home from work that afternoon he found that the city could rise to the occasion. A telegram signed by the City Manager went as follows:

> "Garbage smells.
> Your rhyme does too.
> But I've sent for your hog-feed
> P. D. Q!"

The poet went to his backdoor and looked out. The refuse was gone.

AMERICAN CITY

❧

POOR ROBIN'S ALMANAC, 1760

The first of April, some do say,
Is set apart for All Fool's Day;
But why the people call it so,
Nor I, nor they themselves, do know.

❧

VIOLETS.

Welcome, maids of honor!
  You do bring
  In the Spring,
And wait upon her.

She has virgins many,
  Fresh and fair;
  Yet you are
More sweet than any.

Y' are the maiden Posies,
  And, so graced,
  To be placed
'Fore damask roses.

Yet thou thus respected,
  By and By
  Ye do lie
Poor girls, neglected.

ROBERT HERRICK, 1591 - 1674

SIGNS OF RAIN

FORTY REASONS FOR NOT ACCEPTING AN IN-VITATION OF A FRIEND TO MAKE AN EXCURSION WITH HIM.

1. The hollow winds begin to blow,
2. The clouds look black, the glass is low;
3. The soot falls down, the spaniels
  sleep,
4. And spiders from their cobwebs peep.
5. Last night the sun went pale to bed,
6. The moon in halos hid her head;
7. The boding shepherd heaves a sigh,
8. For see, a rainbow spans the sky!
9. The walls are damp, the ditches smell,
10. Closed is the pink-eyed pimpernel.
11. Hark how the chairs and tables crack!
12. Old Betty's nerves are on the rack;
13. Loud quacks the duck, the peacocks
  cry,
14. The distant hills are seeming nigh.
15. How restless are the snorting swine!
16. The busy flies disturb the kine;
17. Low o'er the grass the swallow wings,
18. The cricket, too, how sharp he sings!
19. Puss on the hearth, with velvet paws,
20. Sits wiping o'er her whiskered jaws;
21. Through the clear streams the fishes
  rise,
22. And nimbly catch the incautious flies,
23. The glowworms, numerous and light,
24. Illumed the dewy dell last night;
25. At dusk the squalid toad was seen,
26. Hopping and crawling o'er the green;
27. The whirling dust the wind obeys,
28. And in the rapid eddy plays;
29. The frog has changed his yellow vest,
30. And in a russet coat is dressed.
31. Though June, the air is cold and still,
32. The mellow blackbird's voice is shrill;
33. My dog, so altered in his taste,
34. Quits mutton bones on grass to feast;
35. And see yon rooks, how odd their
  flight!
36. They imitate the gliding kite,
37. And seem precipitate to fall,
38. As if they felt the piercing ball.
39. 'T will surely rain; I see with sorrow,
40. Our jaunt must be put off to-morrow.

DR. EDWARD JENNER, 1803 - 1872

❧

I would rather be sick than idle.

SENECA

THE AMERICAN CREED

I believe in the United States of America as a government of the people, by the people, for the people; whose just powers are derived from the consent of the governed; a democracy in a republic, a sovereign nation of many sovereign states; a perfect union, one and inseparable; established upon those principles of freedom, equality, justice, and humanity for which American patriots sacrificed their lives and fortunes.

I therefore believe it is my duty to my country to love it; to support its Constitution; to obey its laws; to respect its flag, and to defend it against all enemies.

WILLIAM TYLER PAGE, 1868 - 1942

(Accepted, April 3, 1918, by the House of Representatives on behalf of the American People)

First woman member of Congress, Miss Jeannette Rankin of Montana, in a roll call on declaring war on Germany in April 1917 did not answer, moving nervously in her seat. In a second roll-call to give opportunity for voting for any who had come in late, all eyes turned to this unhappy Congresswoman. She rose finally, and said, "I want to stand by my country, but I cannot vote for war .."

I think this is the most extraordinary collection of talent, of human knowledge, that has ever been gathered together at the White House, with the possible exception of when Thomas Jefferson dined alone.

PRESIDENT JOHN F. KENNEDY, 1917 - 1963
Address, White House dinner and reception honoring Nobel Prize winners [April 1962]

ᎦᏯᎢ

It takes your enemy and your friend working together, to hurt you: the one to slander you, and the other to bring you the news.

MARK TWAIN

ᎦᏯᎢ

The worst waste of breath, next to playing a saxophone, is advising a son.

FRANK MCKINNEY (KIN HUBBARD), 1868 -1930

CONGRESS IS ASKED TO DECLARE WAR

... It is a fearful thing to lead this great peaceful people into war, into the most terrible and disastrous of all wars, civilization itself seeming to be in the balance. But the right is more precious than peace, and we shall fight for the things which we have always carried nearest our hearts—for democracy, for the right of those who submit to authority to have a voice in their own governments, for the rights and liberties of small nations, for a universal dominion of right by such a concert of free peoples as shall bring peace and safety to all nations and make the world itself at last free.

To such a task we can dedicate our lives and our fortunes, everything that we are and everything that we have, with the pride of those who know that the day has come when America is privileged to spend her blood and her might for the principles that gave her birth and happiness and the peace which she has treasured. God helping her, she can do no other.

WOODROW WILSON, 1856 - 1924
From Address to Congress, April 2, 1917

ᎦᏯᎢ

from "PUDD'NHEAD WILSON"

The holy passion of Friendship is of so sweet and steady and loyal and enduring a nature that it will last through a whole lifetime, if not asked to lend money.

MARK TWAIN

ARBOR DAY, APRIL 22nd

This date was selected as it is the birthday of J. Sterling Morton, "father" of Arbor Day.

❧

Through the grass at his feet crept
    maidens sweet,
    To gather the dew of May.
And on that day to the rebeck gay
    They frollicked with lovesome swains;
They are gone, they are dead, in the
    churchyard laid
    But the tree it still remains.
        HENRY FOTHERGILL CHORLEY, 1808 - 1872

❧

Solitude would be ideal if you could pick the people to avoid.
        KARL KRAUS

❧

Two paradises 'twere in one, To live in Paradise alone.
        ANDREW MARVELL, 1621 - 1678

❧

CRABBED AGE AND YOUTH

Crabbed Age and Youth
Cannot live together:
Youth is full of pleasance,
Age is full of care;
Youth like summer morn,
Age like winter weather;
Youth like summer brave,
Age like winter bare.
Youth is full of sport,
Age's breath is short;
Youth is nimble, Age is lame;
Youth is hot and bold,
Age is weak and cold;
Youth is wild, and Age is tame.
Age I do abhor thee;
Youth I do adore thee;
O, my Love, my Love is young!
Age, I do defy thee:
O, sweet shepherd, hie thee!
For methinks thou stay'st too long.

Often attributed to Shakespeare.

THE BRAVE OLD OAK

A song to the oak, the brave old oak,
    Who hath ruled in the greenwood long;
Here's health and renown to his broad
        green crown,
    And his fifty arms so strong!
There's fear in his frown till the sun goes
        down,
    And the fire in the West fades out;
And he showeth his might on a wild
        midnight,
    When the storms through his branches
        shout.

    Then here's to the oak, the brave old
        oak,
        Who stands in his pride alone;
    And still flourish he, a hale green
        tree,
        When a hundred years are gone!

❧

You can always tell a real friend: when you've made a fool of yourself, he doesn't feel you've done a permanent job.

from TREE PLANTER

Who does his duty is a question
    Too complex to be solved by me,
But he, I venture the suggestion
    Does part of his that plants a tree.

What though his memory shall have
    vanished,
    Since the good deed he did survives?
It is not wholly to be banished
    Thus to be part of many lives.
        JAMES RUSSELL LOWELL, 1819 - 1891

This is my seventieth birthday, and I wonder if you all rise to the size of that proposition, realizing all the significance of that phrase, seventieth birthday.

The seventieth birthday! It is the time of life when you arrive at a new and awful dignity; when you may throw aside the decent reserves which have oppressed you for a generation and stand unafraid and unabashed upon your seven-terraced summit and look down and teach—unrebuked. You can tell the world how you got there. It is what they all do. You shall never get tired of telling by what delicate arts and deep moralities you climbed up to that great place. You will explain the process and dwell on the particulars with senile rapture. I have been anxious to explain my own system this long time, and now at last I have the right.

I have achieved my seventy years in the usual way: by sticking strictly to a scheme of life which would kill anybody else. It sounds like an exaggeration, but that is really the common rule for attaining to old age. When we examine the programme of any of these garrulous old people we always find that the habits which have preserved them would have decayed us; that the way of life which enabled them to live upon the property of their heirs so long, as Mr. Choate says, would have put us out of commission ahead of time. I will offer here, as a sound maxim, this: That we can't reach old age by another man's road.

I will now teach, offering my way of life to whomsoever desires to commit suicide by the scheme which has enabled me to beat the doctor and the hangman for seventy years. Some of the details may sound untrue but they are not. I am not here to deceive; I am here to teach.

We have no permanent habits until we are forty. Then they begin to harden, presently they petrify, then business begins. Since forty I have been regular about going to bed and getting up—and that is one of the main things, I have made it a rule to go to bed when there wasn't anybody left to sit up with; and I have made it a rule to get up when I had to. This has resulted in an unswerving regularity of irregularity. It has saved me sound but it would injure another person.

In the matter of diet—which is another main thing—I have been persistently strict in sticking to the things which didn't agree with me until one or the other of us got the best of it. Until lately I got the best of it myself. But last spring I stopped frolicking with mince-pie after midnight; up to then I had always believed it wasn't loaded. For thirty years I have taken coffee and bread at eight in the morning, and no bite or sup until seven-thirty in the evening. Eleven hours. That is all right for me, and is wholesome, because I have never had a headache in my life, but headachy people would not reach seventy comfortably by that road, and they would be foolish to try it. And I wish to urge upon you this—which I think is wisdom—that if you find you can't make seventy by any but an uncomfortable road, don't you go. When they take off the Pullman and retire you to the rancid smoker, put on your things, count your checks, and get out at the first way station where there's a cemetery.

I have made it a rule never to smoke more than one cigar at a time. I have no other restriction as regards smoking. I do not know just when I began to smoke, I only know that it was in my father's lifetime, and that I was discreet.

MARK TWAIN

From an address at a dinner given for him at Delmonico's December 5, 1905.

FOUR SWEET MONTHS

First, April, she with mellow showers
Opens the way for early flowers;
Then after her comes smiling May,
In a more rich and sweet array;
Next enters June, and brings us more
Gems than those two, that went before:
Then, lastly, July comes, and she
More wealth brings in than all those three.
ROBERT HERRICK, 1591 - 1674

❧

Repose is a good thing, but boredom is its brother.
VOLTAIRE, 1694 - 1778

❧

In springtime the whippoorwill's first song tells all children, they can now go barefoot—was the rule in earlier days. For adults, if they quickly turned a somersault, no backache would they have that summer.

❧

Reason is the life of the law.
SIR EDWARD COKE, 1552 - 1634

❧

When you get in a tight place and everything goes against you, till it seems as though you could not hold on a minute longer, never give up then, for that is just the place and time that the tide will turn.
HARRIETT BEECHER STOWE

❧

THE DOG IN THE MANGER

A dog was lying upon a manger full of hay. An Ox, being hungry came near, and offered to eat of the hay; but the envious ill-natured cur, getting up and snarling at him, would not suffer him to touch it. Upon which the Ox, in the bitterness of his heart, said, "A curse light on thee, for a malicious wretch, who wilt neither eat hay nor suffer others to do it."
from AESOP'S FABLES

TWELVE ARTICLES

Lest it may more quarrels breed,
I will never hear you read.

By disputing, I will never,
To convince you once endeavor.

When a paradox you stick to,
I will never contradict you.

When I talk and you are heedless,
I will show no anger needless.

When your speeches are absurd,
I will ne'er object a word.

When you furious argue wrong,
I will grieve and hold my tongue.

Not a jest or humorous story
Will I ever tell before ye:
To be chidden for explaining,
When you quite mistake the meaning.

Never more will I suppose,
You can taste my verse or prose.

You no more at me shall fret,
While I teach and you forget.

You shall never hear me thunder,
When you blunder on, and blunder.

Show your poverty of spirit,
And in dress place all your merit;
Give yourself ten thousand airs:
That with me shall break no squares.

Never will I give advice,
Till you please to ask me thrice:
Which if you in scorn reject,
'T will be just as I expect.

Thus we both shall have our ends
And continue special friends.
JONATHAN SWIFT, 1667 - 1745

❧

CHERRY TREE

Oh fair to see
Bloom-laden cherry tree,
  Arrayed in sunny white,
  An April day's delight;
Oh fair to see!

Oh fair to see
Fruit-laden cherry tree,
  With balls of shining red
  Decking a leafy head;
Oh fair to see!
CHRISTINA ROSSETTI, 1830 - 1894

In sober verity I will confess a truth to thee, reader. I love a Fool—as naturally as if I were of kith and kin to him. When a child, with childlike apprehensions, that dived not below the surface of the matter, I read those Parables—not guessing at the involved wisdom—I had more yearnings towards that simple architect, that built his house upon the sand, than I entertained for his more cautious neighbor; I grudged at the hard censure pronounced upon the quiet soul that kept his talent; and—prizing their simplicity beyond the more provident and, to my apprehension, somewhat unfeminine wariness of their competitors—I felt a kindness, that almost amounted to a tendre, for those five thoughtless virgins. I have never made an acquaintance since that lasted, or a friendship that answered, with any that had not some tincture of the absurd in their characters.

I venerate an honest obliquity of understanding. The more laughable blunders a man shall commit in your company, the more tests he giveth you that he will not betray or overreach you. I love the safety which a palpable hallucination warrants, the security which a word out of season ratifies. And take my word for this, reader, and say a fool told it you, if you please, that he who hath not a dram of folly in his mixture hath points of much worse matter in his composition. It is observed that "the foolisher the fowl, or fish, woodcocks, dotterels, cod's head, etc.,—the finer the flesh thereof;" and what are commonly the world's received fools but such whereof the world is not worthy? And what have been some of the kindliest patterns of our species, but so many darlings of absurdity, minions of the goddess, and her white boys? Reader, if you wrest my words beyond their fair construction, it is you, and not I, that are the April Fool.

CHARLES LAMB, 1775 - 1834

A man who is always looking for a helping hand can always find one - attached to his arm.

CROSSING THE BAR

Sunset and evening star,
And one clear call for me!
And may there be no moaning of the bar,
When I put out to sea,

But such a tide as moving seems asleep,
Too full for sound and foam,
When that which drew from out the
boundless deep
Turns again home.

Twilight and evening bell,
And after that the dark!
And may there be no sadness of farewell,
When I embark;

For though from out our bourne of Time
and Place
The flood may bear me far,
I hope to see my Pilot face to face
When I have crossed the bar.

ALFRED TENNYSON, 1809 - 1892

When bees stay close to the hive Rain is near.

You may paddle all day long, but it is when you come back at nightfall, and look in at the familiar room, that you find Love or Death awaiting you beside the stove; and the most beautiful adventures are not those we go to seek.

STEVENSON

MATURITY IN CHARACTER

Faith without credulity,
Conviction without bigotry,
Charity without condescension,
Courage without pugnacity,
Self-respect without vanity,
Humility without obsequiousness,
Love of humanity without sentimentality,
Meekness with power.

CHARLES EVANS HUGHES, 1862 - 1948

APRIL RAIN

The April rain, the April rain,
Comes slanting down in fitful showers,
   Then from the furrow shoots the grain,
And banks are edged with nestling flowers;
And in gray shaw and woodland bowers
   The cuckoo through the April rain
      Calls once again.

The April sun, the April sun,
Glints through the rain in fitful splendor,
   And in gray shaw and woodland dun
The little leaves spring forth and tender
Their infant hands, yet weak and slender,
   For warmth towards the April sun,
      One after one.

And between shower and shine hath
      birth
The rainbow's evanescent glory;
   Heaven's light that breaks on mist of
      earth!
Frail symbol of our human story,
It flowers through showers where,
      looming hoary,
   The rain-clouds flash with April
      mirth,
      Like Life on earth.
                    MATHILDE BLIND, 1841 - 1896

❦

To Madame Helvetius who inquired when
he would visit her, Benjamin Franklin
writes:

Madame, I am waiting till the nights are
longer.

❦

Ignorant people think it's the noise which
fighting cats make that is so aggravating,
but it ain't so; it's the sickening grammar
they use.
                              MARK TWAIN

❦

   Syntax must be bad, having both sin
and tax in it.
                              WILL ROGERS

❦

The owl is an ungrammatical bird who
always hoots *to who* instead of *to whom.*

TO NIGHT

Mysterious Night! when our first parent
      knew
   Thee from report divine, and heard thy
      name,
Did he not tremble for this lovely frame,
   This glorious canopy of light and blue?
Yet 'neath a curtain of translucent dew,
   Bathed in the rays of the great setting
      flame,
Hesperus with the host of heaven came,
   And lo! creation widened in man's view.
Who could have thought such darkness lay
      concealed,
   Within thy beams, O Sun! or who could
      find,
Whilst fly, and leaf, and insect stood
      revealed,
   That to such countless orbs thou mad'st
      us blind!
Why do we then shun Death with anxious
      strife?
   If light can thus deceive, wherefore not
      life?
                    JOSEPH BLANCO WHITE, 1775 - 1841

❦

The night—

Is the Sabbath of all mankind, To rest the
body and the mind.
                              SAMUEL BUTLER

❦

—is long that never finds the day.—

                    WILLIAM SHAKESPEARE
Macbeth

❦

Watchman what of the night?
                              ISAIAH, XXI, 11

❦

Shows stars and women in a better light.
                    GEORGE GORDEN BYRON, 1788 - 1824

❦

WEATHER LORE:

When the sheep collect and huddle
Tomorrow will become a puddle.

SPRING

Now fades the last long streak of snow,
   Now burgeons every maze of quick
   About the flowering squares, and thick
By ashen roots the violets blow.

Now rings the woodland loud and long,
   The distance takes a lovelier hue,
   And drowned in yonder living blue
The lark becomes a sightless song.

Now dance the lights on lawn and lea,
   The flocks are whiter down the vale,
   And milkier every milky sail,
On winding stream or distant sea;

Where now the seamew pipes, or dives
   In yonder greening gleam, and fly
   The happy birds, that change their sky
To build and brood, that live their lives.

From land to land; and in my breast
   Spring wakens too; and my regret
   Becomes an April violet,
And buds and blossoms like the rest.

      ALFRED LORD TENNYSON, 1809 - 1892

The glory is not in never failing, but in rising every time you fail.

      CHINESE PROVERB

It is one life whether we spend it laughing or weeping.

THE JEWEL

There is a jewel which no Indian mines can
   buy,
No chymic art can counterfeit;
It makes men rich in greatest poverty,
Makes water wine, turns wooden cups to
   gold,
The homely whistle to sweet music's
   strain;
Seldom it comes, to few from Heaven
   sent,
That much in little, all in naught—
   Content.

      JOHN WILBYE, 1598 - 1614

CARELESS CONTENT

I am content, I do not care,
   Wag as it will the world for me!
When fuss and fret was all my fare
   It got no ground that I could see;
So when away my caring went
I counted cost and was content.

With more of thanks and less of thought
   I strive to make my matters meet;
To seek what ancient sages sought,
   Physic and food in sour and sweet;
To take what passes in good part
And keep the hiccups from the heart.

With good and gently-humored hearts
   I choose to chat where'er I come,
Whate'er the subject be that starts;
   But if I get among the glum
I hold my tongue to tell the troth,
And keep my breath to cool my broth.

I suit not where I shall not speed,
   Nor trace the turn of every tide.
If simple sense will not succeed
   I made no bustling, but abide.
For shining wealth or scaring woe
I force no friend, I fear no foe.

With whom I feast I do not fawn,
   Nor if the folks should flout me, faint.
If wonted welcome be withdrawn
   I cook no kind of a complaint.
With none disposed to disagree,
I like them best who best like me.

Not that I rate myself the rule
   How all my betters should behave;
But fame shall find me no man's fool,
   Nor to a set of men a slave;
I love a friendship free and frank,
But hate to hang upon a hank.

Now taste and try this temper, sirs,
   Mood it and brood it in your breast;
Or, if ye ween for worldly stirs
   That man does right to mar his rest,
Let me be deft and debonair,
I am content, I do not care!

      JOHN BYROM, 1692 - 1763

The first and best victory is to conquer self; to be conquered by self is, of all things, the most shameful and vile.

      PLATO

from SWEET WILD APRIL

O sweet wild April
  Came over the hills,
He skipped with the winds
  And he tripped with the rills;
His raiment was all
  Of the daffodils.

    Sing hi,
    Sing hey,
    Sing ho!

O sweet wild April
  Came down the lea,
Dancing along
  With his sisters three:
Carnation, and Rose,
  And tall Lily.

    Sing hi,
    Sing hey,
    Sing ho!

O sweet wild April,
  On pastoral quill
Came piping in moonlight
  By hollow and hill,
In starlight at midnight,
  By dingle and rill.

    Sing hi,
    Sing hey,
    Sing ho!

O sweet wild April,
  Farewell to thee!
And a deep sweet sleep
  To thy sisters three,—
Carnation, and Rose,
  And tall Lily.

    Sing hi,
    Sing hey,
    Sing ho!

WILLIAM FORCE STEAD

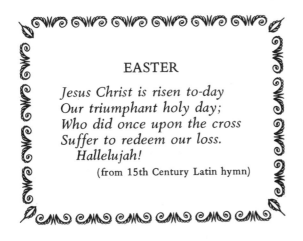

EASTER

Jesus Christ is risen to-day
Our triumphant holy day;
Who did once upon the cross
Suffer to redeem our loss.
  Hallelujah!

(from 15th Century Latin hymn)

from an EASTER HYMN

Awake, thou wintry earth—
  Fling off thy sadness!
Fair vernal flowers, laugh forth
  Your ancient gladness.
    Christ is risen.

THOMAS BLACKBURN

There is no death! What seems so is a transition.

HENRY WADSWORTH LONGFELLOW

When belief is painful, we are slow to believe.

OVID, 43 B.C. - 17 A.D.

from CHRIST THE LORD IS RISEN

"Christ the Lord is risen to-day,"
Sons of men and angels say:
Raise your joys and triumphs high;
Sing, ye heavens, and earth, reply.

CHARLES WESLEY, 1707 - 1788

SPRING

When daisies pied and violets blue,
  And lady-smocks all silver-white,
And cuckoo-buds of yellow hue
  Do paint the meadows with delight,
The cuckoo then, on every tree,
Mocks married men; for thus sings he,
    Cuckoo!
Cuckoo, cuckoo!—O word of fear,
Unpleasing to a married ear!

When shepherds pipe on oaten straws,
  And merry larks are ploughman's clocks,
When turtles tread, and rooks, and daws,
  And maidens bleach their summer
    smocks
The cuckoo then, on every tree,
Mocks married men; for thus sings he,
    Cuckoo!
Cuckoo, cuckoo!—O word of fear,
Unpleasing to a married ear!

WILLIAM SHAKESPEARE

THERE ARE ONLY FOUR KINDS OF READERS

The first is like the hour-glass; their reading being as the sand, it runs in and runs out, and leaves no vestige behind.

The second is like the sponge, which imbibes everything, and returns it in nearly the same state, only a little dirtier.

A third is like a jelly-bag, allowing all that is pure to pass away, retaining only the refuse and dregs.

And the fourth is like the slaves in the diamond mines, who, casting aside all that is worthless, retain only pure gems.

SAMUEL T. COLERIDGE, 1772 - 1834

Books are the blessed chloroform of the mind.

ROBERT CHAMBERS, 1802 - 1871

READING—

Some books are to be tasted, others to be swallowed, and some few to be chewed and digested: that is, some books are to be read only in parts, others to be read, but not curiously, and some few to be read wholly, and with diligence and attention.

FRANCIS BACON, 1561 - 1626
from HIS ESSAYS

CHOOSE:

Of all crazes, the craze to be forever reading new books is one of the oddest.

AUGUSTINE BIRRELL, 1850 - 1933

THE BOSTON ANTHENAEUM

For books are more than books; they are the life
The very heart and core of ages past,
The reason why men lived and worked and died,
The essence and quintessence of their lives.

AMY LOWELL, 1874 - 1925

Some read old books, as if there were no new valuable truths to be discovered in modern publications.

ISAAC D'ISRAELI, 1766 - 1848

INSCRIPTION, DATING FROM 1578

This book is one thing, the halter another; He that stealeth the one may be sure of the other.

Dear little child, this little book
Is less a primer than a key
To sunder gates where wonder waits
Your "Open Sesame!"
RUPERT HUGHES, 1872 - 1948
With a First Reader.

from PILGRIM'S PROGRESS

The Author's Apology for his Book. If that thou wilt not read, let it alone; Some love the meat, some love to pick the bone.

JOHN BUNYAN, 1628 - 1688

from "BOOKS AND LIBRARIES"

Have you ever rightly considered what the mere ability to read means? That it is the key which admits us to the whole world of thought and fancy and imagination? To the company of saint and sage, of the wisest and the wittiest at their wisest and wittiest moment? That it enables us to see with the keenest eyes, hear with the finest ears, and listen to the sweetest voices of all time?

JAMES RUSSELL LOWELL, 1819 - 1891

THE OLD LOG CABIN

It is only shallow minded pretenders who either make distinguished origin a matter of personal merit, or obscure origin a matter of personal reproach. Taunts and scoffing at the humble condition of early life affect nobody in America but those who are foolish enough to indulge in them; and they are generally sufficiently punished by public rebuke. A man who is not ashamed of himself need not be ashamed of his early condition. It did not happen to me to be born in a log cabin; but my elder brothers and sisters were born in a log cabin, raised among the snowdrifts of New Hampshire, at a period so early, that when the smoke first rose from its rude chimney and curled over the frozen hills, there was no similar evidence of a white man's habitation between it and the settlements on the rivers of Canada.

Its remains still exist. I make to it an annual visit. I carry my children to it to teach them the hardships endured by the generations gone before them. I love to dwell on the tender recollections, the kindred ties, the early affections, and the touching narratives and incidents which mingle with all I know of this primitive family abode. I weep to think that none of those who inhabited it are now among the living; and if ever I am ashamed of it, or if ever I fail in affectionate veneration for him who reared it, and defended it against savage violence and destruction, cherished all the domestic virtues beneath its roof, and through the fire and blood of a seven years' revolutionary war, shrank from no danger, no toil, no sacrifice, to serve his country, and to raise his children to a condition better than his own, may my name, and the name of my posterity, be blotted from the memory of mankind!

DANIEL WEBSTER, 1782 - 1852

One may live as a conqueror, a king or a magistrate; but he must die as a man.

DANIEL WEBSTER

THE HAPPY WARRIOR

Who is the happy Warrior? Who is he
That every man in arms should wish to be?
—It is the generous Spirit, who, when brought
Among the tasks of real life, hath wrought
Upon the plan that pleased his boyish thought:
Whose high endeavors are an inward light
That makes the path before him always bright:
Who, with a natural instinct to discern
What knowledge can perform, is diligent to learn;
Abides by this resolve, and stops not there,
But makes his moral being his prime care;
Who, doomed to go in company with Pain,
And Fear, and Bloodshed, miserable train!
Turns his necessity to glorious gain;
In face of these doth exercise a power
Which is our human nature's highest dower;
Controls them and subdues, transmutes, bereaves
Of their bad influence, and their good receives:
By objects, which might force the soul to abate
Her feeling, rendered more compassionate;
Is placable—because occasions rise
So often that demand such sacrifice;
More skillful in self-knowledge, even more pure,
As tempted more; more able to endure,
As more exposed to suffering and distress;
Thence also, more alive to tenderness.
—'Tis he whose law is reason; who depends
Upon that law as on the best of friends;
Whence, in a state where men are tempted still
To evil for a guard against worse ill,
And what in quality or act is best
Doth seldom on a right foundation rest,
He labors good on good to fix, and owes
To virtue every triumph that he knows: ...
Finds comfort in himself and in his cause;
And, while the mortal mist is gathering, draws
His breath in confidence of Heaven's applause:
This is the happy Warrior; this is He
That every Man in arms should wish to be.

WILLIAM WORDSWORTH, 1770 - 1850

FROM THE PRINCIPLES OF PSYCHOLOGY, 1890

Could the young but realize how soon they will become mere walk-
ing bundles of habits, they would give more heed to their conduct while
in the plastic stage. We are spinning our own fates, good or evil, and
never to be undone. Every smallest stroke of virtue or of vice leaves it
never so little scar. The drunken Rip Van Winkle, in Jefferson's play,
excuses himself from every fresh dereliction by saying "It won't count
this time!" Well, he may not count it, and a kind Heaven may not count
it, but it is being counted none the less. Down among his nerve-cells
and fibers the molecules are counting it, registering and storing it up to
be used against him when the next temptation comes. Nothing we ever
do is, in strict scientific literalness, wiped out. Of course, this has its
good side as well as its bad one. As we become permanent drunkards by
so many separate drinks, so we become saints in the moral, and
authorities and experts in the practical and scientific spheres, by so
many separate acts and hours of work. Let no youth have any anxiety
about the upshot of his education, whatever the line of it may be. If he
keep faithfully busy each hour of the working day, he may safely leave
the final result to itself. He can with perfect certainty count on waking
up some fine morning, to find himself one of the competent ones of his
generation, in whatsoever pursuit he may have singled out. Silently,
between all the details of his business, the power of judging in all that
class of matter will have built itself up within him as a possession that
will never pass away. Young people should know this truth in advance.
The ignorance of it has probably engendered more discouragement and
faint-heartedness in youths embarking on arduous careers than all other
courses put together.

WILLIAM JAMES, 1842 - 1910

MAY

"As it fell upon a day
    In the merry month of May . . ."

THE GOLDEN MEAN

Receive, dear friend, the truths I teach,
So shalt thou live beyond the reach
    Of adverse Fortune's power;
Not always tempt the distant deep,
Nor always timorously creep
    Along the treacherous shore.

He that holds fast the golden mean,
And lives contentedly between
    The little and the great,
Feels not the wants that pinch the poor,
Nor plagues that haunt the rich man's door,
    Imbittering all his state.

The tallest pines feel most the power
Of wintry blasts; the loftiest tower
    Comes heaviest to the ground;
The bolts, that spare the mountain's side,
His cloud-capped eminence divide,
    And spread the ruin round.

The well-informed philosopher
Rejoices with a wholesome fear,
    And hopes, in spite of pain
If Winter bellow from the north,
Soon the sweet Spring comes dancing
        forth,
    And nature laughs again.

            After Horace, WILLIAM COWPER, 1731 - 1800

The creation of a thousand forests is in one acorn.

RED

Any color, so long as it's red,
    Is the color that suits me best,
Though I will allow there is much to be
        said
    For yellow and green and the rest;
But the feeble tints which some affect
    On the things they make or buy
Have never—I say it with all respect—
    Appealed to my critical eye.

There's that in red that warmeth the blood,
    And quickeneth a man within,
And bringeth to speedy and perfect bud
    The germs of original sin;
So, though I am properly born and bred,
    I'll own, with a certain zest,
That any color, so long as it's red,
    Is the color that suits me best.

            EUGENE FIELD, 1850 - 1895

MAY

May! queen of blossoms,
    And fulfilling flowers,
With what pretty music
    Shall we charm the hours?
Wilt thou have pipe and reed,
    Blown in the open mead?
Or to the lute give heed
    In the green bowers?

Thou hast no need of us,
    Or pipe or wire;
Thou hast the golden bee
    Ripened with fire;
And many thousand more
Songsters, that thee adore,
Filling earth's grassy floor
    With new desire.

Thou hast thy mighty herds,
    Tame and free-livers;
Doubt not, thy music too
    In the deep rivers;
And the whole plumy flight
Warbling the day and night—
Up at the gates of light,
    See, the lark quivers!

            EDWARD HOWELL-THURLOW, 1781 - 1829

I'M NOBODY! WHO ARE YOU?

I'm nobody! Who are you?
Are you nobody, too?
Then there's a pair of us—don't tell!
They'd banish us, you know.

How dreary to be somebody!
How public, like a frog
To tell your name the livelong day
To an admiring bog!

            EMILY DICKINSON, 1830 - 1886

THE SOLDIER

If I should die, think only this of me:
That there's some corner of a foreign field
That is forever England. There shall be
In that rich earth a richer dust concealed;
A dust whom England bore, shaped, made
    aware,
Gave, once, her flowers to love, her ways
    to roam;
A body of England's, breathing English
    air,
Washed by the rivers, blest by suns of
    home.
And think, this heart, all evil shed away,
A pulse in the eternal mind, no less
Gives somewhere back the thoughts by
    England given;
Her sights and sounds; dreams happy as
    her day;
And laughter, learnt of friends; and
    gentleness,
In hearts at peace, under an English
    heaven.

RUPERT BROOKE, 1887 - 1915

❦

How shall I a habit break?
As you did that habit make.
As you gathered, you must lose;
As you yielded, now refuse.
Thread by thread the strands we twist
Till they bind us, neck and wrist.
Thread by thread the patient hand
Must untwine, ere free we stand.
As we builded stone by stone
We must toil, unhelped, alone,
Till the wall is overthrown.

JOHN BOYLE O'REILLY, 1844 - 1890

❦

A BABY'S EYES

A baby's eyes, ere speech begin,
    Ere lips learn words or sighs,
Bless all things bright enough to win
    A baby's eyes.

Love, while the sweet thing laughs and lies
    And sleep flows out and in,
Sees perfect in them Paradise!

Their glance might cast out pain and sin,
    Their speech make dumb the wise,
By mute glad godhead felt within
    A baby's eyes.

A. C. SWINBURNE, 1837 - 1909

HABITS:

from AUTOCRAT OF THE BREAKFAST TABLE

Habit is the approximation of the animal system to the organic. It is a confession of failure in the highest function of being, which involves a perpetual self-determination, in full view of all existing circumstances.

O. W. HOLMES

❦

That which has become habitual becomes, as it were, a part of our nature; in fact, habit is something like nature, for the difference between "often" and "always" is not great, and nature belongs to the idea of "always," habit to that of "often."

ARISTOTLE

❦

We sow our thoughts, and we reap our action; we sow our actions, and we reap our habits; we sow our habits and we reap our characters; we sow our characters, and we reap our destiny.

CHARLES A. HALL

English writer

❦

Ever' once in a while some feller without a single bad habit gets caught.

FRANK McKINNEY (KIN) HUBBARD
1868 - 1930

❦

Ill habits gather by unseen degrees. As brooks make river, rivers run to seas.

HANNAH MORE, 1745 - 1833

❦

We first make our habits, and then our habits make us.

JOHN DRYDEN, 1631 - 1700

❦

Cultivate only the habits that you are willing should master you.

ELBERT HUBBARD, 1859 - 1915

❦

Man is a bundle of habits.

JOHN RAY

English proverb

from THE COMPLEAT ANGLER

No man is born an angler.

Angling may be said to be so like the mathematics
that it can never be fully learnt.

Angling is somewhat like poetry, men are to be born so.

It is an art worthy the knowledge and
patience of a wise man.

> *Oh the brave Fisher's life,*
> *It is the best of any,*
> *'Tis full of pleasure, void of strife,*
> *And 'tis belov'd of many:*
> > *Other joys Are but toys;*
> > *Only this Lawful is,*
> > *For our skill Breeds no ill*
> *But content and pleasure.*

> *The Angler's Song:*
> *The first men that our Saviour dear*
> *Did choose to wait upon Him here,*
> *Blest fishers were; and fish the last*
> *Food was, that He on earth did taste;*
> *I therefore strive to follow those,*
> *Whom He to follow Him hath chose.*

I have laid aside business and gone a-fishing.

IZAAK WALTON, 1593 - 1683

TO SLEEP

A flock of sheep that leisurely pass by,
One after one; the sound of rain, and bees
Murmuring; the fall of rivers, winds and
  seas,
Smooth fields, white sheets of water, and
  pure sky;
I've thought of all by turns, and yet do
  lie
Sleepless; and soon the small birds'
  melodies
Must hear, first uttered from my orchard
  trees;
And the first cuckoo's melancholy cry.
Even thus last night, and two nights more,
  I lay,
And could not win thee, Sleep! by any
  stealth:
So do not let me wear to-night away:
Without Thee what is all the morning's
  wealth?
Come, blessed barrier between day and
  day,
Dear mother of fresh thoughts and joyous
  health!

WILLIAM WORDSWORTH, 1770 - 1850

❦

Now blessing light on him that first invented sleep! It covers a man all over,
thoughts and all, like a cloak; 'tis meat
for the hungry, drink for the thirsty, heat
for the cold, and cold for the hot. 'tis the
current coin that purchases all the pleasures of the world cheap; and the balance
that sets the king and the shepherd, the
fool and the wise men even.

MIGUEL DE CERVANTES, 1547 - 1616

School is over,
  Oh, what fun!
Lessons finished,
  Play begun.
Who'll run fastest,
  You or I?
Who'll laugh loudest?
  Let us try.
KATE GREENAWAY, 1845 - 1901

from THE BATTLE OF BLENHEIM

And everybody praised the Duke
  Who this great fight did win.
"But what good came of it at last?"
  Quoth little Peterkin.
"Why, that I cannot tell," said he
"But 'twas a famous victory."

ROBERT SOUTHEY, 1774 - 1843

❦

Sleep, to the homeless thou art home;
the friendless find in thee friend.

EBENEZER ELLIOT

❦

"SISTER, AWAKE!"

Sister, awake! close not your eyes!
  The day her light discloses,
And the bright morning doth arise
  Out of her bed of roses.

See ,the clear sun, the world's bright eye,
  In at our window peeping:
Lo, how he blusheth to espy
  Us idle wenches sleeping!

Therefore awake! make haste, I say,
  And let us, without staying,
All in our gowns of green so gay
  Into the park a-maying!

❦

THE TASK

Come, Evening, once again, season of
  peace;
Return, sweet Evening, and continue long!
Methinks I see thee in the streaky west,
With matron-step slow-moving, while the
  night
Treads on thy sweeping train; one hand
  employed
In letting fall the curtain of repose
On bird and beast, the other charged for
  man
With sweet oblivion of the cares of day.

WILLIAM COWPER, 1731 - 1800

96

❧

A MADRIGAL

The trickling rain doth fall
Upon us one and all;
The south-wind kisses
The saucy milkmaid's cheek,
The nun's, demure and meek,
Nor any misses.

E. C. STEDMAN, 1833 - 1908

❧

PHILOMEL

As it fell upon a day
In the merry month of May,
Sitting in a pleasant shade
Which a grove of myrtles made,
Beasts did leap and birds did sing,
Trees did grow and plants did spring;
Everything did banish moan
Save the Nightingale alone:
She, poor bird, as all forlorn
Leaned her breast up-till a thorn,
And there sung the doleful'st ditty,
That to hear it was great pity.
Fie, fie, fie! now would she cry;
Tereu, Tereu! by and by;
That to hear her so complain
Scarce I could from tears refrain;
For her griefs so lively shown
Made me think upon mine own.

RICHARD BARNFIELD, 1574 - 1627

HOW TO LIVE—

Many men knows the laws of mathematics and are skilled in the arts, but most men know very little about the laws governing life, the art of living. One may be able to build an airplane and circle the globe, and yet be entirely ignorant of the simple art of how to be happy, successful and content. When studying the arts, place first upon the list, the art of living.

❧

A RECEIPT FOR COURTSHIP

Two or three dears, and two or three
*   sweets;*
Two or three balls, and two or three
*   treats;*
Two or three serenades, given as a lure;
Two or three oaths, how much they
*   endure;*
Two or three messages sent in one day;
Two or three times led out from the
*   play;*
Two or three soft speeches made by the
*   way,*
Two or three tickets for two or three
*   times;*
Two or three letters writ in all rhymes,
Two or three months keeping strict to
*   these rules*
Can never fail making a couple of fools.

JONATHAN SWIFT, 1667 - 1745

❧

SONG ON A MAY MORNING

Now the bright morning star, day's
*   harbinger,*
Comes dancing from the east, and leads
*   with her*
The flowery May, who from her green lap
*   throws*
The yellow cowslip and the pale primrose.
Hail, bounteous May, that dost inspire
Mirth and youth and warm desire!
Woods and groves are of thy dressing,
Hill and dale doth boast thy blessing.
Thus we salute thee with our early song,
And welcome thee, and wish thee long.

JOHN MILTON, 1608 - 1674

FORGET AND REMEMBER

Forget each kindness that you do
As soon as you have done it;
Forget the praise that falls to you
The moment you have won it.
Forget the slander that you hear
Before you can repeat it;
Forget each slight, each spite, each sneer,
Wherever you may meet it.

Remember every kindness done
To you, whate'er its measure;
Remember praise by others won,
And pass it on with pleasure;
Remember every promise made,
And keep it to the letter;
Remember those who lend you aid,
And be a grateful debtor.

❦

ALFRED E. SMITH, 1873 - 1944 when asked about the New Deal, replied that he wanted nothing to do with it—"No matter how thin you slice it, it's still baloney."

❦

from ADVENTURES OF IDEAS

. . But civilization is more than the appreciation of the Fine Arts. We must not tie it down to museums and studios.

I put forward as a general definition of civilization, that a civilized society is exhibiting the five qualities of Truth, Beauty, Adventure, Art, Peace.

ALFRED NORTH WHITEHEAD, 1861 - 1947

❦

ALWAYS FINISH

If a task is once begun
Never leave it till it's done
Be the labor great or small,
Do it well or not at all.

❦

from ANIMAL FARM

All animals are equal. The single Commandment: But some animals are more equal than others.

GEORGE ORWELL (Eric Hugh Blair)
1903 - 1950

APPARITIONS

Such a starved bank of moss
Till, that May-morn,
Blue ran the flash across:
Violets were born!

Sky—what a scowl of cloud
Till, near and far,
Ray on ray split the shroud:
Splendid, a star!

World—how it walled about
Life with disgrace
Till God's own smile came out:
That was thy face!

ROBERT BROWNING, 1812 - 1889

How sweet, how passing sweet, is Solitude!
But grant me still a friend in my retreat,
Whom I may whisper, Solitude is sweet.

WILLIAM COWPER, 1731 - 1800

❦

MAY

Come walk with me along this willowed
lane,
Where, like lost coinage from some
miser's store,
The golden dandelions more and more
Glow, as the warm sun kisses them again!
For this is May! who with a daisy chain
Leads on the laughing Hours; for now is
o'er
Long winter's trance. No longer rise and
roar
His forest-wrenching blasts. The hopeful
swain,
Along the furrow, sings behind his team;
Loud pipes the redbreast—troubadour of
spring,
And vocal all the morning copses ring;
More blue the skies in lucent lakelets
gleam;
And the glad earth, caressed by
murmuring showers,
Wakes like a bride, to deck herself with
flowers!

HENRY SYLVESTER CORNWELL, 1831 - 1886

from THALABA

How beautiful is night!
A dewey freshness fills the silent air
No mist obscures, nor cloud, nor speck,
  nor stain
Breaks the serene of heaven;
In full-orbed glory yonder moon divine
Rolls through the dark blue depths.
  Beneath her steady ray
  The desert-circle spreads
Like the round ocean, girdled with the
  sky.
How beautiful is night!

ROBERT SOUTHEY, 1774 - 1843

THE DAY IS DONE

The day is done, and the darkness
  Falls from the wings of Night,
As a feather is wafted downward
  From an eagle in his flight.

I see the lights of the village
  Gleam through the rain and the mist,
And a feeling of sadness comes o'er me,
  That my soul cannot resist:

A feeling of sadness and longing,
  That is not akin to pain,
And resembles sorrow only
  As the mist resembles the rain.

Then read from the treasured volume
  The poem of thy choice,
And lend to the rhyme of the poet
  The beauty of thy voice.

And the night shall be filled with music,
  And the cares that infest the day,
Shall fold their tents like the Arabs,
  And silently steal away.

HENRY WADSWORTH LONGFELLOW

from SUMMER LONGINGS

Ah! my heart is weary waiting,
  Waiting for the May,—
Waiting for the pleasant rambles
Where the fragrant hawthorn-brambles,
  With the woodbine alternating,
  Scent the dewy way.
Ah! my heart is weary waiting,
  Waiting for the May.

Waiting sad, dejected, weary,
  Waiting for the May:
Spring goes by with wasted warnings,—
Moonlit evenings, sunbright mornings,—
  Summer comes, yet dark and dreary
  Life still ebbs away;
Man is ever weary, weary,
  Waiting for the May!

DENIS FLORENCE MacCARTHY, 1817 - 1882

For what power is there, in the name of gods and men! who would wish to be surrounded by unlimited wealth and to abound in every material blessing, on condition that he love no one and that no one love him? Such indeed is the life of tyrants—a life, I mean, in which there can be no faith, no affection, no trust in the continuance of good will, and where friendship has no place.

CICERO

They, who are of the opinion that Money will do everything, may very well be suspected to do everything for Money.

GEORGE SAVILE, 1633 - 1695

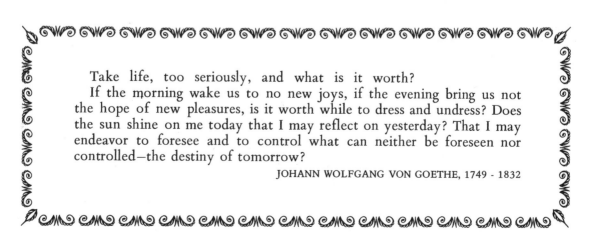

Take life, too seriously, and what is it worth?
If the morning wake us to no new joys, if the evening bring us not the hope of new pleasures, is it worth while to dress and undress? Does the sun shine on me today that I may reflect on yesterday? That I may endeavor to foresee and to control what can neither be foreseen nor controlled—the destiny of tomorrow?

JOHANN WOLFGANG VON GOETHE, 1749 - 1832

THE PHYSICIAN'S OATH

I swear by Apollo Physician, by Asclepius, by Health, by Panacea, and by all the gods and goddesses, making them my witnesses, that I will carry out, according to my ability and judgment, this oath and this indenture. To hold my teacher in this art equal to my own parents; to make him partner in my livelihood; when he is in need of money to share mine with him; to consider his family as my own brothers, and to teach them this art, if they want to learn it, without fee or indenture ... I will use treatment to help the sick according to my ability and judgment, but never with a view to injury and wrongdoing ... I will keep pure and holy both my life and my art ... In whatsoever houses I enter, I will enter to help the sick, and I will abstain from all intentional wrongdoing and harm, especially from abusing the bodies of man or woman, bond or free. And whatsoever I shall see or hear in the course of my profession in my intercourse with men, if it be what should not be published abroad, I will never divulge, holding such things to be holy secrets. Now if I carry out this oath, and break it not, may I gain forever reputation among all men for my life and for my art; but if I transgress it and forswear myself, may the opposite befall me.

HIPPOCRATES, 460 - 400 B.C.

❦

I wonder why ye can always read a doctor's bill an ye niver can read his purscription.

FINLEY PETER DUNNE (MR. DOOLEY), 1867 - 1936

❦

In a good surgeon, a hawk's eye: a lion's heart: and a lady's hand.

LEONARD WRIGHT
16th century

❦

All that I am or hope to be, I owe to my angel mother.

ABRAHAM LINCOLN

THE HUMAN SEASONS

Four Seasons fill the measure of the year;
There are four seasons in the mind of
* man:*
He has his lusty Spring, when fancy clear
Takes in all beauty with an easy span:

He has his Summer, when luxuriously
Spring's honeyed cud of youthful thought
* he loves*
To ruminate, and by such dreaming high
Is nearest unto Heaven: quiet coves

His soul has in its Autumn, when his
* wings*
He furleth close; contented so to look
On mists in idleness—to let fair things
Pass by unheeded as a threshold brook:—

He has his Winter too of pale misfeature,
Or else he would forego his mortal nature.

JOHN KEATS, 1795 - 1821

SCYTHE SONG

Mowers, weary and brown, and blithe,
* What is the word methinks ye know,*
Endless over-word that the Scythe
* Sings to the blades of the grass below?*
Scythes that swing in the grass and clover,
* Something, still, they say as they pass;*
What is the word that, over and over,
* 'Sings the Scythe to the flowers and*
*   grass?*

Hush, ah hush, the Scythes are saying,
* Hush, and heed not, and fall asleep;*
Hush, they say to the grasses swaying,
* Hush, they sing to the clover deep!*
Hush—'tis the lullaby Time is singing—
* Hush, and heed not, for all things pass,*
Hush, ah hush! and the Scythes are
*   swinging*
* Over the clover, over the grass!*

ANDREW LANG, 1844 - 1912

A Resolution was introduced in the House of Representatives May 7, 1914 providing that the second Sunday in May be designated "Mother's Day". The Senate approved it the next day, and President Woodrow Wilson issued a proclamation asking the public to display the American flag "as a public expression of our love and reverence for the mothers of our country."

Every year since has seen a greater or wider observance of Mother's Day. And although gifts, flowers, messages and dinner out, have become a way of expressing thought of one's mother, it is now an American custom!

✦

All that I am my mother made me.

JOHN QUINCY ADAMS

Another Mother's Day that's authentic but not nationally observed is the day school reopens in September.

✦

MRS. DARLING: Peter . . . . let me adopt you . . . .
PETER: Would you send me to school?
MRS. DARLING: Yes.
PETER: And then to an office?
MRS. DARLING: I suppose so.
PETER: Soon I should be a man?
MRS. DARLING: Very soon.
PETER: I don't want to go to school and learn solemn things. No one is going to catch me, lady, and make me a man. I want always to be a little boy and to have fun.

JAMES M. BARRIE, 1860 - 1937

Peter Pan (Act V)

WOMAN IN THE GARDEN

Now, there is my corn, two or three inches high this 18th of May, and apparently having no fear of a frost. I was hoeing it this morning for the first time—it is not well usually to hoe corn until about the 18th of May—when Polly came out to look at the Lima beans. She seemed to think the poles had come up beautifully. I thought they did look well: they are a fine set of poles, large and well grown, and stand straight. They were inexpensive too. The cheapness came about from my cutting them on another man's land, and he did not know it. I have not examined this transaction in the moral light of gardening; but I know people in this country take great liberties at the polls. Polly noticed that the beans had not themselves come up in any proper sense, but that the dirt had got off from them, leaving them uncovered. She thought it would be well to sprinkle a slight layer of dirt over them; and I, indulgently, consented. It occurred to me, when she had gone, that beans always come up that way—wrong end first; and that what they wanted was light, and not dirt.

Observation.—Woman always did, from the first, make a muss in a garden.

CHARLES DUDLEY WARNER
[My Summer in a Garden: 1st Week]

THE WHISTLE

When I was a child of seven years old, my friends on a holiday filled my little pocket with halfpence. I went directly to a shop where they sold toys for children; and being charmed with the sound of a whistle that I saw by the way, in the hands of another boy, I voluntarily offered and gave all my money for it. When I came home, whistling all over the house, much pleased with my whistle, but disturbing all the family; my brothers, sisters, and cousins, understanding the bargain I had made, told me I had given four times as much for it as it was worth; put me in mind what good things I might have bought with the rest of the money; and laughed at me so much for my folly, that I cried with vexation; and the reflection gave me more chagrin than the whistle gave me pleasure.

"This however was afterwards of use to me, the impression continuing on my mind so that often, as I grew up and came into the world, and observed the actions of men, I thought I met many, 'who gave too much for the whistle.'

"When I met a man of pleasure, sacrificing every laudable improvement of his mind or of his fortune, to mere material satisfactions, and ruining his health in their pursuit, 'Mistaken man,'' say I, 'you are providing pain for yourself instead of pleasure; you pay too much for your whistle.'—If I see one fond of appearance only, of fine clothes, fine houses, fine furniture, all above his fortune, for which he contracts debts, and ends his career in prison, 'Alas!' say I, 'he has paid dear, very dear, for his whistle.'

"In short, I conceived that great part of the miseries of mankind were brought upon them by the false estimates they have made of the value of things, and by their 'giving too much for their whistles.'"

BENJAMIN FRANKLIN, 1706 - 1790

ⓒⓌⓢ

When the meek inherit the earth, they will have little left after paying inheritance, capital gains and other taxes.

"The cost of a thing," says Thoreau, "is the amount of what I will call life which is required to be exchanged for it, immediately or in the long run." I have been accustomed to put it to myself, perhaps more clearly, that the price we have to pay for money is paid in liberty. Between these two ways of it, at least, the reader will probably not fail to find a third definition of his own, and it follows, on one or other, that a man may pay too dearly for his livelihood by giving in Thoreau's terms, his whole life for it, or, in mine, bartering for it the whole of his available liberty, and becoming a slave till death. There are two questions to be considered—the quality of what we buy, and the price we have to pay for it. Do you want a thousand a year, a two thousand a year or a ten thousand a year, livelihood? and can you afford the one you want? It is a matter of taste; it is not in the least degree a question of duty, though commonly supposed so. But there is no authority for that view anywhere. It is nowhere in the Bible. It is true that we might do a vast amount of good if we were wealthy, but it is also highly improbable; not many do; and the art of growing rich is not only quite distinct from that of doing good, but the practice of the one does not at all train a man for practising the other. "Money might be of great service to me," writes Thoreau, "but the difficulty now is that I do not improve my opportunities, and therefore I am not prepared to have my opportunities increased." It is a mere illusion that, above a certain income, the personal desires will be satisfied and leave a wider margin for the generous impulse. It is as difficult to be generous, or anything else, except perhaps a member of Parliament, on thirty thousand as on two thousand a year.

ROBERT LOUIS STEVENSON, 1850 - 1894

ⓒⓌⓢ

The best things in life are free but it costs a lot of time and money before you find this out.

ⓒⓌⓢ

In every business there is a constant struggle between the head and the overhead.

THE GREAT LOVER

These I have loved:
White plates and cups, clean-gleaming,
Ringed with blue lines; and feathery, faery
*   dust;*
Wet roofs, beneath the lamplight; the
*   strong crust*
Of friendly bread; and many-tasting food;
Rainbows; and the blue bitter smoke of
*   wood;*
And radiant raindrops couching in cool
*   flowers;*
And flowers themselves, that sway
*   through sunny hours,*
Dreaming of moths that drink them under
*   the moon;*
Then, the cool kindliness of sheets, that
*   soon*
Smooth away trouble; and the rough male
*   kiss*
Of blankets; grainy hair; live hair; that is
Shining and free; blue-massing clouds; the
*   keen*
Unpassioned beauty of a great machine;
The benison of hot water; furs to touch;
The good smell of old clothes; and others
*   such—*
The comfortable smell of friendly fingers,
Hair's fragrance, and the musty reek that
*   lingers*
About dead leaves and last year's ferns.

RUPERT BROOKE, 1887 - 1915

FLOWER IN THE CRANNIED WALL

Flower in the crannied wall,
I pluck you out of the crannies,
I hold you here, root and all, in my hand,
Little flower—but if I could understand
What you are, root and all, and all in all,
I should know what God and man is.

ALFRED TENNYSON, 1809 - 1892

SONG

The feathers of the willow
Are half of them grown yellow
*   Above the swelling stream;*
And ragged are the bushes,
And rusty now the rushes,
*   And wild the clouded gleam.*

The thistle now is older,
His stalk begins to moulder,
*   His head is white as snow;*
The branches all are barer,
The linnet's song is rarer,
*   The robin pipeth now.*

RICHARD WATSON DIXON, 1833 - 1900

The world of the future belongs to the optimists—to those who seek for right solutions of difficult problems and who are confident that they will achieve success.

The things that were hardest to hear are sweetest to remember.

SENECA A. D. 50

The art of saying appropriate words in a kindly way is one that never goes out of style, never ceases to please, and is within the reach of the humblest.

Friendship is the melody and fragrance of life.

There are persons so radiant, so genial, so kind, so pleasure-bearing, that you instinctively feel in their presence that they do you good; whose coming into a room is like the bringing of a lamp there.

HENRY WARD BEECHER

A PSALM OF LIFE

Tell me not, in mournful numbers,
    Life is but an empty dream!
For the soul is dead that slumbers,
    And things are not what they seem.

Life is real! Life is earnest!
    And the grave is not its goal;
Dust thou art, to dust returnest,
    Was not spoken of the soul.

Not enjoyment, and not sorrow,
    Is our destined end or way;
But to act, that each to-morrow
    Finds us farther than to-day,

Art is long, and Time is fleeting,
    And our hearts, though stout and brave,
Still, like muffled drums, are beating
    Funeral marches to the grave.

In the world's broad field of battle,
    In the bivouac of Life,
Be not like dumb, driven cattle!
    Be a hero in the strife!

Trust no Future, howe'er pleasant!
    Let the dead Past bury its dead!
Act,—act in the living Present!
    Heart within, and God o'erhead;

Lives of great men all remind us
    We can make our lives sublime,
And, departing, leave behind us
    Footprints on the sands of time—

Footprints, that perhaps another,
    Sailing o'er life's solemn main,
A forlorn and shipwrecked brother,
    Seeing, shall take heart again.

Let us, then, be up and doing,
    With a heart for any fate;
Still achieving, still pursuing,
    Learn to labor and to wait.

HENRY WADSWORTH LONGFELLOW, 1807 - 1882

THE BROWN THRUSH

There's a merry brown thrush sitting up in
    the tree.
"He's singing to me! He's singing to me!"
    And what does he say, little girl, little
        boy?
    "Oh, the world's running over with joy!
        Don't you hear? Don't you see?
        Hush! Look! In my tree,
        I'm as happy as happy can be!"

So the merry brown thrush sings away in
    the tree,
To you and to me, to you and to me;
    And he sings all the day, little girl, little
        boy,
    "Oh, the world's running over with joy!
        But long it won't be,
        Don't you know? Don't you see?
        Unless you're as good as can be."

LUCY LARCOM, 1824 - 1893

Happy the man, and happy he alone,
He, who can call to-day his own:
He who, secure within, can say:
"To-morrow do thy worst, for I have
    liv'd today."

HORACE, 65-8 B.C.

No civilization is complete which does not include the dumb and defenseless of God's creatures within the sphere of charity and mercy.

QUEEN VICTORIA

Better late than never.

DIONYSIUS

WORDS TO THE WISE

Thrift to some people means worrying about what became of last month's income.

For age and want, save while you may, No morning lasts a whole day.

BENJAMIN FRANKLIN

❧

To refute that we are easily satisfied, Justice Holmes wrote this satirical verse:

"MAN WANTS BUT LITTLE HERE BELOW"

Little I ask, my wants are few,
*   I only wish a hut of stone,*
(A very plain brownstone will do)—
*   That I may call my own.*
I care not much for gold or land,
*   Give me a mortgage here and there*
Some good bank stock, some note of hand
*   Or trifling railroad share.*

Jewels and baubles?—'tis a sin
*   To care for such unfruitful things.*
One good-sized diamond in a pin,
*   Some not so large, in rings,*
A ruby and a pearl or so will do for me.
*   I laugh at show . . .*

Thus humbly, let me live and die
*   Nor long for Midas' golden touch*
If heaven, more generous gifts deny
*   I shall not miss them—much;*
Too grateful for the blessing lent
*   Of simple tastes and much content!*

OLIVER WENDELL HOLMES, 1809 - 1894

A PRAYER AS WE GROW OLDER

Keep me from the fatal habit of thinking that I must say something on every subject and on every occasion.

Release me from craving to straighten out everybody's affairs.

Make me thoughtful but not moody; helpful but not bossy. With my vast store of wisdom, it seems a pity not to use it all—but Thou knowest, Lord, that I want a few friends at the end.

Keep my mind from the recital of endless details—give me wings to get to the point.

Seal my lips on my aches and pains. They are increasing and love of rehearsing them is becoming sweeter as the years go by.

I dare not ask for grace enough to enjoy the tales of others but help me to enjoy them with patience.

I dare not ask for improved memory but a growing humility and lessening cocksureness when my memory seems to clash with the memory of others.

Teach me the glorious lesson that occasionally I may be mistaken.

Keep me reasonably sweet. I do not want to be a saint—some of them are hard to live with—but a sour old person is one of the crowning works of the devil.

Give me the ability to see good things in unexpected places and talents in unexpected people. Give me the grace to tell them so.

❧

All I have seen teaches me to trust the Creator for all I have not seen.

RALPH WALDO EMERSON

RECIPROCITY

With the May blossoms, cheery and bold,
  Came the oriole's song to his mate;
  And he sang to her early and late
The one theme that can never grow old;
  While after-notes too eager to wait,
  All regardless of measure and date,
Were at any odd season outrolled,
When she thought his whole story was
    told.

Serene in her golden-hued gown sat she,
  With no sign of assent or demur
  To the rhapsodies showered upon her
By the flamelet aloft in the tree.
  That her love was awake and astir
  With his jubilant music and whir,
She could trust such a wooer to see.
"Nothing sweeter than silence," sang he.

D. H. INGHAM

from ON A FLY DRINKING OUT OF A
CUP OF ALE

Busy, curious, thirsty fly,
Drink with me, and drink as I;
Freely welcome to my cup,
Couldst thou sip and sip it up.
Make the most of life you may;
Life is short and wears away.
Both alike are mine and thine,
Hastening quick to their decline;
Thine's a summer, mine no more,
Though repeated to three-score;
Three-score summers, when they've gone,
Will appear as short as one.

WILLIAM OLDYS, 1696 - 1761

If one suffers a hundred bee stings, one
will never have rheumatism.

FLIGHT

A flea and a fly in a flue
Were imprisoned, so what could they do?
  Said the fly, "Let us flee,"
  Said the flea, "Let us fly,"
So they flew through a flaw in the flue.

BUSY BEE

How doth the little busy bee
  Improve each shining hour,
And gather honey all the day
  From every opening flower!

How skillfully she builds her cell!
  How neat she spreads her wax!
And labors hard to store it well
  With the sweet food she makes.

In works of labor or of skill,
  I would be busy too;
For Satan finds some mischief still
  For idle hands to do.

In books, or work or beautiful play,
  Let my first years be passed,
That I may give for every day
  Some good account of last.

ISAAC WATTS, 1674 - 1748

from THE MAN AND THE FLEA

"I cannot raise my worth too high;
Of what vast consequence am I!"
"Not of the importance you suppose,"
Replies a flea upon his nose;
"Be humble, learn thyself to scan;
Know, pride was never made for man."

JOHN GAY, 1685 - 1782

The chief objection to gardening is that
by the time your back gets used to it,
your enthusiasm is gone.

WHAT IS GOOD?

"What is the real good?"
I ask in musing mood.

"Order," said the law court;
"Knowledge," said the school;
"Truth," said the wise man;
"Pleasure," said the page;
"Love," said the maiden;
"Beauty," said the page;
"Freedom," said the dreamer;
"Home," said the sage;
"Fame," said the soldier;
"Equity," said the seer.
Spake my heart fully sad:
"The answer is not here."

Then within my bosom
Softly this I heard:
"Each heart holds the secret:
'Kindness' is the word."

JOHN BOYLE O'REILLY, 1844 - 1890

It might be a good idea if the various countries of the world would occasionally swap history books, just to see what other people are doing with the same set of facts.

BILL VAUGHAN

from THE WATER BABIES

When all the world is young, lad,
And all the trees are green;
And every goose a swan, lad,
And every lass a queen;
Then hey for boot and horse, lad,
And round the world away:
Young blood must have its course, lad,
And every dog his day.

When all the world is old, lad,
And all the trees are brown;
And all the sport is stale, lad,
And all the wheels run down;
Creep home, and take your place there,
The spent and maimed among:
God grant you find one face there,
You loved when all was young.

CHARLES KINGSLEY, 1819 - 1875

I don't know who my grandfather was: I am much more concerned to know what his grandson will be.

Every man over forty is responsible for his face—to a cabinet member when Lincoln was taken to account for turning down a job applicant because he didn't like his face.

He reminds me of the man who murdered both his parents, and then, when sentence was about to be passed, pleaded for mercy on the grounds he was an orphan.

No man has a good enough memory to be a successful liar.

ABRAHAM LINCOLN, 1809 - 1865

Fools can make money.
It takes a wise man to tell how to spend it.

ENGLISH PROVERB

"NO!"

Learn to speak this little word
In its proper place;
Let no timid doubt be heard,
Clothed with sceptic grace;
Let thy lips, without disguise,
Boldly pour it out;
Though a thousand dulcet lies
Keep hovering about.
For be sure our lives would lose
Future years of woe,
If our courage could refuse
The present hour with "No."

ELIZA COOK, 1818 - 1889

THIS LAND AND FLAG

What is the love of country for which our flag stands? Maybe it begins with love of the land itself. It is the fog rolling in with the tide at Eastport, or thru the Golden Gate and among the towers of San Francisco. It is the sun coming up behind the White Mountains, over the Green, throwing a shining glory on Lake Champlain and above the Adirondacks. It is the storied Mississippi rolling swift and muddy past St. Louis, rolling past Cairo, pouring down past the levees of New Orleans. It is lazy noontide in the pines of Carolina, it is a sea of wheat rippling in Western Kansas, it is the San Francisco peaks far north across the glowing naked-ness of Arizona, it is the Grand Canyon and a little stream coming down out of a New England ridge, in which are trout.

It is men at work. It is the storm-tossed fisherman coming into Gloucester and Provincetown and Astoria. It is the farmer riding his great machine in the dust of harvest, the dairyman going to the barn before sunrise, the lineman mending the broken wire, the miner drilling for the blast. It is the servants of fire in the mur-ky splendor of Pittsburgh, between the Allegheny and the Monogahela, the trucks rumbling thru the night, the locomotive engineer bringing the train in on time, the pilot in the clouds, the riveter running along the beam a hundred feet in air. It is the clerk in the office, the housewife doing the dishes and sending the children off to school. It is the teacher, doctor, and parson tending and helping, body and soul, for small reward.

It is small things remembered, the little corners of the land, the houses, the people that each one loves. We love our country because there was a little tree on a hill, and grass thereon, and a sweet val-ley below; because the hurdy-gurdy man came along on a sunny morning in a city street; because a beach or a farm or a lane or a house that might not seem much to others were once, for each of us, made magic. It is voices that are remembered only, no longer heard. It is parents, friends, the lazy chat of street and store and office, and the ease of mind that makes life tranquil. It is summer and win-ter, rain and sun and storm. These are flesh of our flesh, bone of our bone, blood of our blood, a lasting part of what we are, each of us and all of us together.

It is stories told. It is the Pilgrims dying in their first dreadful winter. It is the Minute Man standing his ground at Con-cord Bridge, and dying there. It is the army in rags, sick, freezing, starving at Valley Forge. It is the wagons and the men on foot going westward over Cum-berland Gap, floating down the great rivers, rolling over the great plains. It is the settler hacking fiercely at the primeval forest on his new, his own lands. It is Thoreau at Walden Pond, Lincoln at Cooper Union, and Lee riding home from Appomattox. It is corruption and dis-grace, answered always by men who would not let the flag lie in the dust, who have stood up in every generation to fight for the old ideals and the old rights, at risk of ruin or of life itself.

It is a great multitude of people on pil-grimage, common and ordinary people, charged with the usual human failings, yet filled with such a hope as never caught the imaginations and the hearts of any na-tion on earth before. The hope of liberty. The hope of justice. The hope of a land in which a man can stand straight, with-out fear, without rancor.

The land and the people and the flag—the land a continent, the people of every race, the flag a symbol of what humanity may aspire to when the wars are over and the barriers are down; to these each gener-ation must be dedicated and consecrated anew, to defend with life itself, if need be, but, above all, in friendliness, in hope, in courage, to live for.

THE NEW YORK TIMES
Editorial Jan. 14, 1940.

BATTLE HYMN OF THE REPUBLIC

Mine eyes have seen the glory of the coming of the Lord:
He is trampling out the vintage where the grapes of wrath are stored;
He hath loosed the fateful lightning of His terrible swift sword:
   His truth is marching on.
I have seen Him in the watch-fires of a hundred circling camps;
They have builded Him an altar in the evening dews and damps;
I can read His righteous sentence by the dim and flaring lamps:
   His day is marching on.
I have read a fiery gospel, writ in burnished rows of steel:
"As ye deal with my contemners, so with you my grace shall deal;
Let the Hero, born of woman, crush the serpent with His heel, Since
   God is marching on."
He has sounded forth the trumpet that shall never call retreat;
He is sifting out the hearts of men before His judgment-seat:
O, be swift, my soul, to answer Him! Be jubilant, my feet!
   Our God is marching on.
In the beauty of the lilies Christ was born across the sea,
With the glory in His bosom that transfigures you and me;
As He died to make men holy, let us die to make men free,
   While God is marching on.

                                             JULIA WARD HOWE, 1819 - 1910

HERE RESTS IN
HONORED GLORY
AN AMERICAN
SOLDIER
KNOWN BUT TO GOD

Inscription on Tomb of Unknown Soldier, Arlington
Cemetery, Washington, D.C.

from THE BIVOUAC OF THE DEAD

The muffled drum's sad roll has beat
   The soldier's last tattoo;
No more on Life's parade shall meet
   That brave and fallen few.
On Fame's eternal camping-ground
   Their silent tents are spread,
And Glory guards, with solemn round,
   The bivouac of the dead.

Yon marble minstrel's voiceless stone
   In deathless song shall tell,
When many a vanished age hath flown,
   The story how ye fell;
Nor wreck, nor change, nor winter's blight,
   Nor Time's remorseless doom,
Shall dim one ray of glory's light
   That gilds your deathless tomb.

        THEODORE O'HARA, 1820 - 1867

"HOW SLEEP THE BRAVE"

How sleep the brave, who sink to rest
By all their country's wishes blest!
When Spring, with dewy fingers cold,
Returns to deck their hallowed mould,
She there shall dress a sweeter sod
Than Fancy's feet have ever trod.

By fairy hands their knell is rung;
By forms unseen their dirge is sung;
There Honor comes, a pilgrim gray,
To bless the turf that wraps their clay;
And Freedom shall awhile repair
To dwell, a weeping hermit, there!

        WILLIAM COLLINS, 1721 - 1759

I have heard something said about allegiance to the South. I know no South, no North, no East, no West to which I owe any allegiance.. The gentleman speaks of Virginia being my country. The Union, sir, is my country.

        HENRY CLAY, 1777 - 1852
        Speech in the Senate, 1848

A THOUGHT

If all the harm that women have done
Were put in a bundle and rolled into one,
 Earth would not hold it,
 The sky could not enfold it,
It could not be lighted nor warmed by
  the sun;
 Such masses of evil
 Would puzzle the devil
And keep him in fuel while Time's wheels
  run.

But if all the harm that's done by men
Were doubled and doubled and doubled
  again,
And melted and fused into vapor and then
Were squared and raised to the power of
  ten,
There wouldn't be nearly enough, not
  near,
To keep a small girl for the tenth of a
  year.

      JAMES KENNETH STEPHEN, 1859 - 1892

Ailments of a hypochondriac are not only chronic, but chronicles!

An advertisement in a Pennsylvania paper attracted a great deal of notice, especially as it was headed "Mother's Day Special." It read: "Don't Kill Your Wife. Let Our Washing Machine Do the Dirty Work."

A REASONABLE AFFLICTION

On his death-bed poor Lubin lies:
 His spouse is in despair;
With frequent cries, and mutual sighs,
 They both express their care.

"A different cause," says Parson Sly,
 "The same effect may give:
Poor Lubin fears that he may die;
 His wife, that he may live."

      MATTHEW PRIOR, 1664 - 1721

A lifetime of happiness! No man alive could bear it: It would be hell on earth.

      G.B. SHAW, 1856 - 1950

A VERY NICE PAIR

Two magpies sat on a garden wall,
 As it might be Wednesday week;
And one little magpie wagged his tail
 In the other little magpie's beak.

And doubling like a fist his little claw-
  hand,
 Said this other: "Upon my word,
This is more than flesh and blood can
  stand,
 Of magpie or any other bird."

So they picked and they scratched each
  other's little eyes,
 Till all that was left on the rail
Was the beak of one of the little magpies,
 And the other little magpie's tail.

"A GOOD, LONG WAIT"

My granddad, viewing earth's worn cogs,
Said things were going to the dogs;
His granddad in his house of logs
Said things were going to the dogs;
His granddad in the Flemish bogs
Said things were going to the dogs;
His granddad in his old skin togs
Said things were going to the dogs;
There's one thing that I have to state—
The dogs have had a good long wait.

JUNE

"And what is so rare as a day in June?
Then, if ever, come perfect days . ."

from
THE VISION OF SIR LAUNFAL

And what is so rare as a day in June?
  Then, if ever, come perfect days;
Then Heaven tries earth if it be in tune,
  And over it softly her warm ear lays;
Whether we look or whether we listen,
We hear life murmur, or see it glisten;
Every clod feels a stir of might,
  An instinct within it that reaches and
    towers,
And, groping blindly above it for light,
  Climbs to a soul in grass and flowers;
The flush of life may well be seen
  Thrilling back over hills and valleys;
The cowslip startles in meadows green,
  The buttercup catches the sun in its
    chalice,
And there's never a leaf nor a blade too
    mean
  To be some happy creature's palace;
The little bird sits at his door in the sun,
  Atilt like a blossom among the leaves,
And lets his illumined being o'errun
  With the deluge of summer it receives;
His mate feels the eggs beneath her wings,
And the heart in her dumb breast flutters
    and sings;
He sings to the wide world and she to her
    nest—
In the nice ear of Nature, which song is
    the best?

Now is the high-tide of the year,

And whatever of life hath ebbed away
Comes flooding back with a ripply cheer,
  Into every bare inlet and creek and bay;
Now the heart is so full that a drop overfills
    it,
We are happy now because God wills it;
No matter how barren the past may have
    been,
'Tis enough for us now that the leaves are
    green;
We sit in the warm shade and feel right
    well
How the sap creeps up and the blossoms
    swell;
We may shut our eyes, but we cannot help
    knowing
That skies are clear and grass is growing;
The breeze comes whispering in our ear,
That dandelions are blossoming near,
  That maize has sprouted, that streams
    are flowing,
That the river is bluer than the sky,
That the robin is plastering his house hard
    by;
And if the breeze kept the good news
    back,
For other couriers we should not lack;
  We could guess it all by yon heifer's
    lowing,—
And hark! how clear bold chanticleer,
Warmed with the new wine of the year,
  Tells all in his lusty crowing!

JAMES RUSSELL LOWELL, 1819 - 1891

❧❧❧❧❧❧❧❧❧❧❧❧❧❧❧

Memory is the treasury and guardian of all things.

CICERO 80 B.C.

Justice is as strictly due between neighbor nations as between neighbor citizens. A highwayman is as much a robber when he plunders in a gang as when single; and a nation that makes an unjust war is only a *great gang*.

BENJAMIN FRANKLIN

A nail is driven out by another nail, habit is overcome by habit.

ERASMUS, 1465 - 1536

Decoration Day, which later became Memorial Day, since 1868 has been observed on May 30th. Some authorities state this date was chosen as it was the date of the discharge of the last Union volunteers.

On June 28, 1968 a Congressional bill was signed into effect which provides uniform annual observances of certain legal holidays on Monday. Affected by this new act was Memorial Day, henceforth observed on the last Monday in May.

My cup runneth over.

OLD TESTAMENT
Psalms xxiii, 5.

ALMA MATER, FORGET ME

Twice a year,
    Chatty and blithe,
Letters requesting
    My old school tithe:

Twice a year
    It's "Dear Alumnus,
Don't we have
    Something com'n' us?

"Remember the class
    Of nineteen-o-;
It's time to pass
    The old chapeau."

Billets-doux
    To tous the alumni;
We are the stars
    They set their sum by.

This importuning
    Makes me bridle;
I get alma
    Matricidal.

Take the chapel
    Bell and hock it;
I'm tired of being
    Out of pocket.

Take the football
    Team and sell it;
Or save money—
    Just expel it.

I'm all paid up
    For my education;
Why don't you try
    The Ford Foundation?

And please forget
    The undersigned;
He'd like to cut
    The tithes that bind.

WILLIAM COLE

My Dearest Betsy, yesterday I received Letters from some of our Friends at the Camp informing me of the Engagement [Bunker Hill] between American troops and the Rebel Army in Charlestown. I can not but be greatly rejoyced at the tryed Valor of your Countrymen, who, by all Accounts behaved with an intrepidity becoming those who fought for their Liberties against the mercenary Soldiers of a Tyrant.

It is painful to me to reflect on the terror I must suppose you were under on hearing the Noise of War so near. Favor me, my dear, with an Account of your Apprehensions at that time, under your own hand . . . . . .

Mr. Pitts and Dr. Church inform me that my dear Son has at length escaped from the Prison at Boston . . . . Remember me to my dear Hannah and sister Polly and to all Friends.

Let me know where good old Swory is. Gage [the British General] has made me respectable by naming me first among those who are to receive no favor [of pardon] from him. I thoroughly despise him and his [amnesty] Proclamation . . . . The Clock is now striking twelve. I therefore wish you a good Night. Yours most affectionately,

SAMUEL ADAMS, 1722 - 1803
(Letter to his Wife, June 28th, 1775)

A SPRING LILT

Through the silver mist
    Of the blossom-spray
Trill the orioles: list
    To their joyous lay!
"What in all the world,
    in all the world,"
        they say,
"Is half so sweet, so sweet, is half so
        sweet as May?"

"June! June! June!"
    Low croon
The brown bees in the clover,
    "Sweet! sweet! sweet!"
Repeat
The robins, nested over.

from
THE ALHAMBRA BY MOONLIGHT

The moon has gradually gained upon the nights, and now rolls in full splendor above the towers, pouring a flood of tempered light into every court and hall. The garden beneath my window is gently lighted up; the orange and citron trees are tipped with silver; the fountain sparkles in the moonbeams, and even the blush of the rose is faintly visible.

I have sat for hours at my window inhaling the sweetness of the garden, and musing on the chequered features of those whose history is dimly shadowed out in the elegant memorials around. Sometimes I have issued forth at midnight when every thing was quiet, and have wandered over the whole building. Who can do justice to a moonlight night in such a climate, and in such a place! The temperature of an Andalusian midnight, in summer, is perfectly ethereal. We seem lifted up into a purer atmosphere; there is a serenity of soul, a buoyancy of spirits, and elasticity of frame, that render mere existence enjoyment. The effect of moonlight, too, on the Alhambra has something like enchantment. Every rent and chasm of time, every mouldering tint and weather stain disappears; the marble resumes its original whiteness; the long colonnades brighten in the moonbeams; the halls are illuminated with a softened radiance, until the whole edifice reminds one of the enchanted palace of an Arabian tale.

Sometimes I would hear the faint sounds of castanets from some party of dancers lingering in the Alameda; at other times I have heard the dubious tones of a guitar and the notes of a single voice rising from some solitary street and have pictured to myself some youthful cavalier serenading his lady's window, a gallant custom of former days, but now sadly on the decline, except in the remote towns and villages of Spain. Such were the scenes that have detained me for many an hour loitering about the courts and balconies of the castle, enjoying that mixture of reverie and sensation which steal away existence in a southern climate, and it has been almost morning before I have retired to my bed and been lulled to sleep by the falling waters of the fountain of Lindaraxa."

WASHINGTON IRVING, 1783 - 1859

HOW SWEET THE MOONLIGHT

How sweet the moonlight sleeps upon this
  bank!
Here we will sit and let the sounds of
  music
Creep in our ears: soft stillness and the
  night
Become the touches of sweet harmony.
Sit, Jessica. Look how the floor of heaven
Is thick inlaid with patines of bright gold:
There's not the smallest orb which thou
  behold'st
But in his motion like an angel sings,
Still quiring to the young-eyed cherubins.
Such harmony is in immortal souls;
But whilst this muddy vesture of decay
Doth grossly close it in, we cannot hear it.
  WILLIAM SHAKESPEARE

From The Merchant of Venice.

There exists no cure for a heart wounded with the sword of separation.

HITOPADESA

Love is the delusion that one woman differs from another.

H. L. MENCKEN

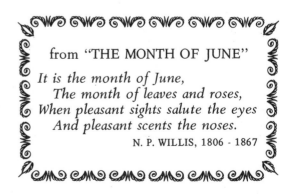

from "THE MONTH OF JUNE"

It is the month of June,
  The month of leaves and roses,
When pleasant sights salute the eyes
  And pleasant scents the noses.
  N. P. WILLIS, 1806 - 1867

THE JOYS OF MARRIAGE

How uneasy is his life,
Who is troubled with a wife!
Be she ne'er so fair or comely,
Be she ne'er so foul or homely,
Be she ne'er so young and toward,
Be she ne'er so old and froward,
Be she kind, with arms enfolding,
Be she cross, and always scolding,
Be she blithe or melancholy,
Have she wit, or have she folly,
Be she wary, be she squandering,
Be she staid, or be she wandering,
Be she constant, be she fickle,
Be she fire, or be she ickle;
Be she pious or ungodly,
Be she chaste, or what sounds oddly:
Lastly, be she good or evil,
Be she saint, or be she devil,—
Yet, uneasy is his life
Who is married to a wife.

CHARLES COTTON, 1630 - 1687

from WITNESS TO THE TRUTH

There is a field where all wonderful perfections of microscope and telescope fail, all exquisite niceties of weights and measures, as well as that which is behind them, the keen and driving power of the mind. No facts however indubitably detected, no effort of reason however magnificently maintained, can prove that Bach's music is beautiful.

EDITH HAMILTON, 1867 - 1963

LIVING

To touch the cup with eager lips and taste,
*   not drain it;*
To woo and tempt and court a bliss—and
*   not attain it;*
To fondle and caress a joy, yet hold it
*   lightly,*
Lest it become necessity and cling too
*   tightly;*
To watch the sun set in the west without
*   regretting;*
To hail its advent in the east—the night
*   forgetting;*
To smother care in happiness and grief in
*   laughter;*
To hold the present close—not questioning
*   hereafter;*
To have enough to share—to know the joy
*   of giving;*
To thrill with all the sweets of life—is
*   living.*

from "JUNE SONG"

O you poor folk in cities,
A thousand, thousand pities!
Heaping the fairy gold that withers and
*   dies;*
One field in June weather
Is worth all the gold ye gather,
One field in June weather - one Paradise.

KATHERINE TYNAN (HINKSON), 1861 - 1931
Irish poet and novelist.

I was born an American; I live an American; I shall die an American; and I intend to perform the duties incumbent upon me in that character to the end of my career. I mean to do this with absolute disregard of personal consequences. What are the personal consequences? What is the individual man, with all the good or evil that may betide him, in comparison with the good or evil which may befall a great country, and in the midst of great transactions which concern that country's fate? Let the consequences be what they will, I am careless. No man can suffer too much, and no man can fall too soon, if he suffer, or if he fall, in the defense of the liberties and constitution of his country.

DANIEL WEBSTER, 1782 - 1852

SO LONG! SON

A famous writer speaks here for all fathers whose sons
go off to war.

There was no band, no flags, no ceremonial. It wasn't even dramatic. A car honked outside and he said: "Well, I guess that's for me." He picked up his little bag, and his mother said: "You haven't forgotten your gloves?"

He kissed his mother and held out his hand to me. "Well, so long," he said. I took his hand but all I could say was "Good luck."

The door slammed and that was that—another boy gone to war.

I had advised waiting for the draft—waiting at least until he was required to register. I had pointed out that he was not yet of age. He had smiled at that, and assured me that his mind was made up. He wanted peace, he said. Without peace, what good was living?

There was finality in the way he said this—a finality at once grim and gentle. I said no more about waiting.

After the door closed behind him I went upstairs. I went to what had been his room. It was in worse chaos than usual. His bureau was littered—an incredible collection of things, letters, keys, invitations to parties he would not attend.

Clothing was scattered about—dancing pumps, a tennis racket, his precious collection of phonograph records, his trumpet, gleaming in its case.

I went then to my room. On the wall was a picture of a little boy, his toothless grin framed in tawny curls—the same boy who had just taken my hand and said: "Well, so long."

Not much time, I thought, between the making of that picture and the slamming of the front door. Not much more than a decade.

Suddenly, a queer thing happened. Objects came alive—whispered to me. The house was full of soft voices. They led me up to the attic—to a box of toy soldiers, a broken music rack, a football helmet, a homemade guitar, schoolbooks, class pictures, a stamp album, a penny bank with the lid pried off . . . ancient history, long hidden under dust.

The voices led me on to a filing case and a folder stuffed with papers—report cards, letters—among them the wail of an exasperated teacher: "Though he looks like an angel . . ."—telegrams, passports, a baptismal certificate, a ribbon won in a track meet, faded photographs—one taken on the memorable first day of long pants—a bit of golden hair.

I sat down and thought how time had flown. Why, it was only yesterday when I had held him in my arms! That, somehow, made me remember all the scoldings I had given him, the preachments, the exhortation to a virtue and wisdom I did not myself possess . . . .

I thought, too, of that last inarticulate "good luck," that last perfunctory handclasp; and I wished that I had somehow been able to tell him how much I really loved him. Had he perhaps penetrated my brusque reserve? Had he perhaps guessed what was in my heart?

And then I thought: what fools we are with our children—always plotting what we shall make of them, always planning for a future that never comes, always intent on what they may be, never accepting what they are.

Well, curly-head—you're a man now, bearing your bright new shield and spear. I hated to see you go out of my house and close the door behind you; but I think I would not have halted you if I could. I salute you, sir. I cannot pretend that I am not sad; but I am proud, too. So long.

HOWARD VINCENT O'BRIEN, 1888 - 1947
Some months later the son was killed in combat.

THE AMERICAN BOY

What we have a right to expect of the American boy is that he shall turn out to be a good American man. The boy can best become a good man by being a good boy—not a goody-goody boy, but just a plain good boy. I do not mean that he must love only the negative virtues; I mean that he must love the positive virtues also. "Good," in the largest sense, should include whatever is fine, straight forward, clean, brave, and manly. The best boys I know—the best men I know—are good at their studies or their business, fearless and stalwart, hated and feared by all that is wicked and depraved, incapable of submitting to wrongdoing, and equally incapable of being aught but tender to the weak and helpless. Of course the effect that a thoroughly manly, thoroughly straight and upright boy can have upon the companions of his own age, and upon those who are younger, is incalculable. If he is not thoroughly manly, then they will not respect him, and his good qualities will count for but little; while, of course, if he is mean, cruel or wicked, then his physical strength and force of mind merely make him so much the more objectionable a member of society. He can not do good work if he is not strong and does not try with his whole heart and soul to count in any contest; and his strength will be a curse to himself and to every one else if he does not have a thorough command over himself and over his own evil passions, and if he does not use his strength on the side of decency, justice and fair dealing.

In short, in life, as in a football-game, the principle to follow is: Hit the line hard; don't foul and don't shirk, but hit the line hard.

THEODORE ROOSEVELT, 1858 - 1919

PIPPA'S SONG

The year's at the spring;
The day's at the morn;
Morning's at seven;
The hillside's dew-pearled;
The lark's on the wing;
The snail's on the thorn;
God's in His Heaven—
All's right with the world!

ROBERT BROWNING

TO A CHILD

Small service is true service while it lasts:
Of humblest friends, bright creature! scorn
   not one:
The daisy, by the shadow that it casts,
Protects the lingering dewdrop from the
   sun.

WILLIAM WORDSWORTH, 1770 - 1850

LITTLE THINGS

Little drops of water,
   Little grains of sand,
Make the mighty ocean
   And the pleasant land.

So the little moments,
   Humble though they be,
Make the mighty ages
   Of eternity.

So our little errors
   Lead the soul away
From the path of virtue,
   Far in sin to stray.

Little deeds of kindness,
   Little words of love,
Help to make earth happy
   Like the heaven above.

JULIA FLETCHER CARNEY, 1823 - 1908

from "THE FIRST TOOTH"

O there was a baby, he sat on my knee,
With a pearl in his mouth that was precious
    to me,
His little dark mouth like my cave of the
    sea!

I said to my heart, "And my jewel is bright!
He blooms like a primrose! He shines like a
    light!"
Put your hand in his mouth! Do you feel?
    He can bite!

WILLIAM BRIGHTY RANDS, 1823 - 1882

⚜

At five years of age your son is your master, at ten your slave, at fifteen your double, and after that your friend or foe.

Here we have a baby. It is composed of a bald head and a pair of lungs.

EUGENE FIELD, 1850 - 1895

⚜

from "SOMEWHERE"

Whenever a little child is born
All night a soft wind rocks the corn;
One more buttercup wakes to the morn,
Somewhere, Somewhere

AGNES CARTER MASON, 1835 - 1908

⚜

WEATHER LORE:

When the dew is on the grass,
Rain will never come to pass.
When the grass is dry at morning light,
Look for rain before the night.

⚜

JOSH BILLINGS said—
    There iz two things in this life for which we are never fully prepared; and this iz twins.

HENRY WHEELER SHAW, 1818 - 1885

TO MY DAUGHTER

To You
Because I see you
in blue ribbons
starched dresses
and skinned knees
rag curls
frilly petticoats
dressed up—
young vanity, so pleased
I see you run - then
wait for me
or walk sedately
on our strolls
—just you and me
or playing grown-up
with tea
Finding paper dolls
in your favorite chair
or watching you "be hostess"
when company was there
Gold curls—wide eyes
a steadiness with grace
were promises of
the woman
in some future time in space
I see in you
the qualities
I wish that I possessed
and then I know for sure
He heard
—and gave
—and blessed
So many happy memories
come back
and live with me
and I treasure every moment
and hoard them lovingly
For you're a very special picture
that only I can see
and wonder
by what magic
you always stay
just three
to me.

PEARL HILTNER

THE AMERICAN FLAG

Its red for love, and its white for law;
And its blue for the hope that our fathers
*   saw,*
Of a larger liberty.

ᏀᏔᎣ

A thoughtful mind, when it sees a nation's flag, sees not the flag only, but the nation itself; and ... he reads chiefly in the flag the government, the principles, the truths, the history which belongs to the nation that set it forth.

HENRY WARD BEECHER, 1813 - 1887

ᏀᏔᎣ

OUR FLAG

I love to see the starry flag
That floats above my head.
I love to see its waving folds
With stripes of white and red.
"Be brave," say the red stripes,
"Be pure," say the white.
"Be true," say the bright stars,
"And stand for the right."

ᏀᏔᎣ

When I think of the flag .. I see alternate strips of parchment upon which are written the rights of liberty and justice, and stripes of blood to vindicate those rights, and then, in the corner, a prediction of the blue serene into which every nation may swim which stands for these great things ... The lines of red are lines of blood, nobly and unselfishly shed by men who loved the liberty of their fellowmen more than they loved their own lives and fortunes. God forbid that we should have to use the blood of America to freshen the color of the flag. But if it should ever be necessary, that flag will be colored once more, and in being colored will be glorified and purified.

WOODROW WILSON, 1856 - 1924
24th President of United States
from address 17 May 1915

RESOLUTION OF THE CONTINENTAL CONGRESS JUNE 14, 1777:

The flag of the thirteen United States be thirteen stripes, alternate red and blue; that the union be thirteen stars, white in a blue field, representing a new constellation.

ᏀᏔᎣ

I am not the flag; not at all. I am but its shadow. I am whatever you make me, nothing more. I am your belief in yourself, your dream, of what a People may become .. I am the day's work of the weakest man, and the largest dream of the most daring .. I am the clutch of an idea, and the reasoned purpose of resolution. I am no more than you believe me to be and I am all that you believe I can be. I am whatever you make me, nothing more.

FRANKLIN K. LANE, 1864 - 1921
American Secretary of the Interior under Wilson.

ᏀᏔᎣ

It speaks of equal rights; of the inspiration of free institutions exemplified and vindicated; of liberty under law intelligently conceived and impartially administered. There is not a thread in it but scorns selfindulgence, weakness, and rapacity. It is eloquent of our common destiny.

CHARLES EVANS HUGHES, 1862 - 1948

THE TIRED WOMAN'S EPITAPH

Here lies a poor woman, who always was
tired;
She lived in a house where help was not
hired,
Her last words on earth were: "Dear
friends, I am going
Where washing ain't done, nor sweeping,
nor sewing;
But everything there is exact to my wishes;
For where they don't eat there's no
washing of dishes.
I'll be where loud anthems, will always be
ringing,
But, having no voice, I'll be clear of the
singing.
Don't mourn for me now; don't mourn
for me never—
I'm going to do nothing for ever and ever."

❧

PORTRAIT BY A NEIGHBOR

Before she has her floor swept
Or her dishes done,
Any day you'll find her
A-sunning in the sun!

It's long after midnight
Her key's in the lock,
And you never see her chimney smoke
Till past ten o'clock!

She digs in her garden
With a shovel and a spoon,
She weeds her lazy lettuce
By the light of the moon.

She walks up the walk
Like a woman in a dream,
She forgets she borrowed butter
And pays you back cream!

Her lawn looks like a meadow,
And if she mows the place
She leaves the clover standing
And the Queen Anne's lace!

EDNA·ST. VINCENT MILLAY, 1892 - 1950

❧

It is better to wear out than to rust out.
BISHOP GEORGE HORNE Sermon
1730 - 1792

from a SERMON

The only war I ever approved of was
the Trojan war; it was fought over a
woman and the men knew what they
were fighting for.
WILLIAM LYON PHELPS, 1865 - 1943
Riverside Church, New York City, June 25, 1933.

❧

'Tis better to have loved and lost than
never to have loved at all—better for the
florist and the jeweler.

❧

There was a young lady of Lynn,
Who was so excessively thin,
That when she asseyed to drink lemonade,
She slipped through the straw and fell in.

❧

Legend tells that at a banquet
Cleopatra gave for Marc Antony, she took
off a pearl eardrop and dissolved it in
wine and drank to the health of her guest.
And it is also told that Sir Thomas
Gresham at the London Royal Exchange
when he entertained Elizabeth the Ist of
England, pledged her health in a cup of
wine in which a pearl valued at 15,000 £
had been placed. However, as it takes
"stronger than vinegar or wine" to dissolve pearls, not much credence can be
placed in the pearls dissolving.

❧

EPITAPH, MEOLE CHURCHYARD

She took the cup of life to sip,
Too bitter 'twas to drain;
She meekly put it from her lip,
And went to sleep again.

❧

Glamour is what makes a man ask for
your telephone number, and a woman ask
for the name of your dressmaker.

LILLY DACHE

THE IDEAL HUSBAND TO HIS WIFE

We've lived for forty years, dear wife,
　And walked together side by side,
And you to-day are just as dear
　As when you were my bride.
I've tried to make life glad for you,
　One long, sweet honeymoon of joy,
A dream of marital content,
　Without the least alloy.
I've smoothed all boulders from our path,
　That we in peace might toil along,
By always hastening to admit
　That I was right and you were wrong.

No mad diversity of creed
　Has ever sundered me from thee;
For I permit you evermore
　To borrow your ideas of me.
And thus it is, through weal or woe,
　Our love forevermore endures;
For I permit that you should take
　My views and creeds and make them
　　yours.
And thus I let you have my way,
　And thus in peace we toil along,
For I am willing to admit
　That I am right and you are wrong.

And when our matrimonial skiff
　Strikes snags in love's meandering
　　stream,
I lift our shallop from the rocks,
　And float as in a placid dream.
And well I know our marriage bliss
　While life shall last will never cease;
For I shall always let thee do,
　In generous love, just what I please.
Peace comes, and discord flies away,
　Love's bright day follows hatred's
　　night;
For I am ready to admit
　That you are wrong and I am right.
　　　　　SAM WALTER FOSS, 1858 - 1911

from A MINUET ON REACHING
THE AGE OF FIFTY

Old age, on tiptoe, lays her jeweled hand
lightly in mine.
　　　　　GEORGE SANTAYANA, 1863 - 1952

A TOAST from "School for Scandal"

Here's to the maiden of bashful fifteen;
Here's to the widow of fifty;
Here's to the flaunting, extravagant queen,
And here's to the house-wife that's
　　thrifty.
　Let the toast pass;
　Drink to the lass;
I'll warrant she'll prove an excuse for the
　　glass.
　　　　RICHARD BRINSLEY SHERIDAN, 1751 - 1816

from "THE ESSAYS OF MONTAIGNE"

And there is nothing more remarkable in
the life of Socrates than that he found
time in his old age to learn to dance and
play on instruments, and thought it time
well spent.
　　　　　MICHEL DE MONTAIGNE, 1533 - 1592

The older I grow the more I distrust the
familiar doctrine that age brings wisdom.
　　　　　H. L. MENCKEN, 1880 - 19

from
TO MRS. M. B. ON HER BIRTHDAY

Is that a birthday? 'tis, alas! too clear;
'Tis but the funeral of the former year.
　　　　　ALEXANDER POPE, 1688 - 1744

ON HIS 75th BIRTHDAY

I strove with none, for none was worth
　my strife,
Nature I loved, and next to nature, art;
I warmed both hands before the fire of
　life,
It sinks, and I am ready to depart.
　　　　　WALTER SAVAGE LANDOR, 1875 - 1964

George Washington wrote his wife, Martha, from Philadelphia where the second Continental Congress was in session. This letter repeats his belief "I do not think myself equal to the command . . " Two weeks later, he accepted command of the Army:

Philadelphia, June 18, 1775

My Dearest: I am now set down to write to you on a subject, which fills me with inexpressible concern, and this concern is greatly aggravated and increased, when I reflect upon the uneasiness I know it will give you. It has been determined in Congress, that the whole army raised for the defence of the American cause shall be put under my care, and that it is necessary for me to proceed immediately to Boston to take upon me the command of it.

You may believe me, my dear Patsy, when I assure you, in the most solemn manner that, so far from seeking this appointment, I have used every endeavor in my power to avoid it, not only from my unwillingness to part with you and the family, but from a consciousness of its being a trust too great for my capacity, and that I should enjoy more real happiness in one month with you at home, than I have the most distant prospect of finding abroad, if my stay were to be seven times seven years. But as it has been a kind of destiny, that has thrown me upon this service, I shall hope that my undertaking it is designed to answer some good purpose. You might, and I suppose did perceive, from the tenor of my letters, that I was apprehensive I could not avoid this appointment, as I did not pretend to intimate when I should return. That was the case. It was utterly out of my power to refuse this appointment, without exposing my character to such censures, as would have reflected dishonor upon myself, and given pain to my friends. This, I am sure, could not, and ought not, to be pleasing to you, and must have lessened me considerably in my own esteem. I shall rely, therefore, confidently on that Providence, which has heretofore preserved and been bountiful to me, not doubting but that I shall return safe to you in the fall. I shall feel no pain from the toil or the danger of the campaign; my unhappiness will flow from the uneasiness I know you will feel from being left alone. I therefore beg, that you will summon your whole fortitude, and pass your time as agreeably as possible. Nothing will give me so much sincere satisfaction as to hear this, and to hear it from your own pen. My earnest and ardent desire is, that you would pursue any plan that is most likely to produce content, and a tolerable degree of tranquillity; as it must add greatly to my uneasy feelings to hear, that you are dissatisfied or complaining at what I really could not avoid.

As life is always uncertain, and common prudence dictates to every man the necessity of settling his temporal concerns, while it is in his power, and while the mind is calm and undisturbed, I have, since I came to this place (for I had not time to do it before I left home) got Colonel Pendleton to draft a will for me, by the directions I gave him, which will I now enclose. The provision made for you in case of my death will, I hope, be agreeable.

I shall add nothing more, as I have several letters to write, but to desire that you will remember me to your friends, and to assure you that I am, with the most unfeigned regard, my dear Patsy, your affectionate, & c.

123

GENERAL EISENHOWER'S D DAY
ORDER OF THE DAY

June 6, 1944

Soldiers, sailors, and airmen of the Allied Expeditionary Force: You are about to embark upon a great crusade toward which we have striven these many months. The eyes of the world are upon you. The hopes and prayers of liberty-loving peoples everywhere march with you.

You will bring about the destruction of the German war machine, the elimination of Nazi tyranny over the oppressed peoples of Europe, and security for ourselves in a free world.

Your task will not be an easy one. Your enemy is well trained, well equipped, and battle-hardened. He will fight savagely.

But this is the year 1944. Much has happened since the Nazi triumphs of 1940-41.

The United Nations have inflicted upon the Germans great defeat in open battle man to man. Our air offensive has seriously reduced their strength in the air and their capacity to wage war on the ground.

Our home fronts have given us an overwhelming superiority in weapons and munitions of war and placed at our disposal great reserves of trained fighting men.

The tide has turned.

The free men of the world are marching together to victory. I have full confidence in your courage, devotion to duty, and skill in battle.

We will accept nothing less than full victory.

Good luck, and let us all beseech the blessings of Almighty God upon this great and noble undertaking.

DWIGHT D. EISENHOWER, 1890 - 1968

People of Western Europe: A landing was made this morning on the coast of France by troops of the Allied Expeditionary Force. This landing is part of the concerted United Nations plan for the liberation of Europe made in conjunction with our great Russian allies . . . I call upon all who love freedom to stand with us now. Together we shall achieve victory.

GENERAL DWIGHT D. EISENHOWER
broadcast June 4, 1944

The mission of this Allied Force was fulfilled at 3 A.M., local time, May 7, 1945.

EISENHOWER

(telegram to Combined Chiefs of Staff, at end of World War II, Europe.)

SOMEBODY

Somebody's courting somebody
Somewhere or other to-night;
Somebody's whispering to somebody,
Somebody's listening to somebody,
    Under this clear moonlight.

Near the bright river's flow,
Running so still and slow,
Talking so soft and low,
    She sits with somebody.

Pacing the ocean's shore,
Edged by the foaming roar,
Words never used before
    Sound sweet to somebody,
Under the maple tree
Deep though the shadow be,
Plain enough they can see,
    Bright eyes has somebody.

No one sits up to wait,
Though she is out so late,
All know she's at the gate,
    Talking with somebody,

Tiptoe to parlor door,
Two shadows on the floor,
Moonlight, reveal no more,
    Susy and somebody.

Somewhere, somebody
Makes love to somebody
    Tonight.

Memory is the power to gather roses in the Winter.

THE FIRST DANDELION

Simple and fresh and fair from winter's
    close emerging,
As if no artifice of fashion, business,
    politics, had ever been,
Forth from its sunny nook of sheltered
    grass—innocent, golden, calm as the
    dawn,
The spring's first dandelion shows its
    trustful face.

                    WALT WHITMAN, 1819 - 1892

At this Revolutionary Battle, the Irish, red-haired, freckle faced Molly Pitcher was carrying water to her cannoneer husband. He was killed at his post. Molly Pitcher seized his rammer, and took his place, serving with skill and courage during the battle.

The next morning when presented by General Greene to Washington, a sergeant's commission was conferred on her.

MOLLY PITCHER

'Twas hurry and scurry at Monmouth
    town,
    For Lee was beating a wild retreat;
The British were riding the Yankees
    down,
    And panic was pressing on flying feet.

Galloping down like a hurricane
    Washington rode with his sword swung
    high,
Mighty as he of the Trojan plain
    Fired by a courage from the sky.

"Halt, and stand to your guns!" he cried.
    And a bombardier made swift reply.
Wheeling his cannon into the tide,
    He fell 'neath the shot of a foeman
    nigh.

Molly Pitcher sprang to his side,
    Fired as she saw her husband do.
Telling the king in his stubborn pride
    Women like men to their homes are
    true.

Washington rode from the bloody fray
    Up to the gun that a woman manned.
"Molly Pitcher, you saved the day,"
    He said, as he gave her a hero's hand.

He named her sergeant with manly praise,
    While her war-brown face was wet with
    tears—
A woman has ever a woman's ways,
    And the army was wild with cheers.
                    KATE BROWNLEE SHERWOOD, 1841 - 1914

from OLD AGE

A woman is as old as she looks to a man that likes to look at her.

                    FINLEY PETER DUNNE, 1867 - 1936

KNEE-DEEP IN JUNE

Tell you what I like the best—
  'Long about knee-deep in June,
'Bout the time strawberries melts
On the vine,—some afternoon
Like to jes' git out and rest,
  And not work at nothin' else!

Orchard's where I'd ruther be—
Needn't fence it in for me!—
  Jes' the whole sky overhead,
And the whole airth underneath—
Sort o' so's a man kin breathe
  Like he ort, and kind o' has
Elbow room to keerlessly
  Sprawl out len'thways on the grass
    Where the shadders thick and soft
  As the kivvers on the bed
    Mother fixes in the loft
    Allus, when they's company!

Jes' a-sort o' lazin' there—
  S'lazy, 'at you peek and peer
Through the wavin' leaves above,
Like a feller 'ats in love
  And don't know it, ner don't keer!
Ever'thing you hear and see
  Got some sort o' interest—
  Maybe find a bluebird's nest
  Tucked up there conveenently
  Fer the boy 'at's ap' to be
  Up some other apple-tree!
Watch the swallers skootin' past
  'Bout as peert as you could ast;
    Er the Bob-white raise and whiz
    Where some other's whistle is.

Lay out there and try to see
Jes' how lazy you kin be!—
  Tumble round and souse yer head
  In the clover-bloom, er pull
  Yer straw hat acrost yer eyes
  And peek through it at the
    skies,
  Thinkin' of old chums 'at's dead,
  Maybe smilin' back at you
I betwixt the beautiful
    Clouds o' gold and white and
    blue!—
  Month a man kin railly love—
  June, you know, I'm talkin' of!

March ain't never nothin' new!—
Aprile's altogether too
  Brash fer me! and May—I jes'
  'Bominate its promises,—
Little hints o' sunshine and
Green around the timber-land—
  A few blossoms, and a few
Chip-birds, and a sprout er two,—
  Drap asleep, and it turns in
  'Fore daylight and snows ag'in!—

But when June comes—Clear my throat
  With wild honey!—Rench my hair
In the dew! and hold my coat!
  Whoop out loud! and throw my hat!—
June wants me, and I'm to spare!
Spread them shadders anywhere,
I'll get down and waller there,
  And obleeged to you at that!

JAMES WHITCOMB RILEY, 1849 - 1916

HIAWATHA'S CHILDHOOD

By the shores of Gitche Gumee,
By the shining Big-Sea-Water,
Stood the wigwam of Nokomis,
Daughter of the Moon, Nokomis.
Dark behind it rose the forest,
Rose the black and gloomy pine-trees,
Rose the firs with cones upon them;
Bright before it beat the water,
Beat the clear and sunny water,
Beat the shining Big-Sea-Water.

There the wrinkled old Nokomis
Nursed the little Hiawatha,
Rocked him in his linden cradle,
Bedded soft in moss and rushes,
Safely bound with reindeer sinews;
Stilled his fretful wail by saying,
"Hush! the Naked Bear will hear thee!"
Lulled him into slumber, singing,
"Ewa-yea! my little owlet!
Who is this that lights the wigwam?
With his great eyes lights the wigwam?
Ewa-yea! my little owlet!"

At the door, on summer evenings,
Sat the little Hiawatha;
Heard the whispering of the pine-trees,
Heard the lapping of the water,
Sounds of music, words of wonder;
"Minnie-wawa!" said the pine-trees,
"Mudway-aushka!" said the water;
Saw the fire-fly, Wah-wah-taysee,
Flitting through the dusk of evening,
With the twinkle of its candle
Lighting up the brakes and bushes,
And he sang the song of children.

Saw the moon rise from the water
Rippling, rounding from the water,
Saw the flecks and shadows on it,
Whispered, "What is that, Nokomis?"
And the good Nokomis answered:
"Once a warrior, very angry,
Seized his grandmother, and threw her
Up into the sky at midnight;
Right against the moon he threw her;
'Tis her body that you see there."

Saw the rainbow in the heaven,
In the eastern sky, the rainbow,
Whispered, "What is that, Nokomis?"
And the good Nokomis answered:
"'Tis the heaven of flowers you see there;
All the wild-flowers of the forest,
All the lilies of the prairie,
When on earth they fade and perish,
Blossom in that heaven above us."

When he heard the owls at midnight,
Hooting, laughing in the forest,
"What is that?" he cried, in terror;
"What is that," he said, "Nokomis?"

And the good Nokomis answered:
"That is but the owl and owlet,
Talking in their native language,
Talking, scolding at each other."

Then the little Hiawatha
Learned of every bird its language,
Learned their names and all their secrets,
How they built their nests in summer,
Where they hid themselves in winter,
Talked with them whene'er he met them,
Called them "Hiawatha's Chickens."

Of all beasts he learned the language,
Learned their names and all their secrets,
How the beavers built their lodges,
Where the squirrels hid their acorns,
How the reindeer ran so swiftly,
Why the rabbit was so timid,
Talked with them whene'er he met them,
Called them "Hiawatha's Brothers."

HENRY W. LONGFELLOW

THE SIOUX

Now what in the world shall we dioux
With the bloody and murderous Sioux
    Who some time ago
    Took an arrow and bow
And raised such a hellabelioux?

EUGENE FIELD, 1850 - 1895

127

A FAREWELL

My fairest child, I have no song to give
you;
No lark could pipe to skies so dull and
gray:
Yet, if you will, one quiet hint I'll leave
you
For every day.

I'll tell you how to sing a clearer carol
Than lark who hails the dawn on breezy
down;
To earn yourself a purer poet's laurel
Than Shakespeare's crown.

Be good, sweet maid, and let who will be
clever;
Do noble things, not dream them, all
day long:
And so make Life, and Death, and that
For Ever
One grand sweet song.

CHARLES KINGSLEY, 1819 - 1875

There is quite as much education and true
learning in the analysis of an ear of corn
as in the analysis of a complex sentence;
ability to analyze clover and alfalfa roots
savors of quite as much culture as does
the study of the Latin and Greek roots.

O. H. BENSON

There is nothing more frightful than a
bustling ignorance.

JOHANN WOLFGANG VON GOETHE
1749 - 1832

from RABBI BEN EZRA

Grow old along with me!
The best is yet to be,
The last of life, for which the first was
made:
Our times are in his hand
Who saith "A whole I planned,
Youth shows but half; trust God: see all,
nor be afraid!"

Not that, amassing flowers,
Youth sighed, "Which rose make ours,
Which lily leave and then as best recall?"
Not that, admiring stars,
It yearned, "Nor Jove, nor Mars;
Mine be some figured flame which blends,
transcends them all!"

ROBERT BROWNING, 1812 - 1889

Don't let studies interfere with your
college education.

Often called motto of America's college students.

MY GARDEN

A garden is a lovesome thing, God wot!
Rose plot,
Fringed pool,
Ferned grot—
The veriest school
Of peace; and yet the fool
Contends that God is not—
Not God! in gardens! when the eve is cool?
Nay, but I have a sign
'Tis very sure God walks in mine.

THOMAS EDWARD BROWN, 1830 - 1897

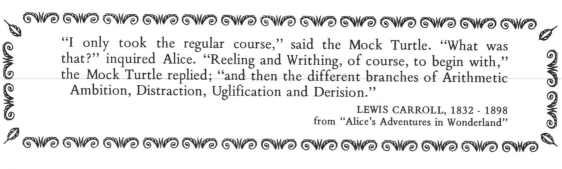

"I only took the regular course," said the Mock Turtle. "What was
that?" inquired Alice. "Reeling and Writhing, of course, to begin with,"
the Mock Turtle replied; "and then the different branches of Arithmetic
Ambition, Distraction, Uglification and Derision."

LEWIS CARROLL, 1832 - 1898
from "Alice's Adventures in Wonderland"

THE USEFUL PLOW

A country life is sweet!
In moderate cold and heat,
  To walk in the air how pleasant and
    fair!
In every field of wheat,
  The fairest of flowers adorning the
    bowers,
And every meadow's brow;
  So that I say, no courtier may
  Compare with them who clothe in gray,
And follow the useful plow.

They rise with the morning lark,
And labor till almost dark,
  Then, folding their sheep, they hasten
    to sleep
While every pleasant park
  Next morning is ringing with birds that
    are singing
On each green, tender bough.
  With what content and merriment
  Their days are spent, whose minds are
    bent
To follow the useful plow.

❧

from JOURNAL

There is no plateau on which Nature rests at mid-summer, but she instantly commences the descent to winter.
                                 HENRY DAVID THOREAU

❧

SING-SONG

The days are clear,
  Day after day,
When April's here,
  That leads to May,

And June
Must follow soon:
  Stay, June, stay!—
If only we could stop the moon
And June!
CHRISTINA GEORGINA ROSSETTI, 1830 - 1894

SIGH NO MORE, LADIES

Sigh no more ladies, sigh no more,
  Men were deceivers ever,
One foot in sea and one on shore,
  To one thing constant never:
Then sigh not so, but let them go,
  And be you blithe and bonny,
Converting all your sounds of woe
  Into Hey nonny, nonny.

Sing no more ditties, sing no more,
  Of dumps so dull and heavy;
The fraud of men was ever so,
  Since summer first was leafy:
Then sigh not so, but let them go,
  And be you blithe and bonny,
Converting all your sounds of woe
  Into Hey nonny, nonny.
                      WILLIAM SHAKESPEARE
from Much Ado About Nothing

❧

Being a woman is a terribly difficult task since it consists principally in dealing with men.

❧

Life would be a perpetual flea hunt if a man were obliged to run down all the innuendoes, inveracities, insinuations and misrepresentations which are uttered against him.

                        HENRY WARD BEECHER

❧

LA CARTE

It takes much art
To choose a la carte
For less than they quote
For the table d'hôte
                          JUSTIN RICHARDSON

THE BAREFOOT BOY

Blessings on thee, little man,
Barefoot boy, with cheek of tan!
With thy turned-up pantaloons,
And thy merry whistled tunes;
With thy red lip, redder still
Kissed by strawberries on the hill;
With the sunshine on thy face,
Through thy torn brim's jaunty grace;
From my heart I give thee joy,—
I was once a barefoot boy!

Oh for boyhood's painless play,
Sleep that wakes in laughing day,
Health that mocks the doctor's rules,
Knowledge never learned of schools,
Of the wild bee's morning chase,
Of the wild flower's time and place,
Flight of fowl and habitude
Of the tenants of the wood;
How the tortoise bears his shell,
How the woodchuck digs his cell,
And the ground-mole sinks his well,
How the robin feeds her young,
How the oriole's nest is hung;

Oh for boyhood's time of June,
Crowding years in one brief moon,
When all things I heard or saw,
Me, their master, waited for.
I was rich in flowers and trees,
Humming-birds and honey-bees;
For my sport the squirrel played,
Plied the snouted mole his spade;
For my taste the blackberry cone
Purpled over hedge and stone;
Laughed the brook for my delight
Through the day and through the night,
Whispering at the garden wall,
Talked with me from fall to fall;
Mine the sand-rimmed pickerel pond
Mine the walnut slopes beyond,
Mine, on bending orchard trees,
Apples of Hesperides!
Still as my horizon grew,
Larger grew my riches too;
All the world I saw or knew
Seemed a complex Chinese toy,
Fashioned for a barefoot boy!

Oh for festal dainties spread,
Like my bowl of milk and bread;

Pewter spoon and bowl of wood,
On the door-stone, gray and rude!
O'er me, like a regal tent,
Cloudy-ribbed, the sunset bent,

Purple-curtained, fringed with gold,
Looped in many a wind-swung fold;
While for music came the play
Of the pied frogs' orchestra;
And, to light the noisy choir,
Lit the fly his lamp of fire.
I was monarch: pomp and joy
Waited on the barefoot boy!

JOHN GREENLEAF WHITTIER, 1807 - 1892

THE EAGLE

He clasps the crag with crooked hands;
Close to the sun in lonely lands,
Ring'd with the azure world, he stands.

The wrinkled sea beneath him crawls;
He watches from his mountain walls,
And like a thunderbolt he falls.

ALFRED TENNYSON, 1809 - 1892

You cannot fly like an eagle with the wings of a wren.

PROVERB

from HIS LETTER TO SARAH BACHE, Jan. 1784

I wish the Bald Eagle had not been chosen as the Representative of our Country; he is a bird of bad moral Character; like those among Men who live by Sharping and Robbing, he is generally poor, and often very lousy. The Turkey is a much more respectable Bird, and withal a true original Native of America.

BENJAMIN FRANKLIN

JULY

"The thunder shower, the clearing sky,
And sunset splendor of July."

TEN COMMANDMENTS OF SUCCESS

1. Work hard. Hard work is the best investment a man can make.

2. Study hard. Knowledge enables a man to work more intelligently and effectively.

3. Have initiative. Ruts often deepen into graves.

4. Love your work. Then you will find pleasure in mastering it.

5. Be Exact. Slipshod methods bring slipshod results.

6. Have the Spirit of Conquest. Thus you can successfully battle and overcome difficulties.

7. Cultivate Personality. Personality is to a man what perfume is to a flower.

8. Help and Share with others: The real test of business greatness lies in giving opportunity to others.

9. Be Democratic. Unless you feel right towards your fellowmen you can never be a successful leader of men.

10. In all things do your best. The man who has done his best has done everything. The man who has done less than his best has done nothing.

CHARLES M. SCHWAB, 1862 - 1939

❧

The difference between intelligence and education is that intelligence will make you a good living.

CHARLES F. KETTERING, 1876 - 1958

❧

ST. SWITHIN DAY

July 15th—

St. Swithin, Bishop of Winchester, is remembered for this rhyme

St. Swithin's Day, if thou dost rain
For forty days it will remain;
St. Swithin's Day, if thou be fair
For forty days 'twill rain na mair.

It is told that a century after his burial, it was decided to move his remains—against his instructions—to a more prominent place in the Cathedral. It rained so for forty days and nights the change had to be abandoned.

THE COUNTRY STORE

Far out beyond the city's lights, away from
din and roar,
The cricket chirps of summer nights
beneath the country store;
The drygoods boxes ricked about afford a
welcome seat
For weary tillers of the ground, who here
on evenings meet.

A swinging sign of ancient make, and one
above the door,
Proclaim that William Henry Blake is
owner of the store;
Here everything from jam to tweed, from
silks to ginghams bright
Is spread before the folk who need from
early morn till night

Tea, sugar, coffee (browned or green),
molasses, grindstones, tar
Suspenders, peanuts, navy beans, and
homemade vinegar,
Fine combs, wash ringers, rakes, false hair,
paints, rice, and looking glasses,
Side saddles, hominy, crockery ware, and
seeds for garden grasses.

Lawn mowers, candies, books to read, corn
planter, household goods,
Tobacco, salt, and clover seed, horsewhips
and knitted hoods,
Canned goods, shoe blacking, lime and
nails, straw hats and carpet slippers,
Prunes, buttons, codfish, bridal veils,
cranberries, clocks, and clippers.

Umbrellas, candles, scythes and hats, caps,
boots and shoes and bacon,
Thread, nutmegs, pins and Rough on Rats,
for cash or produce taken;
Birdseed, face powder, matches, files, ink,
onions and many more,
Are found in heaps and stacks and piles
within the country store.

FOR AGILE TONGUES—

I need not your needles, they're needless
    to me;
For kneading of needles were needless,
    you see;
But did my neat trousers but need to be
    kneed,
I then should have need of your needles
    indeed.

Celia sat beside the seaside,
Quite beside herself was she
For beside her on the leeside
No one sat beside her, see?

Betty Botter bought some butter,
But, she said, the butter's bitter;
If I put it in my batter
It will make my batter bitter,
But a bit of better butter
Will make my batter better.
So she bought a bit of butter
Better than her bitter butter,
And she put it in her batter
And the batter was not bitter.
So 'twas better Betty Botter bought a bit
    of better butter.

PETER PIPER

Peter Piper's Practical Principles of Plain
    and Perfect
Pronunciation to Please the Palates of
    Pretty Prattling Playfellows.
Pray Parents to Purchase this Playful
    Performance, Partly to Pay him for his
    Patience and Pains; Partly to Provide
    for the Printers and Publishers; but
    Principally to Prevent the Pernicious
    Prevalence of Perverse Pronunciation.

Peter Piper picked a peck of pickled
    peppers;
Did Peter Piper pick a peck of pickled
    peppers?
If Peter Piper picked a peck of pickled
    peppers,
Where's the peck of pickled peppers Peter
    Piper picked?

If you and your folks like me and my
    folks
Like me and my folks like you and your
    folks,
Then me and my folks like you and your
    folks
Like you and your folks like me and my
    folks.

OUT OF SIGHT, OUT OF MIND

The oft'ner seen, the more I lust,
The more I lust, the more I smart,
The more I smart, the more I trust,
The more I trust, the heavier heart,
The heavy heart breeds mine unrest,
Thy absence therefore I like best.

The rarer seen, the less in mind,
The less in mind, the lesser pain,
The lesser pain, less grief I find,
The lesser grief, the greater gain,
The greater gain, the merrier I,
Therefore I wish thy sight to fly.

The further off, the more I joy,
The more I joy, the happier life,
The happier life, less hurts annoy,
The lesser hurts, pleasure most rife,
Such pleasures rife shall I obtain
When distance doth depart us train.

BARNABY GOOGE, 1540 - 1594

from MARMION, CANTO VI

Oh what a tangled web we weave
When first we practice to deceive!

SIR WALTER SCOTT, 1771 - 1832

To which J. R. Pope added:

But when we've practiced quite a while
How vastly we improve our style!

J. R. POPE, 1874 - 1937

JOSH BILLINGS said—
Laughing is a sensation of feeling good
all over, and showing it principally in one
spot.

HENRY WHEELER SHAW, 1818 - 1885

THE MAN WITHOUT A COUNTRY

(This short story tells of a young army officer, Philip Nolan, who in a moment of passion during his trial for treason with Aaron Burr, cried, "Damn the United States. I wish I may never hear of the United States again." He was sentenced to the fulfillment of this unfortunate wish, and for 55 years was kept on board ships at sea, never permitted ashore in the U.S. During all that time he never saw his country, and never heard of it until the day of his death.)

. . . At the Cape of Good Hope on Nolan's first voyage, Philip had borrowed a lot of English books. Among them, "The Lay of the Last Minstrel". Nolan was permitted to join the circle one afternoon when a lot of them sat on deck smoking and reading aloud. . In his turn, Nolan took the book and read to the others.

> Breathes there the man, with soul so dead,
> Who never to himself hath said,
> This is my own, my native land?

. . he turned a little pale, but plunged on,

> Whose heart hath ne'er within him burned,
> As home his footsteps he has turned
> From wandering on a foreign strand?
> If such there breathe, go, mark him well;
> High though his titles, proud his name,
> Boundless his wealth as wish can claim:
> The wretch, concentred all in self,
> Living shall forfeit fair renown, . . .

and here the poor fellow choked, could not go on, but started up, swung the book into the sea, vanished into his stateroom . . . As we lay back in the stern sheets . . he said to me: "Youngster, let that show you what it is to be without a family, without a home, and without a country. And if you are ever tempted to say a word or to do a thing that shall put a bar between you and your family, your home, and your country, pray God in his mercy to take you that instant home to his own heaven. Stick by your family, boy; forget you have a self, while you do everything for them. Think of your home, boy; write and send and talk about it. Let it be nearer and nearer to your thought the farther you have to travel from it; and rush back to it when you are free . . . . And for your country, boy," and the words rattled in his throat, "and for that flag," and he pointed to the ship, "never dream a dream but of serving her as she bids you, though the service carry you through a thousand hells. No matter what happens to you, no matter who flatters you or who abuses you, never look at another flag, never let a night pass but you pray God to bless that flag. Remember, boy, that behind all these men you have to do with, behind officers, and

Government, and people even, there is the Country Herself, your Country, and that you belong to Her as you belong to your own mother. Stand by Her, boy, as you would stand by your mother!" I had not thought it was the end. I knew he was happy and I wanted him to be alone.

But in an hour, when the doctor went in gently, he found Nolan had breathed his life away with a smile. He had something pressed to his lips. It was his father's badge of the Order of Cincinnati.

We looked in his Bible, and there was a slip of paper, at the place where he had marked the text: "They desire a country, even a heavenly: wherefore God is not ashamed to be called their God: for he hath prepared for them a city."

On this slip of paper he had written: Bury me in the sea; it has been my home, and I love it. But will not someone set up a stone for my memory at Fort Adams or at Orleans, that my disgrace may not be more than I ought to bear? Say on it:

IN MEMORY OF
PHILIP NOLAN
LIEUTENANT IN THE ARMY OF THE UNITED STATES
He loved his country as no other man has loved her;
but no man deserved less at her hands.

EDWARD EVERETT HALE, 1822 - 1909

(So real was this story, that many thought it a record of actual fact until Dr. Hale stated it was his own invention.)

If there is a country in the world where concord, according to common calculation, would be least expected, it is America. Made up, as it is, of people from different nations, accustomed to different forms and habits of government, speaking different languages, and more different in their modes of worship, it would appear that the union of such a people was impracticable. But by the simple operation of constructing government on the principles of society and the rights of man, every difficulty retires, and the parts are brought into cordial unison.

THOMAS PAINE, 1737 - 1809

PREAMBLE TO THE DECLARATION OF INDEPENDENCE

When, in the course of human events, it becomes necessary for one people to dissolve the political bands which have connected them with another, and to assume among the powers of the earth, the separate and equal station to which the laws of nature and of nature's God entitle them, a decent respect to the opinions of mankind requires that they should declare the causes which impel them to the separation.

We hold these truths to be self-evident: That all men are created equal, that they are endowed by their Creator with certain unalienable rights, that among these are life, liberty, and the pursuit of happiness; that, to secure these rights, Governments are instituted among men, deriving their just powers from the consent of the governed; that, whenever any form of Government becomes destructive of these ends, it is the right of the people to alter or to abolish it, and to institute new Government, laying its foundation on such principles, and organizing its powers in such form, as to them shall seem most likely to effect their safety and happiness.

From The Declaration of Independence (July 4, 1776).

The United States is the only country with a known birthday.

JAMES G. BLAINE, 1830 - 1893

FOURTH OF JULY ODE

Our fathers fought for Liberty,
They struggled long and well,
History of their deeds can tell—
But did they leave us free?

Are we free to speak our thought,
To be happy, and be poor,
Free to enter Heaven's door,
To live and labor as we ought?

Are we then made free at last
From the fear of what men say,
Free to reverence To-day,
Free from the slavery of the Past?

Our fathers fought for liberty,
They struggled long and well,
History of their deeds can tell—
But, ourselves must set us free.

JAMES RUSSELL LOWELL, 1819 - 1891

Summer afternoon—summer afternoon; to me those have always been the two most beautiful words in the English language.

HENRY JAMES, 1843 - 1916
Writing to Edith Wharton.

⌘

JULY

The summer harvest day begun
With cloudless dawn and flaming sun;
Ripe grain the sickle flashes through;
The sweep of scythes in morning dew;
The nooning underneath the trees
Made cool by sea or mountain breeze;
The thunder shower, the clearing sky,
And sunset splendor of July.

Attributed to JOHN GREENLEAF WHITTIER

⌘

E PLURIBUS UNUM
(One from many)

Motto for United States Seal. Adopted June 1872 after selected by Committee of Benjamin Franklin, John Adams and Thomas Jefferson.

⌘

Do what we can, summer will have its flies. If we walk in the woods, we must feed mosquitoes.

RALPH WALDO EMERSON

⌘

When I joined the army, even before the turn of the century, it was the fulfillment of all my boyhood hopes and dreams . . . . I still remember the refrain of one of the most popular barracks ballads of that day, which proclaimed most proudly that old soldiers never die; they just fade away. I now close my military career and just fade away.

DOUGLAS MacARTHUR, 1880 - 1964
Address before a joint meeting of Congress, April 19, 1951.

⌘

from
IN THE GOOD OLD SUMMER TIME

In the good old summer time,
In the good old summer time,
Strolling thro' the shady lanes,
With your baby mine;
You hold her hand and she holds yours,
And that's a very good sign
That she's your tootsey-wootsey
In the good old summer time.

REN SHIELDS

⌘

SANITARY FAIR, BALTIMORE
APRIL 18, 1864

The world has never had a good definition of the word liberty.

ABRAHAM LINCOLN
from an Address

⌘

CUCKOO SONG

Sumer is icumen in,
Lhude sing cuccu!
Groweth sed, and bloweth med,
And springth the wude nu—Sing cuccu!

(probably the oldest song in the English language written circa 1226)

Every man is the builder of a temple called his body. We are all sculptors and painters, and our material is our own flesh and blood and bones. Any nobleness begins at once to refine a man's features, any meanness or sensuality to imbrute them.

HENRY DAVID THOREAU, 1817 - 1862

from SATIRES BOOK 2

Who then is free? The wise man, who is lord over himself, whom neither poverty, nor death, nor bonds affright, who bravely defies his passions, and scorns ambition, who in himself, is a whole, smoothed and rounded, so that nothing from outside can rest on the polished surface, and against whom Fortune in her onset is ever defeated.

HORACE, 65 - 8 B.C.

from THE OLD FLAG

Off with your hat, as the flag goes by!
And let the heart have its say;
You're man enough for a tear in your eye
That you will not wipe away.

HENRY CUYLER BUNNER, 1855 - 1896

There is no freedom on earth or in any star for those who deny freedom to others.

ELBERT HUBBARD, 1859 - 1915

I have seen the glories of art and architecture, and mountain and river; I have seen the sunset on the Jungfrau, and the full moon rise over Mont Blanc; but the fairest vision on which these eyes ever looked was the flag of my country in a foreign land. Beautiful as a flower to those who love it, terrible as a meteor to those who hate it, it is the symbol of the power and glory, and the honor, of fifty millions of Americans.

GEORGE FRISBIE HOAR, 1826 - 1904
Speech.

THE AMERICAN FLAG

When Freedom, from her mountain height,
  Unfurled her standard to the air,
She tore the azure robe of night,
  And set the stars of glory there;
She mingled with its gorgeous dyes
The milky baldric of the skies,
And striped its pure, celestial white
With streakings of the morning light;
Then, from his mansion in the sun,
She called her eagle-bearer down,
And gave into his mighty hand
  The symbol of her chosen land.

Flag of the free heart's hope and home,
  By angel hands to valor given
Thy stars have lit the welkin dome,
  And all thy hues were born in heaven.
Forever float that standard sheet!
  Where breathes the foe but falls before us,
With Freedom's soil beneath our feet,
  And Freedom's banner streaming o'er us?

JOSEPH RODMAN DRAKE, 1795 - 1820

FREEDOM

Men! whose boast it is that ye
Come of fathers brave and free,
If there breathe on earth a slave,
Are ye truly free and brave?
If ye do not feel the chain
When it works a brother's pain,
Are ye not base slaves indeed,
Slaves unworthy to be freed!

Is true Freedom but to break
Fetters for our own dear sake,
And, with leathern hearts, forget
That we owe mankind a debt?
No! True Freedom is to share
All the chains our brothers wear,
And, with heart and hand, to be
Earnest to make others free!

They are slaves who fear to speak
For the fallen and the weak;
They are slaves who will not choose
Hatred, scoffing and abuse,
Rather in silence shrink
From the truth they needs must think:
They are slaves who dare not be
In the right with two or three.

JAMES RUSSELL LOWELL, 1819 - 1891

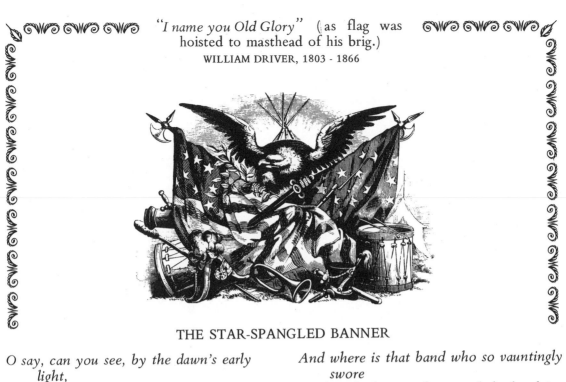

THE STAR-SPANGLED BANNER

O say, can you see, by the dawn's early
   light,
   What so proudly we hailed at the
   twilight's last gleaming—
Whose broad stripes and bright stars,
   through the perilous fight,
   O'er the ramparts we watched were so
   gallantly streaming!
And the rocket's red glare, the bombs
   bursting in air,
Gave proof through the night that our flag
   was still there,
O! say, does that star-spangled banner yet
   wave
O'er the land of the free, and the home of
   the brave?

On that shore dimly seen through the
   mists of the deep
   Where the foe's haughty host in dread
   silence reposes,
What is that which the breeze, o'er the
   towering steep,
   As it fitfully blows, now conceals, now
   discloses?
Now it catches the gleam of the morning's
   first beam,
In full glory reflected now shines on the
   stream;
'Tis the star-spangled banner; O long may
   it wave
O'er the land of the free, and the home of
   the brave!

And where is that band who so vauntingly
   swore
   That the havoc of war and the battle's
   confusion
A home and a country should leave us no
   more?
   Their blood has washed out their foul
   footsteps' pollution.
No refuge could save the hireling and
   slave
From the terror of flight, or the gloom of
   the grave;
And the star-spangled banner in triumph
   doth wave
O'er the land of the free, and the home of
   the brave.

O! thus be it ever, when freemen shall
   stand
   Between their loved homes and the war's
   desolation!
Blest with victory and peace, may the
   heav'n-rescued land
   Praise the power that hath made and
   preserved us a nation.
Then conquer we must, when our cause it
   is just,
And this be our motto,—'In God is our
   trust:'
And the star-spangled banner in triumph
   shall wave
O'er the land of the free, and the home of
   the brave.

FRANCIS SCOTT KEY, 1779 - 1834

Francis Scott Key, was an attorney who
wrote verse as a hobby.

from OUT OF MY LIFE AND THOUGHT

The ethic of Reverence for Life is the ethic of Love widened into universality. It is the ethic of Jesus, now recognized as a necessity of thought.

Objection is made to this ethic that it sets too high a value on natural life. To this it can retort that the mistake made by all previous systems of ethics has been the failure to recognize that life as such is the mysterious value with which they have to deal. All spiritual life meets us within natural life. Reverence for Life, therefore, is applied to natural life and spiritual life alike. In the parable of Jesus, the shepherd saves not merely the soul of the lost sheep but the whole animal. The stronger the reverence for natural life, the stronger grows also that for spiritual life.

The ethic of Reverence for Life is found particularly strange because it establishes no dividing-line between higher and lower, between more valuable and less valuable life. For this omission it has its reasons.

To undertake to lay down universally valid distinctions of value between different kinds of life will end in judging them by the greater or lesser distance at which they seem to stand from us human beings—as we ourselves judge. But that is a purely subjective criterion. Who among us knows what significance any other kind of life has in itself, and as a part of the universe?

Following on such a distinction there comes next the view that there can be life which is worthless, injury to which or destruction of which does not matter. Then in the category of worthless life we come to include, according to circumstances, different kinds of insects, or primitive peoples.

To the man who is truly ethical all life is sacred, including that which from the human point of view seems lower in the scale. He makes distinctions only as each case comes before him, and under the pressure of necessity, as, for example, when it falls to him to decide which of two lives he must sacrifice in order to preserve the other. But all through this series of decisions he is conscious of acting on subjective grounds and arbitrarily, and knows that he bears the responsibility for the life which is sacrificed . . .

I rejoice over the new remedies for sleeping-sickness, which enable me to preserve life, whereas I had previously to watch a painful disease. But every time I have under the miscroscope the germs which cause the disease, I cannot but reflect that I have to sacrifice this life in order to save other life.

. . . I buy from natives a young fish-eagle, which they have caught on a sand-bank, in order to rescue it from their cruel hands. But now I have to decide whether I shall let it starve, or kill every day a number of small fishes, in order to keep it alive. I decide on the latter course, but every day I feel it hard that this life must be sacrificed for the other on my responsibility.

DR. ALBERT SCHWEITZER, 1875 - 1965

A GRAIN OF WHEAT

Perry Hayden, a Quaker miller of Tecumseh, Michigan, set out in 1940 to illustrate the 6th verse of the 3rd chapter of St. Paul's epistle to the Corinthians.

He started with a cubic inch of wheat seed, planted in a plot 4 by 8. A yr later he harvested the wheat, deducting 10% of the wheat as a tithe to the church. He then planted the balance in the following yr. The 2nd, 3rd and 4th years he deducted the tithe and replanted the balance of each crop. Last yr's crop, which was the 5th, had grown from the original cubic inch to 230 acres and netted 5,555 bu's. The 6th and final yr of the demonstration required 2,300 acres of land. "If continued for 9 yrs," said Mr. Hayden, "it would require all the land of W. Va., and in 10 yrs it would cover the U S." It is estimated that the 13th yr would cover the whole globe; all starting with a cubic inch of wheat, a little faith, and God's promise of increase.

EVENING AT THE FARM

Over the hill the farm-boy goes.
His shadow lengthens along the land,
A giant staff in a giant hand;
In the poplar-tree, above the spring,
The katydid begins to sing;
　　The early dews are falling;—
Into the stone-heap darts the mink;
The swallows skim the river's brink;
And home to the woodland fly the crows,
When over the hill the farm-boy goes,
　　Cheerily calling,
　'Co', boss! co', boss! co'! co'! co'!'
Farther, farther, over the hill,
Faintly calling, calling still,

'Co', boss! co', boss! co'! co'!'
Into the yard the farmer goes,
With grateful heart, at the close of day:
Harness and chain are hung away;
In the wagon-shed stand yoke and plow;
The straw's in the stack, the hay in the
　　mow.
　　The cooling dews are falling;—
The friendly sheep his welcome bleat,
The pigs come grunting to his feet,
The whinnying mare her master knows,
When into the yard the farmer goes,
　　His cattle calling.—
　'Co', boss! co', boss! co'! co'! co'!'
While still the cow-boy, far away,
Goes seeking those that have gone
　　astray,—
　'Co', boss! co', boss! co'! co'!'

Now to her task the milkmaid goes.
The cattle come crowding through the
　　gate,
Lowing, pushing, little and great;
About the trough, by the farm-yard
　　pump,

The frolicsome yearlings frisk and jump,
　　While the pleasant dews are falling;—
The new milch heifer is quick and shy,
But the old cow waits with tranquil eye,
And the white stream into the bright pail
　　flows,

When to her task the milkmaid goes,
　　Soothingly calling,
　'So, boss! so, boss! so! so! so!'
The cheerful milkmaid takes her stool,
And sits and milks in the twilight cool,
　　Saying, 'So! so, boss! so! so!'

To supper at last the farmer goes.
The apples are pared, the paper read,
The stories are told, then all to bed.
Without, the crickets' ceaseless song
Makes shrill the silence all night long.
　　The heavy dews are falling.
The housewife's hand has turned the lock;
Drowsily ticks the kitchen clock;

The household sinks to deep repose,
But still in sleep the farm-boy goes,
　　Singing, calling,—
　'Co', boss! co', boss! co'! co'! co'!'
And oft the milkmaid in her dreams,
Drums in the pail with the flashing
　　streams,
　　Murmuring, 'So, boss! so!'
　　　　　JOHN T. TROWBRIDGE, 1827 - 1916

142

As the world now knows, Gordon Cooper composed a prayer while rocketing in orbit around the earth. Here's his prayer, as recorded while in orbit and as reported to Congress:

"Father, thank You, especially for letting me fly this flight. Thank You for the privilege of being able to be in this position; to be up in this wondrous place, seeing all these many startling, wonderful things that You have created.

"Help guide and direct all of us that we may shape our lives to be much better Christians, trying to help one another, and to work with one another rather than fighting and bickering.

"Help us to complete this mission successfully. Help us in our future space endeavors that we may show the world that a democracy can compete, and still be able to do things in a big way, and be able to do research development, and conduct many scientific and very technical programs.

"Be with our families. Give them guidance and encouragement, and let them know that everything will be O.K.

"We ask in Thy name. Amen."

Taking his first step on the Moon from the Module, THE EAGLE, Commander Neil Armstrong said "That's one small step for a man, one giant leap for mankind." So another famous "first" on a very historic occasion, July 20, 1969!

When Commander Charles Conrad of the Apollo XII crew, the third man to step on the surface of the Moon, November 18, 1969, was climbing down the nine rung ladder of the *Intrepid,* he hesitated on the bottom rung, contemplating his three foot leap to the Moon's surface. Conrad, 5 foot 6½ inches, obviously recalled Armstrong who is about six feet tall, and his historic remark. Cracked Commander Conrad, "Man, that may have been a small one for Neil, but that's a long one for me."

Immediately after he was forced to recant his views on the motion of the earth before the Inquisition in 1633: BUT IT DOES MOVE!

GALILEO GALILEI, 1564 - 1642

God gave man an upright countenance to survey the heavens, and to look upward to the stars.

OVID

The church says the earth is flat, but I know that it is round, for I have seen the shadow of the moon, and I have more faith in a shadow than in the church.

MAGELLAN, 1480 - 1521

THE SUN BY DAY, THE MOON
AND STARS BY NIGHT

The pride of the height, the clear firmament, the beauty of heaven, with his glorious shew;

The sun when it appeareth, declaring at his rising a marvelous instrument, the Work of the most High:

At noon it parcheth the country, and who can abide the burning heat thereof?

A man blowing a furnace is in works of heat, but the sun burneth the mountains three times more; breathing out fiery vapours, and sending forth bright beams, it dimmeth the eyes.

Great is the Lord that made it; and at his commandment it runneth hastily.

He made the moon also to serve in her season for a declaration of times, and a sign of the world.

From the moon is the sign of feasts, a light that decreaseth in her perfection.

The month is called after her name, increasing wonderfully in her changing, being an instrument of the armies above, shining in the firmament of heaven;

The beauty of heaven, the glory of the stars, an ornament giving light in the highest places of the Lord.

At the commandment of the Holy One they will stand in their order, and never faint in their watches.

THE APOCRYPHA (Book of Ecclesiasticus)

⌒〰⌒

Everyone is a moon and has a dark side which he never shows to anybody.

MARK TWAIN

⌒〰⌒ ⌒〰⌒ ⌒〰⌒ ⌒〰⌒ ⌒〰⌒ ⌒〰⌒ ⌒〰⌒

There was a young lady named Bright,
Who travelled much faster than light,
She started one day
In the relative way
And returned on the previous night.

⌒〰⌒ ⌒〰⌒ ⌒〰⌒ ⌒〰⌒ ⌒〰⌒ ⌒〰⌒ ⌒〰⌒

WEATHER LORE:

The moon and the weather
  May change together.
But change of the moon
  Does not change the weather.

The pale moon doth rain;
  The red moon doth blow;
The white moon doth
  neither nor snow.

⌒〰⌒

SONG

Go and catch a falling star,
  Get with child a mandrake root;
Tell me where all past years are,
  Or who cleft the Devil's foot;
Teach me to hear Mermaids singing,—
Or to keep off envy's stinging,
    And find
    What wind
Serves to advance an honest mind.

If thou be'st born to strange sights,
  Things invisible go see,
Ride ten thousand days and nights,
  Till age snow white hairs on thee;
Thus, when thou return'st, wilt tell me
All strange wonders that befell thee,
    And swear
    Nowhere
Lives a woman true and fair.

If thou find'st one, let me know;
  Such a pilgrimage were sweet.
Yet do not; I would not go,
  Though at next door we might meet.
Though she were true when you met her,
And last till you write your letter,
    Yet she
    Will be
False, ere I come, to two or three.

JOHN DONNE, 1573 - 1631

from EARLY RISING

"God bless the man who first invented
*   sleep!"*
*   So Sancho Panza said, and so say I:*
And bless him, also, that he didn't keep
*   His great discovery to himself; nor try*
To make it—as the lucky fellow might—
A close monopoly by patent-right!

Yes—bless the man who first invented sleep,
*   (I really can't avoid the iteration;)*
But blast the man, with curses loud and
*   deep,*
*   Whate'er the rascal's name, or age, or*
*   station,*
Who first invented, and went round advising,
That artificial cut-off—Early Rising!

"Rise with the lark, and with the lark to
*   bed,"*
*   Observes some solemn, sentimental owl;*
Maxims like these are very cheaply said;
*   But, ere you make yourself a fool or*
*   fowl,*
Pray just inquire about his rise and fall,
And whether larks have any beds at all!

The time for honest folks to be a-bed
*   Is in the morning, if I reason right;*
And he who cannot keep his precious head
*   Upon his pillow till it's fairly light,*
And so enjoy his forty morning winks,
Is up to knavery; or else—he drinks!

So let us sleep, and give the Maker praise.
*   I like the lad who, when his father*
*   thought*
To clip his morning nap by hackneyed
*   phrase*
*   Of vagrant worm by early songster*
*   caught,*
Cried, "Served him right!—it's not at all
*   surprising;*
The worm was punished, sir, for early
*   rising!"*

              JOHN G. SAXE, 1816 - 1887

THERE WAS AN OLD SOLDIER

O there was an old soldier and he had a
*   wooden leg,*
He had no tobaccy, no tobaccy could he
*   beg.*
Another old soldier was as sly as a fox,
He always had tobaccy in the old tobaccy
*   box.*

Said the one old soldier, "Won't you give
*   me a chew?"*
Said the other old soldier, "I'll be damned
*   if I do.*
Save up your money and put away your
*   rocks,*
And you'll always have tobaccy in the old
*   tobaccy box."*

Well, the same old soldier was feelin' very
*   bad.*
He says, "I'll get even, I will, begad!"
He goes to a corner, takes a rifle from a peg,
And stabs the other soldier with a splinter
*   from his leg.*

There was an old hen and she had a wooden
*   foot,*
And she made her nest by a gooseberry
*   root,*
And she laid more eggs than any on the
*   farm;*
And another wooden foot wouldn't do her
*   any harm.*

from THE CIGAR

Some sigh for this and that,
*   My wishes don't go far.*
The world may wag at will,
*   So I have my cigar.*

              THOMAS HOOD, 1799 - 1845

from MORNING MEDITATIONS

Let Taylor preach, upon a morning breezy
How well to rise while night and larks are
*   flying—*
For my part, getting up seems not so easy
By half as lying!

              THOMAS HOOD, 1799 - 1845

SEEIN' THINGS

I ain't afraid uv snakes or toads, or bugs or
    worms or mice,
An' things 'at girls are skeered uv I think are
    awful nice!
I'm pretty brave I guess; an' yet I hate to go
    to bed,
For, when I'm tucked up warm an' snug an'
    when my prayers are said,
Mother tells me "Happy Dreams" an' takes
    away the light,
An' leaves me lyin' all alone an' seein' things
    at night!

Sometimes they're in the corner, sometimes
    they're by the door,
Sometimes they're all a-standin' in the
    middle uv the floor;
Sometimes they are a-sittin' down,
    sometimes they're walkin' round
So softly and so creepy-like they never
    make a sound!
Sometimes they are as black as ink, an'
    other times they're white—
But color ain't no difference when you see
    things at night!

Once, when I licked a feller 'at had just
    moved on our street,
An' father sent me up to bed without a
    bite to eat,
I woke up in the dark an' saw things standin'
    in a row,
A-lookin at me cross-eyed an' p'intin' at
    me—so!
Oh, my! I wuz so skeered 'at time I never
    slep' a mite—
It's almost alluz when I'm bad I see things
    at night!

Lucky thing I ain't a girl or I'd be skeered to
    death!
Bein' I'm a boy, I duck my head an' hold
    my breath.
An' I am, oh so sorry I'm a naughty boy, an'
    then
I promise to be better an' I say my prayers
    again!
Gran'ma tells me that's the only way to
    make it right
When a feller has been wicked an' sees things
    at night!

An' so when other naughty boys would
    coax me into sin,
I try to skwush the Tempter's voice 'at
    urges me within;
An' when they's pie for supper, or cakes
'at's big an' nice,
I want to—but I do not pass my plate f'r
    them things twice!
No, ruther let Starvation wipe me slowly
    out o' sight
Than I should keep a-livin' on an' seein'
    things at night!

EUGENE FIELD, 1850 - 1895

THREE GATES

If you are tempted to reveal
A tale to you someone has told
About another, make it pass,
Before you speak, three gates of gold.
These narrow gates: First, "Is it true?"
Then, "Is it needful?" In your mind

Give truthful answer. And the next
Is last and narrowest, "Is it kind?"
And if to reach your lips at last
It passes through these gateways three,
Then you may tell the tale, nor fear
What the result of speech may be.

BETH DAY, fl. 1855

from the ARABIAN

ON THE GRASSHOPPER AND CRICKET

The poetry of earth is never dead:
    When all the birds are faint with the hot
        sun,
    And hide in cooling trees, a voice will
        run
From hedge to hedge about the new-mown
    mead!
That is the Grasshopper's—he takes the
    lead
    In summer luxury,—he has never done
    With his delights; for when tired out
        with fun
He rests at ease beneath some pleasant
    weed.
The poetry of earth is ceasing never:
    On a lone winter evening, when the
        frost
    Has wrought a silence, from the stove
        there shrills
The Cricket's song, in warmth increasing
    ever,
    And seems to one in drowsiness half
        lost,
    The Grasshopper's among some grassy
        hills.

JOHN KEATS, 1795 - 1821

from SUMMER

Winter is cold-hearted,
Spring is yea and nay,
Autumn is a weathercock
Blown every way.
Summer days for me
When every leaf is on its tree;

. . .

Before green apples blush,
Before green nuts embrown,
When one day in the country
Is worth a month in town;
Is worth a day and a year
Of the dusty, musty, lag-last fashion
That days drone elsewhere.

CHRISTINA ROSSETTI

❧

RESOLUTION

I was in the Harbor
  Snug as I could be—
Pierrot whistled down the wind—
  "Oh, come out to Sea!"

I was bruised and weary
  With sailing on the Sea:
The Harbor held me in its arms
  And safely cradled me.

I knew all about the Sea
  And what a Harbor meant;
Pierrot whistled down the wind—
  And of course I went!

WIOLAR

❧

A PILGRIM'S GRACE

Give me a good digestion, Lord,
And also something to digest.

❧

AN EPITAPH

Their beer was strong; their wine was port;
Their meal was large; their grace was short.

MATTHEW PRIOR, 1664 - 1721

METHUSELAH

Methuselah ate what he found on his
  plate,
And never, as people do now,
Did he note the amount of the calory
  count:
He ate it because it was chow.
He wasn't disturbed as at dinner he sat,
Devouring a roast or a pie,
To think it was lacking in granular fat
Or a couple of vitamins shy.
He cheerfully chewed each species of food,
Unmindful of troubles or fears
Lest his health might be hurt
By some fancy dessert;
And he lived over nine hundred years.

❧

from "THE TEMPEST"

Where the bee sucks, there suck I:
  In a cowslip's bell I lie;
There I couch when owls do cry.
On the bat's back I do fly
After summer merrily:
  Merrily, merrily, shall I live now,
  Under the blossom that hangs on the
    bough.

WILLIAM SHAKESPEARE, 1564 - 1616

Act V, Scene I

❧

from A DAY OF WISHING

If you wish to grow thinner:
  diminish your dinner,
    And take to light
      claret instead of pale ale;
Look down with an utter contempt upon
    butter,
  And never touch bread till it's toasted—
    or stale.

H. S. LEIGH, 1837 - 1883

❧

Erasmus, referring to his dislike of fish:

My heart is Catholic, but my stomach
Lutheran.

THE AMERICAN STANDARD

Tell them that by way of the shop, the field, the skilled hand, habits of economy and thrift, by way of industrial school and college, we are coming. We are crawling up, working up, yea, bursting up. Often through oppression, unjust discrimination, and prejudice, but through them we are coming up, and with proper habits, intelligence, and property, there is no power on earth that can permanently stay our progress. . . .

While we are thus being tested, I beg of you to remember that wherever our life touches yours, we help or hinder. Wherever your life touches ours, you make us stronger or weaker. No member of your race in any part of our country can harm the meanest member of mine, without the proudest and bluest blood in Massachusetts being degraded. When Mississippi commits crime, New England commits crime, and in so much lowers the standard of your civilization. There is no escape—man drags man down, or man lifts man up.

BOOKER T. WASHINGTON, 1859 - 1915
Speech 1896

BRINGING UP BOYS

We have much speculation over whether the city or the country is the better place to bring up boys. I am prejudiced in behalf of the country, but I should have to admit that much depends on the parents and the surrounding neighborhood. We felt the cold in winter and had many inconveniences, but we did not mind them because we supposed they were the inevitable burdens of existence.

It would be hard to imagine better surroundings for the development of a boy than those which I had. While a wider breadth of training and knowledge could have been presented to me, there was a daily contact with many new ideas, and the mind was given sufficient opportunity thoroughly to digest all that came to it.

Country life does not always have breadth, but it has depth. It is neither artificial nor superficial, but is kept close to the realities.

While I can think of many pleasures we did not have, and many niceties of culture with which we were unfamiliar, yet if I had the power to order my life anew I would not dare to change that period of it. If it did not afford me the best that there was, it abundantly provided the best that there was for me.

A horse is much company, and riding over the fields and along the country roads by himself, where nothing interrupts his seeing and thinking, is a good occupation for a boy. The silences of Nature have a discipline all their own.

In the development of every boy who is going to amount to anything there comes a time when he emerges from his immature ways and by the greater precision of his thought and action realizes that he has begun to find himself. Such a transition finally came to me. It was not accidental but the result of hard work. If I had permitted my failures, or what seemed to me at the time a lack of success, to discourage me I cannot see any way in which I would have ever have made progress. If we keep our faith in ourselves, and what is even more important, keep our faith in regular and persistent application to hard work, we need not worry about the outcome.

CALVIN COOLIDGE, 1872 - 1933
Autobiography, chapters 1 and 2

ON HIS BLINDNESS

When I consider how my light is spent
Ere half my days in this dark world and
    wide,
And that one talent, which is death to
    hide,
Lodged with me useless, though my soul
    more bent
To serve therewith my Maker, and present
My true account, lest He returning chide;
"Doth God exact day-labor, light denied?"
I fondly ask. But Patience, to prevent
That murmur, soon replies, "God doth not
    need
Either man's work or his own gifts; who
    best
Bear his mild yoke, they serve him best;
    his state
Is kingly; thousands at his bidding speed,
And post o'er land and ocean without
    rest;
They also serve who only stand and wait."

                  JOHN MILTON, 1608 - 1674

NIGHTFALL: A PICTURE

Low burns the summer afternoon;
    A mellow lustre lights the scene;
And from its smiling beauty soon
    The purpling shade will chase the
        sheen.

The old, quaint homestead's windows
        blaze;
    The cedars long black pictures show;
And broadly slopes one path of rays
    Within the barn, and makes it glow.

The loft stares out—the cat intent,
    Like carving, on some gnawing rat—
With sun-bathed hay and rafters bent,
    Nooked cobwebbed homes of wasp
        and bat.

The harness, bridle, saddle, dart
    Gleam from the lower, rough expanse;
At either side the stooping cart
    Pitchfork and plow cast looks askance.

White Dobbin through the stable-doors
    Shows his round shape; faint color
        coats
The manger, where the farmer pours,
    With rustling rush, the glancing oats.

A sun-haze streaks the dusky shed;
    Makes spears of seams and gems of
        chinks;
In mottled gloss the straw is spread;
    And the gray grindstone dully blinks.

The sun salutes the lowest west
    With gorgeous tints around it drawn;
A beacon on the mountain's breast,
    A crescent, shred, a star—and gone.

Keep cool: it will be all one a hundred
years hence.

        RALPH WALDO EMERSON, 1803 - 1882
                Montaigne; or, The Skeptic

DORIS

Down the lane and across the fields
    Doris and I were walking.
Past bulging stacks that the harvest yields,
    Doris and I were talking.

"The man I wed," said Doris fair
    (Doris did most of the talking),
"Must be a multimillionaire,"
    I only kept on walking.

"His hair must be yellow, his eyes dark
        blue"
    ('T was Doris doing the talking),
"And he must be a Yale man, too,
    Isn't it lovely walking?"

Now I am poor and my hair is brown
    (I never was much at talking),
And I came from Harvard, in Cambridge
        town
    (I'm really quite good at walking).

But I slipped my arm around Doris sweet
    (She suddenly stopped her talking),
And I hugged her nearly off her feet,
    'T was really a help to walking.

And I said: "I'm sorry I don't suit you."
    (Somehow we'd stopped our walking).
But, "Oh," said Doris, "I guess you'll do."
    For Doris was only talking.

                CLARENCE S. HARPER

SUNSET

The moon is up, and yet it is not night:
Sunset divides the sky with her; a sea
Of glory streams along the Alpine height
Of blue Friuli's mountains; heaven is
   free
From clouds, but of all colors seems to
   be
Melted to one vast Iris of the West,
Where the day joins the past eternity;
While, on the other hand, meek Dian's
   crest
Floats through the azure air, an island of
   the blest.

A single star is at her side, and reigns
With her o'er half the lovely heaven;
   but still
Yon sunny sea heaves brightly, and
   remains
Rolled o'er the peak of the far Rhoetian
   hill,
As day and night contending were until
Nature reclaimed her order: gently
   flows
The deep-dyed Brenta, where their hues
   instill
The odorous purple of a new-born rose,
Which streams upon her stream, and
   glassed within its glows,

Filled with the face of heaven, which,
   from afar,
Comes down upon the waters; all its
   hues,
From the rich sunset to the rising star,
Their magical variety diffuse:
And now they change; a paler shadow
   strews
Its mantle o'er the mountains; parting
   day
Dies like the dolphin, whom each pang
   imbues
With a new color as it gasps away,
The last still loveliest, till 'tis gone—and
   all is gray.
   GEORGE GORDON BYRON, 1788 - 1824
[From "Childe Harolde."]

WHEN YOU ARE OLD

When you are old and gray and full of
   sleep,
And nodding by the fire, take down this
   book,
And slowly read and dream of the soft
   look
Your eyes had once, and of their
   shadows deep;

How many loved your moments of glad
   grace,
And loved your beauty with love false
   or true;
But one man loved the pilgrim soul in
   you,
And loved the sorrows of your changing
   face.

And bending down beside the glowing
   bars
Murmur, a little sadly, how love fled
And paced upon the mountains overhead
And hid his face amid a crowd of stars.
   WILLIAM BUTLER YEATS

All would live long, but none would be
old.

   BENJAMIN FRANKLIN

One hour of life, crowded to the full
with glorious action, and filled with noble
risk, is worth whole years of those mean
observances of paltry decorum, in which
men steal through existence, like sluggish
waters through a marsh, without either
honour or observation.

   SIR WALTER SCOTT, 1771 - 1832

We must get away from employment
policies based on cold arithmetical aver-
ages and take advantage of the skills and
judgment of older people. How hideous a
mockery it would be if, as a result of ad-
vances in medicine, surgery, hygiene and
higher living standards, older people were
kept willing and able to work—but society
deprived them of something useful to do.

   BERNARD BARUCH, 1870 - 1965

AUGUST

"June and July have slipped away
And August's here again."

TECUMSEH
1768 - 1813

The Shawnee Indian chief, Tecumseh, (1768 - 1813), born on Mad Creek (now near Springfield, Ohio) had seen the Whites bring suffering to his people from childhood. He knew they must unite as Indians to resist the whites who were forcing them further and further from their fields and hunting grounds. They formed a confederacy of the Indian tribes and established at the junction of the Tippecanoe and Wabash rivers in northern Indiana, "Prophet's Town"—their headquarters.

In 1809 Gov. William Henry Harrison negotiated the Treaty of Fort Wayne by which some Miami chiefs ceded to the Government about three million acres on both sides of the Wabash river, at a price of about one-third of a cent per acre.

In this speech made in Aug. 12, 1810 Tecumseh claims the chiefs had no right to barter away hunting grounds of all of the Indians for a few gifts and a couple of kegs of liquor. And he warns Harrison there will be no peace between the Indians and the whites until the land is ceded back.

Harrison marched on Prophet's Town and in the bloody battle of Tippecanoe completely defeated the hostile Indians. The next year when the War of 1812 broke out, Tecumseh joined the British where he distinguished himself by his bravery, meeting his death at the Battle of the Thames. He was one of the great American Indians with a superb body, a great mind, and the soul of a hero.

SPEECH AT VINCENNES
Aug. 12

It is true I am a Shawanee. My forefathers were warriors. Their son is a warrior. From them I only take my existence; from my tribe I take nothing. I am the maker of my own fortune; and oh! that I could make that of my red people, and of my country; as great as the conceptions of my mind, when I think of the Spirit that rules the universe. I would not then come to Governor Harrison, to ask him to tear the treaty and to obliterate the landmark; but I would say to him, sir you have liberty to return to your own country. The being within, communing with past ages, tells me that once, nor until lately, there was no white man on this continent. That it then all belonged to red men, children of the same parents, placed on it by the Great Spirit that made them, to keep it, to traverse it, to enjoy its productions, and to fill it with the same race. Once a happy race. Since made miserable by the white people, who are never contented, but always encroaching. The way, and the only way to check and to stop this evil, is for all the red men to unite in claiming a common and equal right in the land as it was at first, and should be yet; for it never was divided, but belongs to all for the use of each. That no part has a right to sell, even to each other, much less to strangers; those who want all, and will not do with less.

The white people have no right to take the land from the Indians, because they had it first; it is theirs. They may sell, but all must join. Any sale not made by all is not valid. The late sale is bad. It was made by a part only. Part do not know how to sell. It requires all to make a bargain for all. All red men have equal rights to the unoccupied land. The right of occupancy is as good in one place as in another. There cannot be two occupations in the same place. The first excludes all others. It is not so in hunting or travelling; for there the same ground will serve many, as they may follow each other all day; but the camp is stationary, and that is occupancy. It belongs to the first who sits down on his blanket or skins which he has thrown upon the ground; and till he leaves it no other has a right.

TECUMSEH, 1768 - 1813

PRESERVING—TIME

All over the land there's a savory smell,
  You meet it abroad or at home;
The days of your childhood come back
    for a spell,
  No matter how far you may roam—
'T is the scent of preserving the strawberry
    red,
  The pineapple, raspberry, plum;
That the gooseberry, currant, and cherry
    must shed
  When the jelly and marmalade come.

For the kitchen's a sight in these summery
    days,
  As the kettles all simmer or steam;
The mountains of sugar we view with
    amaze,
  And the fruits are an epicure's dream;
Abroad through the land goes the savory
    scent
  Made by nieces of good Uncle Sam;
And prosperity's balm with th' odor is
    blent
  Of marmalade, jelly, and jam.

<hr />

These lands are ours. No one has a
right to remove us, because we were the
first owners. The Great Spirit above has
appointed this place for us, on which to
light our fires, and here we will remain.
As to boundaries, the Great Spirit knows
no boundaries, nor will his red children
acknowledge any.

TECUMSEH

Chief of the Shawnees, to the messenger of the
President of the United States, 1810.

from GOOD-BY — GOD BLESS YOU!

I like the Anglo-Saxon speech
  With its direct revealings;
It takes a hold, and seems to reach
  Way down into your feelings;
That some folk deem it rude, I know,
And therefore they abuse it;
But I have never found it so,—
  Before all else I choose it.
I don't object that men should air
  The Gallic they have paid for,
With 'Au revoir,'' "Adieu, ma chere,''
  For that's what French was made for,
But when a crony takes your hand
  At parting, to address you,
He drops all foreign lingo and
  He says, "Good-by God bless you!''

EUGENE FIELD, 1850 - 1895

THE FLEETING VISITANT

These parting words we have to say
  Are painful to endure
Each dollar bill that comes my way
  Seems on its farewell tour.

As long as gray hairs can be counted,
they don't count.

The dogged dog-days had begun to bite.

JOHN TAYLOR, 1580 - 1653

No place is home until two people have
latchkeys.

WHEN IT'S AUGUST HEAT—

Heat, ma'am! It was so dreadful here
that I found there was nothing left for it
but to take off my flesh and sit in my
bones.

SYDNEY SMITH, 1771 - 1845

To lead a people in revolution wisely and successfully, without ambition and without crime, demands indeed lofty genius and unbending virtue. But to build their State amid the angry conflict of passion and prejudice, to peacefully inaugurate a complete and satisfactory government—this is the very greatest service that a man can render to mankind. But this also is the glory of Washington.

With the sure sagacity of a leader of men, he selected at once for the three highest stations the three chief Americans. Hamilton was the head, Jefferson was the heart, and John Jay the conscience of his administration. Washington's just and serene ascendency was the lambent flame in which these beneficent powers were fused; and nothing else than that ascendency could have ridden the whirlwind and directed the storm that burst around him. Party spirit blazed into fury. John Jay was hung in effigy; Hamilton was stoned; insurrection raised its head in the West; Washington himself was denounced. But the great soul was undismayed. Without a beacon, without a chart, but with unwavering eye and steady hand, he guided his country safe through darkness and through storm. He held his steadfast way, like the sun across the firmament, giving life and health and strength to the new nation; and upon a searching survey of his administration, there is no great act which his country would annul; no word spoken, no line written, no deed done by him, which justice would reverse or wisdom deplore.

GEORGE WILLIAM CURTIS, 1824 - 1892

The die was now cast; I had passed the Rubicon. Swim or sink, live or die, survive or perish with my country was my unshakable determination.

JOHN ADAMS

Referring to his signing of the Declaration of Independence, 1776.

The Constitution does not provide for first and second class citizens.

WENDELL L. WILLKIE, 1892 - 1944

Patriotism is not enough. I must have no hatred or bitterness towards anyone.

EDITH CAVELL

In conversation with Rev. Gahan Oct. 1915 before her execution by the Germans.

155

A diner while dining at Crewe
Found quite a large mouse in his stew,
Said the waiter, "Don't shout
  And wave it about,
Or the rest will be wanting one too."

⚜

from Sing Song
MOTHER SHAKE THE CHERRY TREE

Mother shake the cherry-tree,
  Susan catch a cherry;
Oh how funny that will be,
  Let's be merry!

One for brother, one for sister,
  Two for mother more,
Six for father, hot and tired,
  Knocking at the door.

CHRISTINA GEORGINA ROSSETTI, 1830 - 1894

⚜

DRIED APPLE PIES

I loathe, abhor, detest, despise,
Abominate dried-apple pies.
I like good bread, I like good meat,
Or anything that's fit to eat;
But of all poor grub beneath the skies,
The poorest is dried apple pies.
Give me the toothache, or sore eyes,
But don't give me dried apple pies.
The farmer takes his gnarliest fruit,
'Tis wormy, bitter, and hard, to boot;
He leaves the hulls to make us cough,
And don't take half the peeling off.
Then on a dirty cord 'tis strung
And in a garret window hung,
And there it serves as roost for flies,
Until it's made up into pies.
Tread on my corns, or tell me lies,
But don't pass me dried-apple pies.

Lettuce is like conversation: It must be
fresh and crisp, and so sparkling that you
scarcely notice the bitter in it.

CHARLES D. WARNER, 1829 - 1900

⚜

from CONDUCT OF LIFE—BEHAVIOR

There is the best way of doing everything, if it be to boil an egg. Manners are
the happy ways of doing things.

RALPH WALDO EMERSON, 1803 - 1882

⚜

To make a perfect salad—
  There should be a spendthrift for oil
  A miser for vinegar
  A wise man for salt
And a madcap to stir it up.

⚜

It isn't travel that's broadening—it's the
rich foreign food!

⚜

Nowadays the riddle is not why does the
chicken cross the road, but how?

⚜

The best thing you can say about gravy is
that it has no bones.

HARVEST

Sweet, sweet, sweet,
  Is the wind's song,
Astir in the rippled wheat
  All day long,
It hath the brook's wild gayety,
  The sorrowful cry of the sea.
    Oh, hush and hear!
    Sweet, sweet and clear,
    Above the locust's whirr
    And hum of bee
Rises that soft, pathetic harmony.

In the meadow-grass
  The innocent white daisies blow,
The dandelion plume doth pass
  Vaguely to and fro,—
    The unquiet spirit of a flower
    That hath too brief an hour.

Now doth a little cloud all white,
  Or golden bright,
Drift down the warm, blue sky;
  And now on the horizon line,
Where dusky woodlands lie,
  A sunny mist doth shine,
  Like to a veil before a holy shrine,
  Concealing, half-revealing, things divine.

    Sweet, sweet, sweet,
      Is the wind's song,
    Astir in the rippled wheat
      All day long.
    That exquisite music calls
      The reaper everywhere—
      Life and death must share.
    The golden harvest falls.
      ELLEN MACKEY HUTCHINSON CORTISSOZ

BREAD

When music spills from golden throat
  In wild bird reveille,
I push the drab world out in space
  And live in melody.
When color glows in countless ways
  Before my hungry eyes.
I am a gourmand at the feast
  Unmindful of how time flies,
For when this pageantry is spread
I quite forget my daily bread.

When cool waves run to greet the sands
  And whisper deep-sea lore,
I stand, at crimson close of day,
  Enchanted on the shore.
Each season wafts in new delights
  As beauty flames its way,
On rock, and earth, and sky, and sea,
  With respite for the day—
And, oh, my dear, I humbly own
I cannot live by bread alone!
  CHRISTINA GEORGINA ROSSETTI, 1830 - 1894

There is something good in all weathers. If it doesn't happen to be good for my work today, it's good for some other man's today, and will come around for me tomorrow.

CHARLES DICKENS, 1811 - 1870

This is the place! Said by Brigham Young 1801 - 1877 on first seeing the Valley of the Great Salt Lake, July 24, 1847.

1947, July 24, Young's grandson, M. M. Young, noted sculptor, dedicated the "This is the place" Monument.

from NINETY-NINE IN THE SHADE

O for a lodge in a garden of cucumbers!
  O for an iceberg or two at control!
O for a vale which at mid-day the dew
    cumbers!
  O for a pleasure-trip up to the pole!

O for a little one-story thermometer,
  With nothing but zeroes all ranged in a
    row!
O for a big double-barreled hygrometer,
  To measure this moisture that rolls from
    my brow!

O for a soda-fount spouting up boldly
  From every hot lamp-post against the
    hot sky!
O for proud maiden to look on me coldly,
  Freezing my soul with a glance of her
    eye!

Then O for a draught from a cup of cold
    pizen,
  And O for a resting-place in the cold
    grave!
With a bath in the Styx where the thick
    shadow lies on
And deepens the chill of its dark-running
    wave.

ROSSITER JOHNSON, 1840 - 1931

Once upon a time we used to read in the obituary column that so-and-so "completed his education" at such-and-such a college. But the phrase, I am glad to say, has about gone out of use.

We now know that when a man finishes college, his education has just about begun!

EDWARD A. FILENE, 1860 - 1937

from "LADDER OF ST. AUGUSTINE"

The heights by great men reached and
    kept
  Were not attained by sudden flight,
But they, while their companions slept,
  Were toiling upward in the night.

HENRY WADSWORTH LONGFELLOW, 1807 - 1882
(Inscribed on his bust in the Hall of Fame)

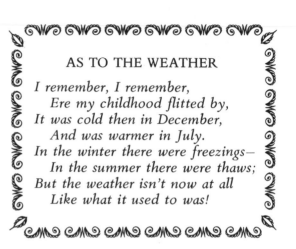

AS TO THE WEATHER

I remember, I remember,
  Ere my childhood flitted by,
It was cold then in December,
  And was warmer in July.
In the winter there were freezings—
  In the summer there were thaws;
But the weather isn't now at all
Like what it used to was!

TWELVE THINGS TO REMEMBER

1. The value of time.
2. The success of perseverance.
3. The pleasure of working.
4. The dignity of simplicity.
5. The worth of character.
6. The power of kindness.
7. The influence of example.
8. The obligation of duty.
9. The wisdom of economy.
10. The virtue of patience.
11. The improvement of talent.
12. The joy of originating.

MARSHALL FIELD

INSTRUCTION TO HIS COURT PHILOSOPHER:

Never instruct me in public; never be in haste to give me advice in private. Wait till I question you; answer in a direct and precise manner. If you see me quitting the path of rectitude, gently lead me back to it, without any harsh expressions; but never address me in equivocal terms.

SARACEN KHALIF-HAROUN AL RASCHILD, 765 - 809 A.D.

THE PROFESSION OF THE LAW

No man has earned the right to intellectual ambition until he has learned to lay his course by a star which he has never seen,—to dig by the divining rod for springs which he may never reach. In saying this, I point to that which will make your study heroic. For I say to you in all sadness of conviction, that to think great thoughts you must be heroes as well as idealists. Only when you have worked alone,—when you have felt around you a black gulf of solitude more isolating than that which surrounds a dying man, and in hope and in despair have trusted to your own unshaken will,—then only will you have achieved. Thus only can you gain the secret isolated joy of the thinker, who knows that, a hundred years after he is dead and forgotten, men who never heard of him will be moving to the measure of his thought,—the subtle rapture of a postponed power, which the world knows not because it has no external trappings, but which to its prophetic vision is more real than that which commands an army. And if this joy cannot be yours, still it is only thus that you can know that you have done what it lay in you to do,—can say that you have lived, and be ready for the end.

JUSTICE OLIVER WENDELL HOLMES, JR., 1841 - 1935

18th CENTURY EPIGRAM:

The law doth punish man or woman
That steals the goose from off the
* common.*
But lets the greater felon loose,
That steals the common from the goose.

My boy, about 75 years ago I learned I was not God. And so, when the people of the various States want to do something and I can't find anything in the Constitution expressly forbidding them to do it, I say, whether I like it or not: "Damn it, let'm do it!"

OLIVER WENDELL HOLMES, JR., 1841 - 1935

Discourage litigation. Persuade your neighbors to compromise whenever you can. As a peacemaker a lawyer has a superior opportunity of being a good man. There will still be business enough.

ABRAHAM LINCOLN
Address on Legal Ethics.

from THE JOLLY TESTATOR

No customer brings so much grist to the
* mill*
As the wealthy old woman who makes her
* own will.*

CHARLES NEAVES, 1800 - 1876

I am not willing that this discussion should close without mention of the value of a true teacher. Give me a log hut, with only a simple bench, Mark Hopkins on one end and I on the other, and you may have all the buildings, apparatus and libraries without him.

JAMES A. GARFIELD, 1831 - 1881
Address in 1871 to Alumni, Williams College.

Deciding that a novel, FOREVER AMBER, was dull, but not obscene, and therefore could be sold in Massachusetts:

This book acts like a soporific rather than an aphrodisiac. While conductive to sleep, it is not conducive to a desire to sleep with a member of the opposite sex.

FRANK J. DONAHUE (1947)

159

from A MAN'S REAL MEASURE

The place to take the true measure of a man is not in the darkest place or in the amen corner, nor the cornfield, but by his own fireside. There he lays aside his mask and you may learn whether he is an imp or an angel, cur or king, hero or humbug. I care not what the world says of him: whether it crowns him boss or pelts him with bad eggs. I care not a copper what his reputation or religion may be: if his babies dread his homecoming and his better half swallows her heart every time she has to ask him for a five-dollar bill, he is a fraud of the first water, even though he prays night and morning until he is black in the face and howls hallelujah until he shakes the eternal hills. But if his children rush to the front door to meet him and love's sunshine illuminates the face of his wife every time she hears his footfall, you can take it for granted that he is pure, for his home is a heaven—and the humbug never gets that near the great white throne of God. He may be a rank atheist and red-flag anarchist, a Mormon and a mugwump; he may buy votes in blocks of five, and bet on the elections; he may deal 'em from the bottom of the deck and drink beer until he can't tell a silver dollar from a circular saw, and still be an infinitely better man than the cowardly little humbug who is all suavity in society but who makes home a hell, who vents upon the helpless heads of his wife and children an ill nature he would inflict on his fellow men but dares not. I can forgive much in that fellow mortal who would rather make men swear than women weep; who would rather have the hate of the whole world than the contempt of his wife; who would rather call anger to the eyes of a king than fear to the face of a child.—

W. C. BRANN, 1855 - 1898

Little fleas have lesser fleas
Upon their backs to bite them,
And these fleas have lesser fleas
Ad infinitum.

Great fleas have greater fleas
Upon their backs to bite them,
And these fleas have greater fleas
And greater fleas and so on.

AUGUSTUS DE MORGAN, 1806 - 1871

In men whom men condemn as ill
I find so much of goodness still,
In men whom men pronounce divine
I find so much of sin and blot,
I do not dare to draw a line
Between the two, where God has not.

JOAQUIN MILLER, 1841 - 1913

❧❦❧

There is so much good in the worst of us,
And so much bad in the best of us
That it hardly becomes any of us
To talk about the rest of us.

Attributed to E. W. Hoch of Kansas, but disclaimed by him.

AUGUST

The yellow goldenrod is dressed
  In gala-day attire;
The glowing redweed by the fence
  Shines like a crimson fire;
And from the hot field's farthest edge
  The cricket's soft refrain
With mellow accent tells the tale
  That August's here again.

The wild hop, from the young elm's
    bough,
  Sways on the languid breeze
And here and there the autumn tints
  Gleam faintly through the trees.
All Nature helps to swell the song
  And chant the same refrain;
July and June have slipped away
  And August's here again.

HELEN MARIA WINSLOW

❧❦❧

from RIP VAN WINKLE

Rip Van Winkle is pictured by Washington Irving as averse to any kind of profitable labor, and sits with his dog "in the shade through a long lazy summer's day, talking listlessly over village gossip, or telling endless sleepy stories about nothing." Dame Van Winkle has for years railed at her shiftless husband:

. . "Times grew worse and worse with Rip Van Winkle as years of matrimony rolled on; a tart temper never mellows with age, and a sharp tongue is the only edged tool that grows keener with constant use."

WASHINGTON IRVING, 1783 - 1859

160

GIVE ME BACK MY YOUTH AGAIN

Then give me back that time of pleasures,
While yet in joyous youth I sang,—
When, like a fount, the crowding measures
Uninterrupted gushed and sprang!
Then bright mist veiled the world before
*   me,*
In opening buds a marvel woke,
As the thousand blossoms broke
Which every valley richly bore me!
I nothing had, and yet enough for youth—
Joy in Illusion, ardent thirst for Truth.
Give unrestrained the old emotion,
The bliss that touched the verge of pain,
The strength of Hate, Love's deep
*   devotion,—*
O, give me back my youth again!
    JOHAN WOLFGANG VON GOETHE, 1749 - 1832

FOR A LITTLE BROWN DOG

For a Little Brown Dog, who "sees" me
*   down*
The hill to the car when I go to town,
And carries my bag with an air of pride,
As he trots sedately by my side,
And waits to see that I'm on all right,
And watches the car till it's out of sight—
*   I thank thee.*

For the way he tears down the hill to
*   meet*
That car at night on his mad little feet—
The car that will bring me, he knows,
*   from town—*
And the joyous greeting, as I step down,
A greeting the passengers hear and see,
Every one of them envying me,
*   I thank thee.*

For the great true heart that is in his eyes,
Tender, and patient, and brave, and wise,
That makes him know when I'm sick, or
*   sad,*
And, knowing, love me the more—dear
*   lad—*
With a love unquestioning, high and fine—
For all of that Little Brown Dog of mine,
*   —I thank thee.*

SMILE

Like a bread without the spreadin',
*   Like a puddin' without sauce,*
Like a mattress without beddin',
*   Like a cart without a hoss,*
Like a door without a latchstring,
*   Like a fence without a stile,*
Like a dry an' barren creek bed—
*   Is the face without a smile.*

Like a house without a dooryard,
*   Like a yard without a flower,*
Like a clock without a mainspring,
*   That will never tell the hour;*
A thing that sort o' makes yo' feel
*   A hunger all the while—*
Oh, the saddest sight that ever was
*   Is a face without a smile!*

So smile an' don't forgit to smile,
*   An' smile, an' smile ag'in;*
'Twill help you all along the way,
*   An' cheer you mile by mile;*
An' so, whatever is your lot,
*   Jes' smile, an' smile, an' smile.*

A DIRGE

Rough wind, that moanest loud
*   Grief too sad for song;*
Wild wind, when sullen cloud
*   Knells all the night long;*

Sad storm, whose tears are vain,
Bare woods, whose branches strain,
Deep caves and dreary main,—
*   Wail, for the world's wrong!*
        PERCY BYSSHE SHELLEY, 1792 - 1822

A smile is a curve that helps to set things straight.

When a dog wags his tail and barks at the same time, how do you know which end to believe?

The nose of a dog has been slanted backwards so he can breathe without letting go.

WINSTON CHURCHILL

SONNET

When in disgrace with fortune and men's
    eyes
I all alone beweep my outcast state,
And trouble deaf heaven with my bootless
    cries,
And look upon myself and curse my fate,
Wishing me like to one more rich in hope,
Featured like him, like him with friends
    possessed,
Desiring this man's art, and that man's
    scope,
With what I most enjoy contented least.
Yet in these thoughts myself almost
    despising,
Haply I think on thee—and then my state,
Like to the lark at break of day arising
From sullen earth, sings hymns at heaven's
    gate,
    For thy sweet love remembered, such
        wealth brings
    That then I scorn to change my state
        with kings.

                    WM. SHAKESPEARE

SONNETS from the PORTUGUESE

How do I love thee? Let me count the
    ways,
I love thee to the depth and breadth and
    height
My soul can reach, when feeling out of
    sight
For the ends of Being and ideal Grace.
I love thee to the level of every day's
Most quiet need, by sun and candle-light.
I love thee freely, as men strive for right;
I love thee purely, as they turn from
    praise.
I love thee with the passion put to use
In my old griefs, and with my childhood's
    faith.
I love thee with a love I seemed to lose
With my lost saints—I love thee with the
    breath,
Smiles, tears, of all my life!—and, if God
    choose,
I shall but love thee better after death.

      ELIZABETH BARRETT BROWNING, 1809 - 1861

THE TIME I'VE LOST IN WOOING

The time I've lost in wooing,
In watching and pursuing
    The light, that lies
    In woman's eyes,
Has been my heart's undoing.
Though Wisdom oft has sought me,
I scorn'd the lore she brought me,
    My only books
    Were woman's looks,
And folly's all they've taught me.

Her smile when Beauty granted,
I hung with gaze enchanted,
    Like him, the sprite,
    Whom maids by night
Oft meet in glen that's haunted.
Like him, too, Beauty won me,
But while her eyes were on me,
    If once their ray
    Was turn'd away,
O! winds could not outrun me.

And are those follies going?
And is my proud heart growing
    Too cold or wise
    For brilliant eyes
Again to set it glowing?
No, vain, alas! th' endeavour
From bonds so sweet to sever;
    Poor Wisdom's chance
    Against a glance
Is now as weak as ever.

          THOMAS MOORE, 1779 - 1852

The Present, the Present is all thou hast
    For thy sure possessing;
Like the patriarch's angel hold it fast
    Till it gives its blessing.
      JOHN GREENLEAF WHITTIER, 1807 - 1892

The greatest test of courage on the earth
is to bear defeat without losing heart.
      ROBERT G. INGERSOLL, 1833 - 1899

THE PINE

The elm lets fall its leaves before the frost,
The very oak grows shivering and sere,
The trees are barren when the summer's
lost:
But one tree keeps its goodness all the
year.

Green pine, unchanging as the days go by,
Thou art thyself beneath whatever sky,
My shelter from all winds, my own
strong pine,
'Tis spring, 'tis summer, still, while thou
art mine.

AUGUSTA WEBSTER, 1837 - 1894

LOVE'S PHILOSOPHY

The fountains mingle with the river
And the rivers with the Ocean,
The winds of Heaven mix for ever
With a sweet emotion;
Nothing in the world is single;
All things by a law divine
In one spirit meet and mingle.
Why not I with thine?—

See the mountains kiss high Heaven
And the waves clasp one another;
No sister-flower would be forgiven
If it disdained its brother;
And the sunlight clasps the earth
And the moonbeams kiss the sea:
What is all this sweet work worth
If thou kiss not me?

PERCY BYSSHE SHELLEY, 1792 - 1822

Pity costs nothing, and ain't worth nothing.

JOSH BILLINGS

LOVE

I love you,
Not only for what you are,
But for what I am
When I am with you.

I love you,
Not only for what
You have made of yourself,
But for what
You are making of me

I love you
For the part of me
That you bring out;
I love you
For putting your hand
Into my heaped-up heart
And passing over
All the foolish, weak things
That you can't help
Dimly seeing there,
And for drawing out
Into the light
All the beautiful belongings
That no one else had looked
Quite far enough to find.

I love you because you
Are helping me to make
Of the lumber of my life
Not a tavern
But a temple;

I don't wanna be a millionaire. I just want to live like one.

TOOTS SHOR

Be like a bird, who
Halting in his flight
On limb too slight
Feels it give way beneath him,
Yet sings
Knowing he hath wings.

VICTOR HUGO, 1802 - 1885

163

THE COMMON PROBLEM

The common problem—yours, mine,
everyone's—
Is not to fancy what were fair in life
Provided it could be; but, finding first
What may be, then find how to make it fair
Up to our means—a very different thing!
My business is not to remake myself
But make the absolute best of what God
made.

ROBERT BROWNING, 1812 - 1889

NONSENSE

Good reader! if you e'er have seen,
When Phoebus hastens to his pillow,
The mermaids, with their tresses green,
Dancing upon the western billow:
If you have seen, at twilight dim,
When the lone spirit's vesper hymn
Floats wild along the winding shore:
If you have seen, through mist of eve,
The fairy train their ringlets weave,
Glancing along the spangled green;—
If you have seen all this, and more,
God bless me! what a deal you've seen!

THOMAS MOORE, 1780 - 1852

SINCERE FLATTERY

The clear cool note of the cuckoo which
has ousted the legitimate nest-holder,
The whistle of the railway guard
dispatching the train to the inevitable
collision,
The maiden's monosyllabic reply to the
polysyllabic proposal,
The fundamental note of the last trump,
which is presumably D natural;
All of these are sounds to rejoice in, yea,
to let your very ribs re-echo with:
But better than all of them is the
absolutely last chord of the apparently
inexhaustible pianoforte player.

JAMES KENNETH STEPHEN, 1859 - 1892

WEATHER LORE:

Winds that swing against the sun
And winds that bring the rain are one.
Winds that swing round with the sun
Keep the rain storm on the run.

Half a loaf is better than no time off.

YOUR AFTERSELF

Your first duty in life is toward your afterself. So live that the man you ought to be may, in his time, be possible, be actual. Far away in the years he is waiting his turn. His body, his brain, his soul, are in your boyish hands. He cannot help himself. What will you leave for him? Will it be a brain unspoiled by lust or dissipation; a mind trained to think and act; a nervous system true as a dial in its response to the truth about you? Will you, Boy, let him come as a man among men in his time? Or will you throw away his inheritance before he has had the chance to touch it? Will you turn over to him a brain distorted, a mind diseased, a will untrained to action, a spinal cord grown thru and thru with "the devil-grass of wild oats"? Will you let him come and take your place, gaining thru your experience, happy in your friendships, hallowed thru your joys, building on them his own? Or will you fling it all away, decreeing, wanton-like, that the man you might have been shall never be? This is your problem in life—the problem which is vastly more to you than any or all others. How will you meet it, as a man or as a fool? It comes before you today and every day, and the hour of your choice is the crisis in your destiny!

DAVID STARR JORDAN, 1851 - 1931

164

SOLILOQUY from "HAMLET"

To be, or not to be; that is the question;
Whether 'tis nobler in the mind to suffer
The slings and arrows of outrageous
    fortune,
Or to take arms against a sea of troubles,
And by opposing end them. To die: to
    sleep:
No more; and by a sleep to say we end
The heart-ache and the thousand natural
    shocks
That flesh is heir to; 'tis a consummation
Devoutly to be wished. To die; to sleep;
To sleep: perchance to dream: aye, there's
    the rub;
For in that sleep of death what dreams
    may come,
When we have shuffled off this mortal coil,
Must give us pause: there's the respect
That makes calamity of so long life;
For who would bear the whips and scorns
    of time,
The oppressor's wrong, the proud man's
    contumely,
The pangs of despis'd love, the law's delay,
The insolence of office, and the spurns
That patient merit of the unworthy takes,
When he himself might his quietus make
With a bare bodkin? Who would fardels
    bear,
To grunt and sweat under a weary life,
But that the dread of something after
    death—
The undiscover'd country from whose
    bourn
No traveler returns—puzzles the will
And makes us rather bear those ills we
    have
Than fly to others that we know not of?
Thus conscience does make cowards of us
    all,
And thus the native hue of resolution
Is sicklied o'er with the pale cast of
    thought,
And enterprises of great pith and moment
With this regard their currents turn awry,
And lose the name of action.

                    WILLIAM SHAKESPEARE

&

"Keep me, my God;
My boat is so small,
And Thy ocean is so wide."
                    BRETON SAILOR'S PRAYER

IF and AND

If you can think
About your work
As being help
To someone else
You soon will find
That that alone
Will make your task
A happier one.
And if you add
To each task done
Some little touch
That goes beyond
What is required,
Your work becomes
A thing of art
And leads you out
Into a realm
Where pleasure lives
And drudgery dies.
And this domain
Of artistry
Has ample room
For hope and dreams
And spreading wings
And lilting song,
To make the day
Eternal dawn.
                    W. P. KING

SEVENTY YEARS OLD!

To be seventy years old is like climbing
the Alps. You reach a snow-crowned summit, and see behind you the deep valley
stretching miles and miles away, and before you other summits higher and whiter,
which you may have strength to climb, or
may not. Then you sit down and meditate
and wonder which it will be.

                    H. W. LONGFELLOW, 1807 - 1882
                    Letter (1877)

165

THE SWING

How do you like to go up in a swing
  Up in the air so blue?
Oh, I do think it the pleasantest thing
  Ever a child can do!

Up in the air and over the wall,
  Till I can see so wide,
Rivers and trees and cattle and all
  Over the countryside—

Till I look down on the garden green,
  Down on the roof so brown—
Up in the air I go flying again,
  Up in the air and down!
ROBERT LOUIS STEVENSON, 1850 - 1894

Indians did a rain dance when they wanted rain; today man just starts out on a picnic.

THE RAIN IT RAINETH

The rain it raineth on the just
  And also on the unjust fella;
But chiefly on the just, because
  The unjust steals the just's umbrella.
LORD BOWEN

UNDER THE LEAVES

Oft have I walked these woodland paths,
  Without the blessed foreknowing
That underneath the withered leaves
  The fairest buds were growing.

To-day the south-wind sweeps away
  The types of autumn's splendor,
And shows the sweet arbutus flowers,—
  Spring's children, pure and tender.

O prophet-flowers!—with lips of bloom,
  Outvying in your beauty
The pearly tints of ocean shells,—
  Ye teach me faith and duty!

Walk life's dark ways, ye seem to say,
  With love's divine foreknowing
That where man sees but withered leaves,
  God sees sweet flowers growing.
ALBERT LAIGHTON, 1829 - 1887

THE TREE

I love thee when thy swelling buds appear,
And one by one their tender leaves unfold,
As if they knew that warmer suns were
  near,
Nor longer sought to hide from winter's
  cold;
And when with darker growth thy leaves
  are seen
To veil from view the early robin's nest,
I love to lie beneath thy waving screen,
With limbs by summer's heat and toil
  oppressed;
And when the autumn winds have stripped
  thee bare,
And round thee lies the smooth, untrodden
  snow,
When naught is thine that made thee once
  so fair,
I love to watch thy shadowy form below,
And through thy leafless arms to look
  above
On stars that brighter beam when most we
  need their love.
JONES VERY, 1813 - 1880

And a thousand recollections
  Weave their air threads into woof,
As I listen to the patter
  Of the rain upon the roof.
COATES KINNEY, 1826 - 1904

WEATHER LORE:

A sunshiny shower won't last half an hour.

MANILA

Oh, dewy was the morning, upon the first
  of May,
And Dewey was the admiral, down in
  Manila Bay;
And dewy were the Regent's eyes, them
  royal orbs of blue,
And dew we feel discouraged? We dew not
  think we dew!

EUGENE F. WARE, 1841 - 1911

SONG

Pious Selinda goes to prayers,
  If I but ask a favour;
And yet the tender fool's in tears,
  When she believes I'll leave her.

Would I were free from this restraint,
  Or else had hope to win her!
Would she could make of me a saint,
  Or I of her a sinner!

WILLIAM CONGREVE, 1670 - 1729

PATRIOTISM
from Lay of the Last Minstrel

Breathes there the man, with soul so dead,
Who never to himself hath said,
  This is my own, my native land?
Whose heart hath ne'er within him burned,
As home his footsteps he hath turned
  From wandering on a foreign strand!
If such there breathe, go, mark him well:
For him no minstrel raptures swell;
High though his titles, proud his name,
Boundless his wealth as wish can claim;
Despite those titles, power and pelf,
The wretch, concentred all in self,
Living, shall forfeit fair renown,
And, doubly dying, shall go down
To the vile dust from whence he sprung,
Unwept, unhonored, and unsung.

SIR WALTER SCOTT, 1771 - 1832

MY MOTHER'S OLD CHECKED APRON

My mother's old checked apron was a
  garment full and wide
It filled its humble mission and a million
  more beside.
'Twas made of six cent gingham, it was
  neither fine nor grand
Just a plain simple pattern fashioned by a
  busy hand.
It had a little cross stich along the bottom
  row
And two long strings that tied behind in a
  hasty half-hitch bow.
It had no lace or ruffles, nor pretty
  applique
But its simple homely usefulness was an
  epic of the day.
'Twas used to shoo the chickens, to dust,
  to shoo the flies
'Twas used to wipe the grimy tears from
  streaming infant's eyes,
'Twas used to fill the kindling box with
  chips or cobs or twigs
And tote the pesky pursley from the
  garden to the pigs.
'Twas used to carry home the eggs
  concealed in leafy bowers,
And bring in half drowned baby chicks
  caught out in sudden showers
'Twas used to snatch hot kettles when no
  pot rag was at hand
And tighten on the fruit jar lids when
  winter stores were canned.
'Twas used to gather garden stuff and
  peaches from the hill
And many a goodly mess of greens did
  Mother's apron fill
Her hands were shielded from the gale,
  beneath its sheltering fold
And tiny bare feet nestled there on
  mornings bleak and cold.
It was a queenly garment and Mother was
  a queen
As memory brings it back, it was a noble
  thing I ween
And when I join the Heavenly throng with
  robes so bright and fair
I'll say this "Old apron is what I want to
  wear."

A MIDSUMMER SONG

O, father's gone to market-town, he was
   up before the day,
And Jamie's after robins, and the man is
   making hay,
And whistling down the hollow goes the
   boy that minds the mill,
While mother from the kitchen-door is
   calling with a will:
     "Polly!—Polly!—The cows are in the
      corn!
     O, where's Polly?"

From all the misty morning air there
   comes a summer sound—
A murmur as of waters from skies and
   trees and ground.
The birds they sing upon the wing, the
   pigeons bill and coo,
And over hill and hollow rings again the
   loud halloo:
     "Polly!—Polly!—The cows are in the
      corn!
     O, where's Polly?"

Above the trees the honey-bees swarm by
   with buzz and boom,
And in the field and garden a thousand
   blossoms bloom.
Within the farmer's meadow a brown-eyed
   daisy blows,
And down at the edge of the hollow a red
   and thorny rose.
     But Polly!—Polly! —The cows are in
      the corn!
     O, where's Polly?

How strange at such a time of day the
   mill should stop its clatter!
The farmer's wife is listening now and
   wonders what's the matter.
O, wild the birds are singing in the wood
   and on the hill,
While whistling up the hollow goes the
   boy that minds the mill.
     But Polly!—Polly!—The cows are in
      the corn!
     O, where's Polly?
       RICHARD WATSON GILDER, 1844 - 1909

KEEN,
FITFUL GUSTS ARE WHISP'RING

Keen, fitful gusts are whisp'ring here and
   there
   Among the bushes half leafless, and dry;
   The stars look very cold about the sky,
And I have many miles on foot to fare.
Yet feel I little of the cool bleak air,
   Or of the dead leaves rustling drearily,
   Or of those silver lamps that burn on
     high,
   Or of the distance from home's pleasant
     lair:
For I am brimfull of the friendliness
   That in a little cottage I have found;
Of fair-hair'd Milton's eloquent distress,
   And all his love for gentle Lycid
     drown'd;
Of lovely Laura in her light green dress,
   And faithful Petrarch gloriously
     crown'd.
       JOHN KEATS, 1795 - 1821

EARLY DAYS

Oh! enviable early days,
   When dancing thoughtless pleasure's
     maze,
    To care, to guilt unknown!
How ill exchanged for riper times
To feel the follies or the crimes
   Of others or my own!
Ye tiny elves that guiltless sport,
   Like linnets in the bush,
Ye little know the ills ye court,
   When manhood is your wish!
       ROBERT BURNS, 1759 - 1796

There once was a maiden of Siam
Who said to her lover, young Kiam,
   "If you kiss me, of course,
   You will have to use force,
But God knows you are stronger than I
   am."

THE NUN

If you become a nun, dear
  A friar I will be;
In any cell you run, dear,
  Pray look behind for me.
The roses all turn pale, too;
The doves all take the veil, too;
  The blind will see the show:
What! you become a nun, my dear!
  I'll not believe it, no.

If you become a nun, dear,
  The bishop Love will be;
The Cupids every one, dear,
  Will chant "We trust in thee";
The incense will go sighing,
The candles fall a dying,
  The water turn to wine:
What! you go take the vows, my dear!
  You may—but they'll be mine.

LEIGH HUNT, 1784 - 1859

RAIN IN SUMMER

How beautiful is the rain!
After the dust and heat,
In the broad and fiery street,
In the narrow lane,
How beautiful is the rain!

How it clatters along the roofs,
Like the tramp of hoofs!
How it gushes and struggles out
From the throat of the overflowing spout!

Across the windowpane
It pours and pours;
And swift and wide,
With a muddy tide,
Like a river down the gutter roars
The rain, the welcome rain!

HENRY WADSWORTH LONGFELLOW, 1807 - 1882

Marilla W. Ricker has often told us that widows are divided into two classes—the bereaved and relieved. She forgot the deceived—the grass widows.

VICTOR ROBINSOLL
in "William Godwin" 1906

REASONS FOR DRINKING

If all be true that I do think
There are five reasons we should drink;
Good wine—a friend—or being dry—
Or lest we should be by and by—
Or any other reason why.

DR. HENRY ALDRICH, 1647 - 1710

TO HIS WIFE

Be life what it has been, and let us hold,
Dear wife, the names we each gave each of
    old;
And let not time work change upon us
    two,
I still your boy, and still my sweetheart
    you.
What though I outlive Nestor? and what
    though
You in your turn a Sibyl's years should
    know?
Ne'er let us know old age or late or soon;
Count not the years, but take of each its
    boon.

DECIMUS MAGNUS ANSONIUS, 310 - 395

Translator (Terrot Reaveley Glover)

TO A GRIEVING HUSBAND

My dear friend,

I have thought much about our meeting last Sunday, and the few words we had together.

May I try to tell you again where your comfort lies? It is not in forgetting the happy past. People bring us well-meant but miserable consolation when they tell us what time will do to our grief. We do not want to lose our grief, because our grief is bound up with our love and we could not cease to mourn without being robbed of our affection.

But if you know, as you do know, that the great and awful change, which has come into your life and brought you such distress, has brought your dear wife the joy of heaven, can you not, in the midst of all your suffering, rejoice for her?

And if knowing she is with God, you can be with God, too, and every day claim His protection and try to do His will, may you not still in spirit be very near to her?

She is not dead, but living, and if you are sure what care is holding her, and educating her, you can be very contentedly with her in spirit, and look forward confidently to the day when you shall also go to God and be with her.

I know that this does not take away your pain. No one can do that. You do not want any one to do that, not even God. But it can help you to bear it, to be brave and cheerful, to do your duty, and to live the pure, earnest, spiritual life which she, in heaven, wishes you to live.

My dear friend, she is yours forever. God never takes away what He has once given. May He make you worthy of her! May He comfort you and make you strong!

Your friend, sincerely,
PHILLIPS BROOKS, 1835 - 1893

"REMEMBER ALL THE BEST"

No funeral gloom, my dears, when I am
gone,
Corpse gazings, tears, black raiment,
graveyard grimness.
Think of me as withdrawn into the
dimness,
Yours still, you mine.
Remember all the best of our past
moments and forget the rest,
And so to where I wait come gently on.

ELLEN TERRY

THE BLUE GENTIANS

The fairest blossoms ever bloom the last;
For fleeting Summer, Mother of the
flowers,
Mindful her joyous, sunny reign will soon
be past,
Has deemed that, moved by beauties
brighter, rarer,
The Chill Destroyer of her happy hours
Might step, perchance, aside and so would
spare her.

Their petals twist at morn and tipped
with dew
To warm noon yield and life a fringe-
lipped and
Pure sapphired chalice of that deep and
richer hue
Than tint of sky or sea, beyond compare,
That sprang to view when God first laid
His hand
Upon the cloud and left the rainbow
there.

They are the Gentians, left alone to face
The unrelenting King of Snow and Rime
By Summer fled and gone; these blossoms
fit to grace
The wondrous gardens washed by southern
seas,
Flung as a hostage to the Wintry Time,
Bend, droop, and wither in the frosty
breeze.

EDWARD RYAN WOODLE

SEPTEMBER

"The pollen-dusted bees search for the honey-lees
That linger in the last flowers of September."

I BELIEVE

I believe in the dignity of labor, whether with head or hand; that the world owes no man a living but that it owes every man an opportunity to make a living.

I believe in the supreme worth of the individual and in his right to life, liberty, and the pursuit of happiness.

I believe that truth and justice are fundamental to an enduring social order.

I believe in the sacredness of a promise, that a man's word should be as good as his bond; that character—not wealth or power or position—is of supreme worth.

I believe that every right implies a responsibility; every opportunity, an obligation; every possession, a duty.

I believe that law was made for man and not man for the law; that government is the servant of the people and not their master.

I believe that thrift is essential to well-ordered living and that economy is a prime requisite of a sound financial structure, whether in government, business or personal affairs.

I believe that the rendering of useful service is the common duty of mankind and that only in the purifying fire of sacrifice is the dross of selfishness consumed and the greatness of the human soul set free.

I believe in an all-wise and all-loving God, named by whatever name, and that the individual's highest fulfillment, greatest happiness, and widest usefulness are to be found in living in harmony with His will.

I believe that love is the greatest thing in the world; that it alone can overcome haste; that right can and will triumph over might.

JOHN D. ROCKEFELLER, JR., 1839 - 1937

LABOR DAY STATEMENT

"I am not a labor leader. I don't want you to follow me or anyone else. If you are looking for a Moses to lead you out of the capitalistic wilderness you will stay right where you are. I would not lead you into the promised land if I could, because if I could lead you in, someone else would lead you out."

EUGENE V. DEBS, 1855 - 1926

Industry must manage to keep wages high and prices low. Otherwise, it will limit the number of its customers. One's own employees should be one's best customers.

HENRY FORD, 1863 - 1947

Labor day is observed throughout the United States in recognition of the dignity of labor, falling on the first Monday in September of each year. Peter J. McGuire, general secretary of the Brotherhood of Carpenters and Joiners, May 18, 1882, at a central Labor Union meeting in New York City, proposed that "a day be set aside as a festive day, during which parade through the streets of the city would permit public tribute to American industry." The motion was adopted and plans for the first Labor Day celebration made.

October 7, 1884, American Federation of Labor meeting at Chicago, A.C. Cameron, member of the Typographical Union 16 introduced the following resolution: "Resolved, That the first Monday in September each year be set aside as a laborers' national holiday, and that we recommend its observance by all wage workers, irrespective of sex, calling or nationality."

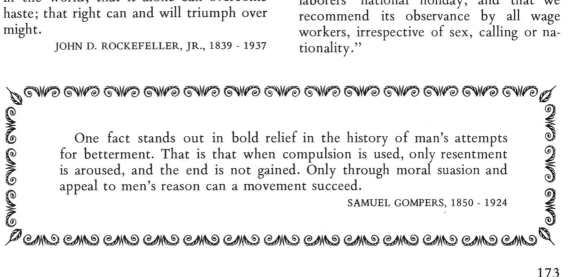

One fact stands out in bold relief in the history of man's attempts for betterment. That is that when compulsion is used, only resentment is aroused, and the end is not gained. Only through moral suasion and appeal to men's reason can a movement succeed.

SAMUEL GOMPERS, 1850 - 1924

SCHOOL-DAYS

School- days, School-Days, dear old Golden
* Rule days,*
Readin' and 'ritin and 'rithmetic,
Taught to the tune of a hick'ry stick;
You were my queen in calico
I was your bashful barefoot beau,
And you wrote on my slate, I love you,
* Joe,*
When we were a couple of kids.

WILL D. COBB, 1876 - 1930

Music was composed by Gus Edwards.

ᏬᏔᎧ

Part of the American myth is that people who are handed the skin of a dead sheep at graduation time, think it will keep their minds alive forever.

JOHN MASON BROWN, 1900 - 1969

ᏬᏔᎧ

Without popular education no government which rests on popular action can long endure; the people must be schooled in the knowledge and if possible in the virtues upon which the maintenance and success of free institutions depend.

WOODROW WILSON, 1856 - 1924

ᏬᏔᎧ

The common school is the greatest discovery ever made by man. In two grand, characteristic attributes, it is supereminent over all others: first, in its universality—for it is capacious enough to receive and cherish in its parental bosom every child that comes into the world; and second, in the timeliness of the aid it proffers—its early, seasonable supplies of counsel and guidance making security antedate danger. Other social organizations are curative and remedial; this is a preventive and an antidote; they come to heal diseases and wounds; this, to make the physical and moral frame invulnerable to them. Let the common school be expanded to its capabilities, let it be worked with the efficiency of which it is susceptible, and nine-tenths of the crimes in the penal code would become obsolete; the long catalog of human ills would be abridged; property, life, and character held by a stronger tenure; all rational hopes respecting the future brightened.

HORACE MANN, 1796 - 1859

from THE PROMISED LAND

Education was free. That subject my father had written about repeatedly, as comprising his chief hope for us children, the essence of American opportunity, the treasure that no thief could touch, not even misfortune or poverty. It was the one thing that he was able to promise us when he sent for us; surer, safer than bread or shelter. On our second day I was thrilled with the realization of what this freedom of education meant. A little girl from across the alley came and offered to conduct us to school. My father was out, but we five between us had a few words of English by this time. We knew the word school. We understood. This child, who have never seen us till yesterday, who could not pronounce our names, who was not much better dressed than we, was able to offer us the freedom of the schools of Boston! No application made, no questions asked, no examinations, rulings, exclusions; no machinations, no fees. The doors stood open for every one of us. The smallest child could show us the way.

This incident impressed me more than anything I had heard in advance of the freedom of education in America. It was a concrete proof—almost the thing itself. One had to experience it to understand it.

MARY ANTIN, 1881 - 1949

ᏬᏔᎧ

Not one student in a thousand breaks down from overwork.

WILLIAM ALLAN NEILSON, 1869 - 1946

ᏬᏔᎧ

The aim of education should be to teach the child to think, not what to think.

JOHN DEWEY, 1859 - 1952

ᏬᏔᎧ

Whom, then, do I call educated? First, those who control circumstances instead of being mastered by them, those who meet all occasions manfully and act in accordance with intelligent thinking, those who are honorable in all dealings, who treat good naturedly persons and things that are disagreeable, and furthermore, those who hold their pleasures under control and not overcome by misfortune, finally those who are not spoiled by success.

ISOCRATES

from ON EDUCATION

The object of what we commonly call education—that education in which man intervenes and which I shall distinguish as artificial education—is to make good these defects in Nature's methods; to prepare the child to receive Nature's education, neither incapably nor ignorantly, nor with wilful disobedience; and to understand the preliminary symptoms of her displeasure, without waiting for the box on the ear.

In short, all artificial education ought to be an anticipation of natural education. And a liberal education is an artificial education which has not only prepared a man to escape the great evils of disobedience to natural laws, but has trained him to appreciate and to seize upon the rewards, which Nature scatters with as free a hand as her penalties.

That man, I think, has had a liberal education, who has been so trained in youth that his body is the ready servant of his will, and does with ease and pleasure all the work that, as a mechanism, it is capable of; whose intellect is a clear, cold, logic engine, with all its parts of equal strength, and in smooth working order; ready, like a steam engine, to be turned to any kind of work, and spin the gossamers as well as forge the anchors of the mind; whose mind is stored with a knowledge of the great and fundamental truths of Nature and of the laws of her operations; one who, no stunted ascetic, is full of life and fire, but whose passions are trained to come to heel by a vigorous will, the servant of a tender conscience; who has learned to love all beauty, whether of Nature or of art, to hate all vileness, and to respect others as himself.

Such an one, and no other, I conceive, has had a liberal education; for he is, as completely as a man can be, in harmony with Nature. He will make the best of her, and she of him. They will get on together rarely; she as his ever beneficent mother; he as her mouthpiece, her conscious self, her minister and interpreter.

THOMAS HUXLEY, 1825 - 1895

☙❦❧

Civilization is a race between education and catastrophe.

H. G. WELLS, 1866 - 1946

The best teacher is not life, but the crystallized and distilled experience of the most sensitive, reflective, and most observant of our human beings, and this experience you will find perserved in our great books and nowhere else.

NATHAN M. PUSEY

☙❦❧

Genius is 1 percent inspiration and 99 percent perspiration.

THOMAS A. EDISON, 1879 - 1931

☙❦❧

There is nothing so stupid as an educated man, if you get off the thing that he was educated in.

WILL ROGERS, 1879 - 1935

☙❦❧

When you educate a man you educate an individual. When you educate a woman, you educate a whole family.

CHARLES D. McIVER

☙❦❧

The things taught in college and schools are not an education, but the means of education.

RALPH WALDO EMERSON, 1803 - 1882

☙❦❧

I have never let my schooling interfere with my education.

The first time that a school boy realizes that a little learning is a dangerous thing is when he first brings home a poor report card.

MARK TWAIN, 1835 - 1910

THE CATERPILLAR

Brown and furry
Caterpillar in a hurry,
Take your walk
To the shady leaf, or stalk,
  Or what not,
Which may be the chosen spot
  No toad spy you,
Hovering bird of prey pass by you;
Spin and die,
To live again as butterfly.

CHRISTINA ROSSETTI, 1830 - 1894

SEPTEMBER

Sweet is the voice that calls
From babbling waterfalls
In meadows where the downy seeds are
  flying;
And soft the breezes blow,
And eddying come and go,
In faded gardens where the rose is dying.

Among the stubbled corn
The blithe quail pipes at morn,
The merry partridge drums in hidden
  places,
And glittering insects gleam
Above the reedy stream,
Where busy spiders spin their filmy laces.

At eve, cool shadows fall
Across the garden wall,
And on the clustered grapes to purple
  turning;
And pearly vapors lie
Along the eastern sky,
Where the broad harvest-moon is redly
  burning.

Ah, soon on field and hill
The winds shall whistle chill,
And patriarch swallows call their flocks
  together
To fly from frost and snow,
And seek for lands where blow
The fairer blossoms of a balmier weather.

The pollen-dusted bees
Search for the honey-lees
That linger in the last flowers of
  September,
While plaintive mourning doves
Coo sadly to their loves
Of the dead summer they so well
  remember.

The cricket chirps all day,
"O fairest summer, stay!"
The squirrel eyes askance the chestnuts
  browning;
The wild fowl fly afar
Above the foamy bar,
And hasten southward ere the skies are
  frowning.

Now comes a fragrant breeze
Through the dark cedar-trees,
And round about my temples fondly
  lingers,
In gentle playfulness,
Like to the soft caress
Bestowed in happier days by loving
  fingers.

Yet, though a sense of grief
Comes with the falling leaf,
And memory makes the summer doubly
  pleasant,
In all my autumn dreams
A future summer gleams,
Passing the fairest glories of the present!

GEORGE ARNOLD, 1834 - 1865

COUNTY FAIR

Tell Me

Tell me, Grandma, when you were a girl,
Did you go to the County fair?

Yes, my child, indeed I did!
Every year I was there.

And did you find such a pretty ring
as the one I found today?

Oh, I guess it was pretty enough
But the gold soon wore away.

And did you ride on the merry-go-round
And look at all the freaks?

Rode the ferris wheel once in the rain
And was sick for several weeks.

Tell me, Grandma, was nothing good
That you got at the county fair?

Well, my dear, I wouldn't say that
I met your grandpa there.

MARY M. LOWE

THE BOYS

Has there any old fellow got mixed with
    the boys?
If there has, take him out without making
    a noise.
Hang the almanac's cheat and the
    catalogue's spite!
Old Time is a liar! We're twenty tonight.

We're twenty! we're twenty! Who says we
    are more?
He's tipsy—Young Jackanapes! Show him
    the door
Gray temples at twenty? Yes! white if we
    please,
Where the snowflakes fall thickest there's
    nothing can freeze!

Was it snowing I spoke of? Excuse the
    mistake
Look close—you will see not a sign of a
    flake!
We want some new garlands for those we
    have shed.
And these are white roses in place of the
    red.

We've a trick, we young fellows, you may
    have been told,
Of talking (in public) as if we were old!
That boy we call "Doctor" and this we
    call "Judge"
It's a neat little fiction—of course it's all
    fudge.

That fellow's the "Speaker," the one on
    the right;
"Mr. Mayor," my young one, how are you
    tonight?
That's our "Member of Congress," we say
    when we chaff;
There's the "Reverend"—what's his
    name?—don't make me laugh.

That boy with the grave, mathematical
    look
Made believe he had written a wonderful
    book,

And the Royal Society thought it was true!
So they chose him right in—a good joke
    it was too!

There's a boy, we pretend, with a three-
    decker brain,
That could harness a team with a logical
    chain;
When he spoke of our manhood in
    syllabled fire
We called him "The Justice," but now he's
    "The Squire."

And there's a nice youngster of excellent
    pith;
Fate tried to conceal him by naming him
    Smith!
But he shouted a song for the brave and
    the free—
Just read on his medal, "My country . . . of
    thee!"

You hear that boy laughing? You think
    he's all fun,
But the angels laugh, too, at the good he
    has done
The children laugh loud as they troop to
    his call,
And the poor man that knows him laughs
    loudest of all.

Yes, we're boys, always playing with
    tongue or with pen,
And I sometimes have asked, shall we
    ever be men?
Shall we always be youthful and laughing
    and gay,
Till the last dear companion drops smiling
    away?

Then here's to our boyhood, its gold and
    its gray!
The stars of its winter, the dews of its
    May!
And when we have done with our
    life-lasting toys,
Dear Father, take care of Thy children,
    the boys.

OLIVER WENDELL HOLMES, 1809 - 1894

THE VOYAGE OF THE MAYFLOWER
1620

Septr. 6. These troubls being blowne over, and now all being compacte togeather in one shipe, they put to sea againe with a prosperus winde, which continued diverce days togeather, which was some incouragemente unto them; yet according to the usual manner many were afflicted with sea-sicknes. . . . .

After they had injoyed faire winds and weather for a season, they were incountred many times with crosse winds, and mete with many feirce stormes, with which the shipe was shroudly shaken, and her upper works made very leakie; and one of the maine beames in the midd ships was bowed & craked, which put them in some fear that the shipe could not be able to performe the vioage. So some of the cheefe of the company, perceiving the mariners to feare the suffisiencie of the shipe, as appeared by their mutterings, they entred into serious consulltation with the mr. & other officers of the ship, to consider in time of the danger; and rather to returne then to cast them selves into a desperate & inevitable perill. And truly ther was great distraction & difference of opinion amongst the mariners them selves; faine would they doe what could be done for their wages sake, (being now halfe the seas over,) and on the other hand they were loath to hazard their lives too desperatly. But in examening of all opinions, the mr. & others affirmed they knew the ship to be stronge & firme under water; and for the buckling of the maine became, ther was a great iron scrue the passengers brought out of Holland, which would raise the beame into his place; the which being done, the carpenter & mr. affirmed that with a post put under it, set firme in the lower deck, & otherways bounde, he would make it sufficiente. And as for the decks & uper workes they would calke them as well as they could, and though with the workeing of the ship they would not longe keepe stanch, yet ther would otherwise be no great danger, if they did not overpress her with sails. So they commited them selves to the will of God, & resolved to proseede. In sundrie of these stormes the winds were so feirce, & the seas so high, as they could not beare a knote of saile, but were forced to hull, for diverce days togither. In all this viage their died but one of the passengers, which was William Butten, a youth, servant to Samuell Fuller, when they drew near the coast. But to omite other things, (that I may be breefe,) after longe beating at sea they fell with that land which is called Cape Cod; the which being made & certainly knowne to be it, they were not a litle joyfull. After some deliberation had amongst them selves & with the mr. of the ship, they tacked aboute and resolved to stande for the southward (the wind & weather being faire) to finde some place aboute Hudsons river for their habitation. But after they had sailed that course aboute halfe the day, they fell amongst deangerous shoulds and roring breakers, and they were so farr intangled ther with as they conceived them selves in great danger; & the wind shrinking upon them withall, they resolved to bear up againe for the Cape, and thought them selves hapy to gett out of those dangers before night overtooke them, as by Gods providence they did. And the next day they gott into the Cape-harbor wher they ridd in saftie. A word or too by the way of this cape; it was thus first named by Capten Gosnole & his company, Anno 1602, and after by Capten Smith was caled Cape James; but it retains the former name amongst seamen. Also that pointe which first shewed those dangerous shoulds unto them, they called Pointe Care, & Tuckers Terrour; but the French & Dutch to this day call it Malabarr, by reason of those perilous shoulds, and the losses they have suffered their.

WILLIAM BRADFORD, 1590 - 1657

Bradford sailed to Plymouth on the Mayflower. He was later governor of the Plymouth Colony for thirty years.

INSCRIPTION ON PLYMOUTH ROCK MONUMENT

Here, under cover of darkness, the fast-dwindling company laid their dead, leveling the earth above them lest the Indians should know how many were the graves. Reader! History records no nobler venture for faith and freedom than of this Pilgrim band. In weariness and painfulness, in watching, often in hunger and cold, they laid the foundations of a state wherein every man, through countless ages, should have liberty to worship God in his own way. May their example inspire thee to do thy part in perpetuating and spreading the lofty ideals of our republic throughout the world!

This monument marks the first burying ground in Plymouth of the passengers of the Mayflower.

November 19, 1620
from the
LANDING OF THE PILGRIM FATHERS

The breaking waves dashed high
On a stern and rock-bound coast;
And the woods against a stormy sky,
Their giant branches tossed;
And the heavy night hung dark
The hills and waters o'er—
When a band of exiles moored their bark
On a wild New England shore.

What sought they thus afar?
Bright jewels of the mine?
The wealth of seas the spoils of war?
They sought a faith's pure shrine!
Aye, call it holy ground,
The soil where first they trod!
They have left unstained what there they
found—
Freedom to worship God!
FELICIA DOROTHEA HEMANS, 1793 - 1835

If fresh meat be wanting to fill up our
dish,
We have carrots and turnips as much as we
wish:
And if there's a mind for a delicate dish
We repair to the clam-banks, and there we
catch fish.
Instead of pottage and puddings and
custards and pies,
Our pumpkins and parsnips are common
supplies;
We have pumpkins at morning and
pumpkins at noon,
If it was not for pumpkins we should be
undone.

If barley be wanting to make into malt,
We must be contented, and think it no
fault;
For we can make liquor to sweeten our
lips,
Of pumpkins and parsnips and walnut-tree
chips.

'Forefathers' Song," in Massachusetts Historical Collection, supposedly taken from the lips of a ninety-six-year-old woman in 1785—but traced back to about 1630.

It is undeniable that the great quest of humanity is happiness. But was the world created to be happy? How many are truly happy? I've studied people in all classes and conditions, and everywhere I have found, when you get below the surface, that it is mostly the insincere individual who says, "I am happy." Nearly everybody wants something he hasn't got, and as things are constructed, what he wants is money—more money than he has in his pocket.

But after all, money can buy only a few things. Why should anyone envy the captains of industry? Their lives are made up of those vast, incessant worries from which the average individual is happily spared. Worry, worry, that is the evil of life.

What do I consider the nearest approximation to happiness of which the present human nature is capable? Why, living on a farm which is one's own, far from the hectic, artificial conditions of the city—a farm where one gets directly from one's own soil what one needs to sustain life, with a garden in front and a healthy, normal family to contribute those small domestic joys which relieve a man from business strain.

THOMAS ALVA EDISON, 1847 - 1931

from SONG OF MYSELF

*There is that in me—I do not know what it
  is—but I know it is in me . .
I do not know it—it is without name—it is a
  word unsaid;
It is not in any dictionary, utterance,
  symbol.
Something it swings on more than the earth
  I swing on.
To it the creation is the friend whose
  embracing awakes me . .
It is not chaos or death—it is form, union,
  plan—it is eternal life—
It is happiness.*

WALT WHITMAN, 1819 - 1892

⌒⌒

THE MOCKINGBIRD

*Listen to that bird! His song—what poet pens
  it?
Brigand of birds, he's stolen every note!
Prince though of thieves—hark! how the
  rascal spends it!
Pours the whole forest from one tiny
  throat!*

EDNAH PROCTOR CLARKE HAYES

from THE SPLEEN

*Happy the man, who, innocent,
Grieves not at ills he can't prevent;
His skiff does with the current glide,
Not puffing, pulled against the tide.
He, paddling by the scuffling crowd,
Sees unconcerned life's wager rowed,
And when he can't prevent foul play,
Enjoys the folly of the fray.*

MATTHEW GREEN, 1696 - 1737

⌒⌒

We exaggerate misfortune and happiness alike. We are never either so wretched or so happy as we say we are.

HONORE DE BALZAC, 1799 - 1850

⌒⌒

from "LIFE SAMUEL JOHNSON"

It is better that some should be unhappy, than that none should be happy, which would be the case in a general state of equality.

JAMES BOSWELL, 1740 - 1795

TODAY

With every rising of the sun
Think of your life as just begun.

The past has cancelled and buried deep
All yesterdays. There let them sleep.

Concern yourself with but Today.
Grasp it, and teach it to obey.
Your will and plan. Since time began
Today has been the friend of man.

You and Today! A soul sublime
And the great heritage of time

With God himself to bind the twain,
Go forth, brave heart! Attain! attain!

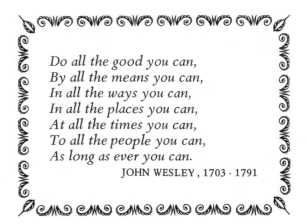

Do all the good you can,
By all the means you can,
In all the ways you can,
In all the places you can,
At all the times you can,
To all the people you can,
As long as ever you can.

JOHN WESLEY, 1703 - 1791

Old Age to me is always fifteen years older than I am!

BERNARD M. BARUCH, 1870 - 1965

To rise at six, to dine at ten,
To sup at six, to sleep at ten,
Makes a man live for ten times ten.

VICTOR HUGO, 1802 - 1885

Inscription over the door of Victor Hugo's study.

Nothing is easier than fault-finding; no talent, no self-denial, no brains, no character are required to set up in the grumbling business.

ROBERT WISE

FOR A FRESH BEGINNING—

This is the first day of the rest of your life!

A SMILE

Let others cheer the winning man,
There's one I hold worth while;
'Tis he who does the best he can
Then loses with a smile.
Beaten he is, but not to stay
Down with the rank and file,
That man will win some other day,
Who loses with a smile.

Make yourself an honest man, and then you may be sure that there is one rascal less in the world.

THOMAS CARLYLE

THE TOUCH OF A HAND

It's the human touch in this world that
counts
The touch of your hand and mine
That means far more to the fainting heart
Than shelter or bread or wine
For shelter is gone when the night is o'er
And bread lasts only a day
But the touch of a hand and the sound of a
voice
Sing on in the soul alway.

Somebody said that it couldn't be done—
But he, with a grin, replied
I'd never be one to say it couldn't be done—
Leastways, not 'til he'd tried.
So he buckled right in, with a trace of a grin;
By golly, he went right to it.
He tackled The Thing That Couldn't Be
Done!
And he couldn't do it.

THE POOR

We have grown literally afraid to be poor. We despise any one who elects to be poor . . .

WILLIAM JAMES, 1842 - 1910

❧

It must be great to be rich and let the other fellow keep up appearances.

KIN HUBBARD, 1868 - 1930

❧

It's no disgrace to be poor, but it might as well be.

KIN HUBBARD, 1868 - 1930

❧

I define a recession as when your neighbor loses his job, but a depression is when you lose your own.

Attributed to Dave Beck and several others.

❧

It has been said that the love of money is the root of all evil. The want of money is so quite as truly.

SAMUEL BUTLER, 1835 - 1902

I'm tired of Love:I'm still more tired of Rhyme.
But money gives me pleasure all the time.

HILLAIRE BELLOC, 1870 - 1953

❧

Remember my son, that any man who is a bear on the future of this country will go broke.

J. P. MORGAN, Dec. 10, 1908

❧

It is wrong to assume that men of immense wealth are always happy.

JOHN D. ROCKEFELLER, 1839 - 1937
To his Sunday School class.

❧

I see one-third of the nation ill-housed, ill-clad, ill-nourished.

FRANKLIN D. ROOSEVELT,
Jan. 20, 1937
Second Inaugural Address.

❧

THE RICH

To secure wealth is an honorable ambition, and is one great test of a person's usefulness to others . . I say, get rich, get rich! . . I won't give in but what I sympathize with the poor, but the number of poor who are to be sympathized with is very small. To sympathize with a man whom God has punished for his sins, thus to help him when God would still continue a just punishment, is to do wrong, no doubt about it.

RUSSELL CONWELL, 1843 - 1925
from "Acres of Diamonds"
Estimated that he gave this talk six thousand times, earning him about $8,000,000.

from FORTY YEARS ON
(Harrow School Song)

Forty years of growing older and older,
Shorter in wind and in memory long,
Feeble of foot and rheumatic of shoulder,
What will it help you that once you were
young.

EDWARD E. BOWEN, 1836 - 1901

⟨W⟩

The atrocious crime of being a young man which the honorable gentleman has with such spirit and decency charged upon me, I shall neither attempt to palliate nor deny; but content myself with wishing that I may be one of their youth, and not of that number who are ignorant in spite of experience.

From a speech by William Pitt, made in March 1741 replying to Horace Walpole. 1717 - 1797

⟨W⟩

The wildest colts make the best horses.

THEMISTOCLES, died 449 B.C.

from I'M GROWING OLD

I'm growing fonder of my staff;
I'm growing dimmer in the eyes;
I'm growing fainter in my laugh;
I'm growing deeper in my sighs;
I'm growing careless of my dress;
I'm growing frugal of my gold;
I'm growing wise, I'm growing—yes,
I'm growing old.

JOHN G. SAXE, 1816 - 1887

Youth is not a time of life—it is a state of mind. It is not a matter of ripe cheeks, red lips and supple knees; it is a temper of the will, a quality of the imagination, a vigor of the emotions; it is a freshness of the deep springs of life.

Youth means a temperamental predominance of courage over timidity, of the appetite of adventure over love of ease. This often exists in a man of fifty, more than in a boy of twenty. Nobody grows old by merely living a number of years; people grow old only by deserting their ideals.

Years wrinkle the skin, but to give up enthusiasm wrinkles the soul.

Worry, doubt, self-distrust, fear and despair—these are the long, long years that bow the head and turn the growing spirit back to dust.

Whether seventy or sixteen, there is in every being's heart the love of wonder, the sweet amazement at the stars and the star-like things and thoughts, the undaunted challenge of events, the unfailing child-like appetite for what next, and the joy and the game of life.

You are as young as your faith, as old as your doubt; as young as your self-confidence, as old as your fear; as young as your hope, as old as your despair.

In the central place of your heart there is a wireless station; so long as it receives messages of beauty, hope, cheer, grandeur, courage and power from the earth, from men and from the Infinite, so long are you young. When the wires are all down and all the central place of your heart is covered with the snows of pessimism and the ice of cynicism, then are you grown old indeed and may God have mercy on your soul.

THE INDIANS

Not many generations ago, where you now sit, encircled with all that exalts and embellishes civilized life, the rank thistle nodded in the wind, and the wild fox dug his hole unscared. Here lived and loved another race of beings. Beneath the same sun that rolls over your head; the Indian hunter pursued the panting deer; gazing on the same moon that smiles for you, the Indian lover wooed his dusky mate.

Here the wigwam blaze beamed on the tender and helpless, and the councilfire glared on the wise and daring. Now, they dipped their noble limbs in yon sedgy lakes, and now, they paddled the light canoe along yon rocky shores. Here they warred; the echoing whoop, the bloody grapple, the defying death-song, all were here; and when the tiger-strife was over, here curled the smoke of peace.

Here, too, they worshiped; and from many a dark bosom went up a fervent prayer to the Great Spirit. He had not written his laws for them on tables of stone, but he had traced them on the tables of their hearts. The poor child of Nature knew not the God of Revelation, but the God of the universe he acknowledged in everything around.

And all this has passed away. Across the ocean came a pilgrim bark, bearing the seeds of life and death. The former were sown for you; the latter sprang up in the path of the simple native.

Here and there, a stricken few remain; but how unlike their bold, untamable progenitors. As a race, they have withered from the land. Their arrows are broken, their springs are dried up, their cabins are in dust. Their council-fire has long since gone out on the shore, and their war cry is fast fading to the untrodden west. Slowly and sadly they climb the distant mountains, and read their doom in the setting sun.

CHARLES SPRAGUE

INDIANS

Savages we call them, because their manners differ from ours.

BENJAMIN FRANKLIN

Onion skins very thin
Mild winter coming in;
Onion skins very tough,
Winter's going to be rough.

THE MODERN HIAWATHA

He killed the noble Mudjokivis,
With the skin he made him mittens,
Made them with the fur side inside,
Made them with the skin side outside,
He, to get the warm side inside,
Put the inside skin side outside:
He, to get the cold side outside,
Put the warm side fur side inside,
That's why he put the fur side inside,
Why he put the skin side outside,
Why he turned them inside outside.

GEORGE A. STRONG, 1832 - 1912

"CALIBAN IN THE COAL MINES"

God, we don't like to complain—
We know that the mine is no lark—
But—there's the pools from the rain;
But—there's the cold and the dark.

God, You don't know what it is—
You, in Your well-lighted sky,
Watch the meteors whizz;
Warm, with the sun always by.

God, if You had but the moon
Stuck in Your cap for a lamp,
Even You'd tire of it soon,
Down in the dark and the damp.

Nothing but blackness above,
And nothing that moves but the cars—
God, if You wish for our love,
Fling us a handful of stars!

LOUIS UNTERMEYER

❦

EPIGRAM

War is not sparing of the brave, but of the cowards.

ANACREON
Greek Poet 563 - 478 B.C.

❦

The physician can bury his mistakes but the architect can only advise his client to plant vines.

FRANK LLOYD WRIGHT, 1869 - 1959

❦

Remarked to R. W. Emerson:
Fulton knocked at the door of Napoleon with steam, and was rejected; and Napoleon lived long enough to know that he had excluded a greater power than his own.

HORATIO GREENOUGH, 1805 - 1852

When Robert Fulton was starting the engines of the *Clermont* Sept. 4, 1807, the crowd cried
She'll Never Run! She'll Never Run! As soon as the steamboat began to move up-river, the crowd on the bank began to shout
She'll Never Stop! She'll Never Stop! To his nervous passengers, Fulton announced "Gentlemen you need not be uneasy; you shall be in Albany before twelve o'clock tomorrow." And they were.

❦

THE AGED STRANGER
(An Incident of the Civil War)

"I was with Grant"—the stranger said;
Said the farmer, "Say no more,
But rest thee here at my cottage porch,
For thy feet are weary and sore."

"I was with Grant"—the stranger said;
Said the farmer, "Nay, no more.
I prithee sit at my frugal board,
And eat of my humble store.

"How fares my boy,—my soldier boy,
Of the old Ninth Army Corps?
I warrant he bore him gallantly
In the smoke and the battle's roar!"

"I know him not," said the aged man,
"And, as I remarked before,
I was with Grant"—"Nay, nay, I know,"
Said the farmer, "say no more.

"He fell in battle,—I see, alas!
Thou'dst smooth these tidings o'er.
Nay, speak the truth, whatever it be,
Though it rend my bosom's core."

"I cannot tell," said the aged man,
"And should have remarked before
That I was with Grant,—in Illinois,—
Three years before the war."

Then the farmer spake him never a word,
But beat with his fist full sore
That aged man, who had worked for Grant
Three years before the war.

BRET HARTE, 1839 - 1902

OLD-FASHIONED LOVE

He struggled to kiss her. She struggled the
*   same*
*   To prevent him so bold and undaunted;*
But, as smitten by lightning, he heard her
*   exclaim,*
*   "Avaunt, Sir!" and off he avaunted.*

Then he meekly approached, and sat down
*   at her feet,*
*   Praying loud, as before he had ranted,*
That she would forgive him, and try to be
*   sweet,*
*   And said "Can't you?" The dear girl*
*   recanted.*

Then softly he whispered, "How could
*   you do so?*
*   I certainly thought I was jilted;*
But come thou with me, to the parson
*   we'll go.*
*   Say, wilt thou, my dear?" And she*
*   wilted.*

⟨W⟩

People who think they can run the
earth should begin with a small garden.

⟨W⟩

MAN—WOMAN

Man's love is of man's life a thing apart,
*   'Tis woman's whole existence. Man may*
*   range.*
The court, camp, church, the vessel and the
*   mart,*
*   Sword, gown, gain, glory, offer in*
*   exchange*
Pride, fame, ambition, to fill up his heart,
*   And few there are whom these cannot*
*   estrange.*
Man have all these resources, we but one,—
To love again, and be again undone.
GEORGE GORDON, LORD BYRON, 1788 - 1824

⟨W⟩

But Woman is rare beyond compare
*   The poets tell us so;*
How little they know of Woman
*   Who only women know!*
CAROLYN WELLS, d. 1942

"WHEN LOVELY WOMAN"
(After Goldsmith)

When lovely woman wants a favor,
*   And finds, too late, that man won't*
*   bend,*
What earthly circumstance can save her
*   From disappointment in the end?*

The only way to bring him over,
*   The last experiment to try,*
Whether a husband or a lover,
*   If he have feeling is—to cry.*
PHOEBE CARY, 1824 - 1871

⟨W⟩

AndI thought to myself, How nice it is
For me to live in a world like this,
Where things can happen, and clocks can
*   strike,*
And none of the people are made alike.
WM. B. RANDS, 1823 - 1883

⟨W⟩

Being an old maid is like death by
drowning, a really delightful sensation
after you cease to struggle.
EDNA FERBER, 1887 - 1968

⟨W⟩

from EPITAPH ON MRS. CORBET

Here rests a Woman, good without
*   pretence,*
Bless'd with plain Reason and with sober
*   sense:*
No Conquests she, but o'er herself desired,
No Arts essay'd but not to be admired ..
So unaffected, so composed, a mind,
So firm, yet soft, so strong, yet so refin'd,
Heav'n as its purest gold, by Tortues
*   tried:*
The Saint sustain'd it, but the Woman
*   died.*
ALEXANDER POPE, 1688 - 1744

FIFTY YEARS HAPPINESS

It only seems like yesterday:
Yet fifty years have passed away
Since at the altar, side by side,
I stood with you, my happy bride.

And now our children's children stand,
Close gathered round, an eager band;
Whilst we recall, with smiles and tears,
The joys and griefs of fifty years.

For we have known the cares of life,
Sweetheart, since we were man and wife:
Yet have not loved each other less
Through fifty years of happiness.

When clouds have threatened storm and
    rain,
The skies have always cleared again,
And fifty years have come and passed,
And brought us sunshine at the last.

And now that we are old and gray,
We trust in Him, our guide and stay,
Our constant and unchanging Friend,
To lead us to our journey's end.

                         J. R. EASTWOOD

⟦❧⟧

A great social success is a pretty girl who
plays her cards as carefully as if she were
plain.

                  F. SCOTT FITZGERALD, 1896 - 1940
Writing to his daughter.

⟦❧⟧

WHAT IS PINK?

What is pink? a rose is pink
By the fountain's brink.
What is red? a poppy's red
In its barley bed.
What is blue? the sky is blue
Where the clouds float thro'
What is white? a swan is white
Sailing in the light.
What is yellow? pears are yellow,
Rich and ripe and mellow.
What is green? the grass is green,
With small flowers between.
What is violet? Clouds are violet
In the summer twilight.
What is orange? Why, an orange,
Just an orange!

            CHRISTINA ROSSETTI, 1830 - 1894

WHAT IS A WOMAN LIKE?

A Woman is like to—but stay—
    What a woman is like, who can say?
    There is no living with or without one.
    Love bites like a fly,
    Now an ear, now an eye,
Buzz, buzz, always buzzing about one.
    When she's tender and kind
    She is like to my mind,
(And Fanny was so, I remember).
    She's like to—Oh, dear!
    She's as good, very near,
As a ripe, melting peach in September.
    If she laugh, and she chat,
    Play, joke, and all that,
And with smiles and good humor she meet
    me,
    She's like a rich dish
    Of venison or fish,
That cries from the table, Come eat me!
    But she'll plague you and vex you,
    Distract and perplex you;
    False-hearted and ranging,
    Unsettled and changing,
    What then do you think, she is like?
        Like sand? Like a rock?
        Like a wheel? Like a clock?
    Ay, a clock that is always at strike.
Her head's like the island folks tell on,
Which nothing but monkeys can dwell on;
Her heart's like a lemon—so nice
She carves for each lover a slice;
    In truth she's to me,
    Like the wind, like the sea,
Whose raging will hearken to no man;
    Like a mill, like a pill,
    Like a flail, like a whale,
    Like an ass, like a glass
Whose image is constant to no man;
    Like a shower, like a flower,
    Like a fly, like a pie,
    Like a pea, like a flea,
    Like a thief, like—in brief,
She's like nothing on earth—but a woman!

⟦❧⟧

No lady is ever a gentleman.
              JAMES BRANCH CABELL, 1879 - 1958

⟦❧⟧

There are three things that are not to
be credited, a woman when she weeps, a
merchant when he swears, nor a drunkard
when he prays.

                  BARNABE RICH, 1540 - 1617

TO THE FRINGED GENTIAN

Thou blossom bright with autumn dew,
And colored with the heaven's own blue,
That openest when the quiet light
Succeeds the keen and frosty night,

Thou comest not when violets lean
O'er wandering brooks and spring unseen,
Or columbines, in purple dressed,
Nod o'er the ground-bird's hidden nest.

Thou waitest late and com'st alone,
When woods are bare and birds are flown,
And frost and shortening days portend
The aged year is near his end.

Then doth thy sweet and quiet eye
Look through its fringes to the sky,
Blue—blue—as if that sky let fall
A flower from its cerulean wall.

I would that thus, when I shall see
The hour of death draw near to me,
Hope, blossoming within my heart,
May look to heaven as I depart.

WILLIAM CULLEN BRYANT, 1794 - 1878

TO A FLOCK OF GEESE

Ye wild, free troopers of the skies
That ride in wedged ranks the blue
And unmarked roads of Paradise,
Who else but God had tutored you
That wind beset and tempest form
To buffet you with mighty sledge,
Ye still sweep onward through the storm
With that unbroken wedge?

Thrill me again, ye serried host,
With that shrill challenge which defies
The strength of whatsoever post
Is set to guard the bending skies
Against such rangers as ye are
That dare with swift and rhythmic
wings
The night unlighted of a star
To guide God's feathered things.

Ye are the joy of being wild,
The sign and symbol of a blest
Estate so sweet and undefiled
It breathes its spirit undistressed
Adown the heights to which have soared
Since Eden was our deepest sighs—
Thrill me again, ye clamant horde,
With your wild-ringing cries.

CLARK McADAMS

If we are ever to enjoy life, now is the time—not tomorrow, nor next year, nor in some future life after we have died. The best preparation for a better life next year is a full, complete, harmonious, joyous life this year. Our beliefs in a rich future life are of little importance unless we coin them into a rich present life. Today should always be our most wonderful day.

THOMAS DREIER

I served with General Washington in the Legislature of Virginia, before the Revolution, and, during it, with Doctor Franklin in Congress. I never heard either of them speak ten minutes at a time, nor to any but the main point, which was to decide the question. They laid their shoulders to the great points, knowing that the little ones would follow of themselves. If the present Congress errs in too much talking, how can it be otherwise, in a body to which the people send one hundred and fifty lawyers, whose trade it is to question everything, yield nothing, and talk by the hour? That one hundred fifty lawyers should do business together ought not to be expected.

THOMAS JEFFERSON, 1743 - 1826

So art has become foolishly confounded with education that all should be equally qualified.

Whereas, while polish, refinement, culture and breeding are in no way arguments for artistic results, it is also no reproach to the most finished scholar or greatest gentleman in the land that he be absolutely without eye for painting or ear for music—that in his heart he prefer the popular print to the scratch of Rembrandt's needle, or the songs of the hall to Beethoven's C minor symphony. Let him have but the wit to say so, and not feel the admission a proof of inferiority.

Art happens—no hovel is safe from it, no Prince may depend upon it, the vastest intelligence can not bring it about, and puny efforts to make it universal end in quaint comedy, and coarse farce.

This is as it should be—and all attempts to make it otherwise are due to the eloquence of the ignorant, the zeal of the conceited.

JAMES McNEILL WHISTLER, 1834 - 1903

The requisites of a singer—a big chest, a big mouth, ninety percent memory, ten percent intelligence, lots of hard work and something in the heart.

ENRICO CARUSO, 1873 - 1921

The true work of art is but a shadow of the divine perfection.

MICHELANGELO, 1475 - 1564

A line is a dot that went for a walk.

PAUL KLEE, 1879 - 1940

There is music in the beauty, and the silent note that Cupid strikes, far sweeter than the sound of an instrument; for there is music wherever there is harmony, order or proportion; and thus far we may maintain the music of the spheres.

SIR THOMAS BROWNE

ON MUSIC

Many love music but for music's sake,
Many because her touches can awake
Thoughts that repose within the breast
*   half-dead,*
And rise to follow where she loves to lead.
What various feelings come from days gone
*   by!*
What tears from far-off sources dim the
*   eye!*
Few, when light fingers with sweet voices
*   play*
And melodies swell, pause, and melt away,
Mind how at every touch, at every tone,
A spark of life hath glistened and has gone.

WALTER SAVAGE LANDOR, 1775 - 1864

Besides theology, music is the only art capable of affording peace and joy of the heart like that induced by the study of the science of divinity . . .

MARTIN LUTHER, 1483 - 1546

Art consists in drawing the line somewhere.

G. K. CHESTERTON, 1874 - 1936

Music that gentlier on the spirit lies,
Than tir'd eyelids upon tir'd eyes:
Music that brings sweet sleep down from
*   the blissful skies.*

ALFRED LORD TENNYSON, 1809 - 1892

When I say beauty of form, I am trying to express not what most people understand by the words, such as beauty of animals or paintings . . . I mean the straight line and the circle and the plane and the solid figures formed from these by turning-lathes and rulers and patterns of angles . . . For I assert that the beauty of these things is not relative like that of other things, but that they are always absolutely beautiful.

PLATO, 428 - 347 B.C.

AUTUMN

The autumn is old;
The sear leaves are flying;
He hath gathered up gold,
And now he is dying:
*   Old age, begin sighing!*

The vintage is ripe;
The harvest is heaping;
But some that have sowed
Have no riches for reaping—
*   Poor wretch, fall a-weeping!*

The year's in the wane;
There is nothing adorning;
The night has no eve,
And the day has no morning;
*   Cold winter gives warning.*

The rivers run chill;
The red sun is sinking;
And I am grown old,
And life is fast shrinking;
*   Here's enow for sad thinking!*

THOMAS HOOD, 1799 - 1845

❦

The greatest of faults, I should say, is to
be conscious of none.—

THOMAS CARLYLE, 1795 - 1881

❦

FRIENDS

It is my joy in life to find
*   At every turning of the road,*
The strong arm of a comrade kind
*   To help me onward with my load.*

And since I have no gold to give,
*   And love alone must make amends,*
My only prayer is while I live—
*   God make me worthy of my friends.*

FRANK D. SHERMAN, 1869 - 1916

FRIENDSHIP

Oh, the comfort—the inexpressible comfort
*   of feeling safe with a person,*
Having neither to weigh thoughts,
Nor measure words—but pouring them
All right out—just as they are—
Chaff and grain together—
Certain that a faithful hand will
Take and sift them—
Keep what is worth keeping—
And with the breath of kindness
Blow the rest away.

DINAH M. M. CRAIK, 1826 - 1887

❦

Work—for some good, be it ever so slowly;
Cherish some flower, be it ever so lowly;
Labor!—all labor is noble and holy!
*   Let thy great deeds be thy prayer to*
*   thy God!*

FRANCES SARGENT OSGOOD, 1811 - 1850

❦

THE HOME

A house is built of bricks and stones
*   Of sills and posts and piers,*
But a home is built of loving deeds,
*   That stand a thousand years.*

VICTOR HUGO, 1802 - 1885

❦

KNOWLEDGE

I have known sorrow—therefore I
May laugh with you, O friend, more
*   merrily*
Than those who never sorrowed upon
*   earth*
And know not laughter's worth.

I have known laughter—therefore I
May sorrow with you far more tenderly
Than those who never knew how sad a
*   thing*
Seems merriment to one heart suffering.

THEODOSIA GARRISON

190

OCTOBER

"Love loveth best of all the year
October's bright blue weather."

OCTOBER'S BRIGHT BLUE WEATHER

O sun and skies and clouds of June,
  And flowers of June together,
Ye cannot rival for one hour
  October's bright blue weather,

When loud the bumblebee makes haste,
  Belated thriftless vagrant,
And goldenrod is dying fast,
  And lanes with grapes are fragrant;

When gentians roll their fingers tight
  To save them for the morning,
And chestnuts fall from satin burrs
  Without a sound of warning;

When on the ground red apples lie
  In piles like jewels shining,
And redder still on old stone walls
  Are leaves of woodbine twining;

When all the lovely wayside things
  Their white-winged seeds are sowing,
And in the fields, still green and fair,
  Late aftermaths are growing;

When springs run low, and on the brooks,
  In idle golden freighting,
Bright leaves sink noiseless in the hush
  Of woods, for winter waiting;

When comrades seek sweet country
    haunts,
  By twos and twos together,
And count like misers, hour by hour,
  October's bright blue weather.

O sun and skies and flowers of June,
  Count all your boasts together,
Love loveth best of all the year
  October's bright blue weather.

HELEN HUNT JACKSON, 1831 - 1885

THE PHEASANT

A pheasant cock sprang into view,
A living jewel, up he flew.

His wings laid hold on empty space,
Scorn bulged his eyeballs out with grace.

He was a hymn from tail to beak
With not a tender note or meek.

Then the gun let out its thunder,
The bird descended struck with wonder.

He ran a little, then, amazed,
Settled with his head upraised.

The fierceness flowed out of his eyes
And left them meek and large and wise.

Gentleness relaxed his head,
He lay in jewelled feathers, dead.

ROBERT P. TRISTRAM COFFIN, 1892 - 1955

SONNET

The world is too much with us; late and
    soon,
Getting and spending, we lay waste our
    powers:
Little we see in Nature that is ours;
We have given our hearts away, a sordid
    boon!
This sea that bares her bosom to the
    moon,
The winds that will be howling at all
    hours,
And are up-gathered now like sleeping
    flowers;
For this, for everything, we are out of
    tune;
It moves us not.—Great God! I'd rather be
A Pagan suckled in a creed outworn;
So might I, standing on this pleasant lea,
Have glimpses that would make me less
    forlorn;
Have sight of Proteus rising from the sea;
Or hear old Triton blow his wreathed
    horn.

WILLIAM WORDSWORTH, 1770 - 1850

193

PEACE FROM AMERICA'S LEADERS—

May we never see another war! For in my opinion there never was a good war or a bad peace.

Benjamin Franklin in letter to Josiah Quincy, Sept. 1783.

Let us pray that peace be now restored to the world, and that God will preserve it always. These proceedings are closed.

General Douglas MacArthur, in speech after surrender of the Japanese aboard the Battleship, *Missouri*, Sept. 2, 1945.

If man does find the solution for world peace, it will be the most revolutionary reversal of his record we have ever known.

General George C. Marshall reporting as Chief of Staff.

from ODE

We are the music-makers,
*   And we are the dreamers of dreams,*
Wandering by lone sea-breakers,
*   And sitting by desolate streams;*
World-losers and world-forsakers,
*   On whom the pale moon gleams:*
Yet we are the movers and shakers
*   Of the world for ever, it seems.*

With wonderful deathless ditties
We build up the world's great cities,
*   And out of a fabulous story*
*   We fashion an empire's glory:*
One man with a dream, at pleasure,
*   Shall go forth and conquer a crown;*
And three with a new song's measure
*   Can trample an empire down.*

ARTHUR O'SHAUGHNESSY, 1844 - 1881

And what's a butterfly? At best,
He's but a caterpillar, drest.

JOHN GAY, 1685 - 1732

Look at that beautiful butterfly! One might wonder where it could live in tempestuous nights, in the whirlwind, or in the stormy day; but I have noticed it is safe and dry under the broad leaf while rivers have been flooded, and the mountain oaks torn up from their roots.

JEREMY TAYLOR, 1613 - 1667

THE BUTTERFLY

The butterfly, an idle thing,
Nor honey makes, nor yet can sing,
*   As do the bee and bird;*
Nor does it like the prudent ant,
Lay up the grain for times of want,
*   A wise and cautious hoard.*

My youth is but a summer's day
Then like the bee and ant I'll lay
*   A store of learning by;*
And though from flower to flower I rove,
My stock of wisdom I'll improve,
*   Nor be a butterfly.*

ADELAIDE O'KEEFE, 1776 - 1855

ENVOI

Fly, white butterflies, out to sea,
Frail pale wings for the wind to try,
Small white wings that we scarce can see,
*   Fly.*

Some fly light as a laugh of glee,
Some fly soft as a low long sigh;
All to the haven where each would be,
*   Fly.*

ALGERNON CHARLES SWINBURNE, 1837 - 1909

THE ART OF LIVING

Many men know the laws of mathematics and are skilled in the arts, but most men know very little about the laws governing life, the art of living. One may be able to build an airplane and circle the globe and yet be entirely ignorant of the simple art of how to be happy, successful and content. When studying the arts, place first upon the list the art of living.

TO CRITICS

When I was seventeen I heard
From each censorious tongue,
"I'd not do that if I were you;
You see you're rather young."

Now that I number forty years,
I'm quite as often told
Of this or that I shouldn't do
Because I'm quite too old.

O carping world! If there's an age
Where youth and manhood keep
An equal poise, alas! I must
Have passed it in my sleep.

WALTER LEARNED, 1847 - 1915

Even the cleverest and most perfect circumstantial evidence is likely to be at fault after all, and therefore ought to be received with great caution. Take the case of any pencil sharpened by any woman; if you have witnesses, you will find she did it with a knife, but if you take simply the aspect of the pencil, you will say she did it with her teeth.

MARK TWAIN

CYNICISM

Meanwhile I inly curse the bore
Of hunting still the same old coon,
And envy him, outside the door,
The golden quiet of the moon.

The winter wind is not so cold
As the bright smile he sees me win,
Nor the host's oldest wine so old
As our poor gabble, sour and thin.

I envy him the rugged prance
By which his freezing feet he warms,
And drag my lady's chains, and dance,
The galley-slave of dreary forms.

Oh, could he have my share of din,
And I his quiet—past a doubt
'Twould still be one man bored within,
And just another bored without.

JAMES RUSSELL LOWELL, 1819 - 1891

SEA—BIRDS

O lonesome sea-gull, floating far
Over the ocean's icy waste,
Aimless and wide thy wanderings are,
Forever vainly seeking rest:—
Where is thy mate, and where thy nest?

'Twixt wintry sea and wintry sky,
Cleaving the keen air with thy breast,
Thou sailest slowly, solemnly;
No fetter on thy wing is pressed:—
Where is thy mate, and where thy nest?

O restless, homeless human soul,
Following for aye thy nameless quest,
The gulls float, and the billows roll;
Thou watchest still, and questionest:—
Where is thy mate, and where thy nest?

ELIZABETH AKERS, 1832 - 1911

A LIFE ON THE OCEAN WAVE

A life on the ocean wave,
    A home on the rolling deep,
Where the scattered waters rave,
    And the winds their revels keep!
Like an eagle caged, I pine
    On this dull, unchanging shore:
Oh! give me the flashing brine,
    The spray and the tempest's roar!

Once more on the deck I stand
    Of my own swift-gliding craft:
Set sail! farewell to the land!
    The gale follows fair abaft.
We shoot through the sparkling foam
    Like an ocean-bird set free;—
Like the ocean-bird, our home
    We'll find far out on the sea.

The land is no longer in view,
    The clouds have begun to frown;
But with a stout vessel and crew,
    We'll say, Let the storm come down!
And the song of our hearts shall be,
    While the winds and the waters rave,
A home on the rolling sea!
    A life on the ocean wave!

EPES SARGENT, 1813 - 1880

⊙W⊙

from EACH AND ALL

The delicate shells lay on the shore;
The bubbles of the latest wave
Fresh pearls to their enamel gave,
And the bellowing of the savage sea
Greeted their safe escape to me.
I wiped away the weeds and foam,
I fetched my sea-born treasures home;
But the poor, unsightly, noisome things
Had left their beauty on the shore,
With the sun and the sand and the wild
    uproar.

RALPH WALDO EMERSON, 1803 - 1882

⊙W⊙

from ROCKED IN THE CRADLE OF THE DEEP

Rocked in the cradle of the deep
I lay me down in peace to sleep;
Secure I rest upon the wave,
For thou, O Lord! hast power to save.

EMMA HART WILLARD

from WITH A NANTUCKET SHELL

I send thee a shell from the oceanbeach;
But listen thou well, for my shell has
    speech.
Hold to thine ear and plain thou'lt hear
    Tales of ships.

CHARLES H. WEBB, 1834 - 1905

⊙W⊙

Ocean: a body of water occupying about two-thirds of a world made for man—who has no gills.

AMBROSE BIERCE, 1842 - 1914

Love the sea? I dote upon it—from the beach.

DOUGLAS JERROLD, 1803 - 1857

One of the best temporary cures for pride and affectation is seasickness: a man who wants to vomit never puts on airs.

MARK TWAIN

⊙W⊙

from CHILDE HAROLD'S PILGRIMAGE
CANTO IV

Roll on, thou deep and dark-blue Ocean,
    roll!
Ten thousand fleets sweep over thee in
    vain;
Man marks the earth with ruin, his control
Stops with the shore; upon the watery
    plain
The wrecks are all thy deed, nor doth
    remain
A shadow of man's ravage, save his own,
When for a moment, like a drop of rain,
He sinks into thy depths with bubbling
    groan,
Without a grave, unknelled, uncoffined
    and unknown.

GEORGE GORDON BYRON, 1788 - 1824

THE NEW COLOSSUS

Not like the brazen giant of Greek fame,
With conquering limbs astride from land to
*   land;*
Here at our sea-washed, sunset gates shall
*   stand*
A mighty woman with a torch, whose
*   flame*
Is the imprisoned lightning, and her name
Mother of Exiles. From her beacon-hand
Glows world-wide welcome; her mild eyes
*   command*
The air-bridged harbor that twin cities
*   frame.*

"Keep, ancient lands, your storied pomp!"
*   cries she*
With silent lips. "Give me your tired, your
*   poor,*
Your huddled masses yearning to breathe
*   free,*
The wretched refuse of your teeming
*   shore.*
Send these, the homeless, tempest-tost to
*   me,*
I lift my lamp beside the golden door!"

EMMA LAZARUS, 1849 - 1887

Written in 1883 and graven on a tablet in the pedestal
on which the Goddess stands. The Statue of Liberty was
unveiled in October, 1886.

Symbol of freedom to the
oppressed everywhere,

The giant Statue of Liberty, stands on Bedloe's Island in New York
Harbor, its uplifted torch guiding the "homeless, tempest-tost" to the
new world. It was a gift from the people of France commemorating the
alliance of the two nations during the Revolutionary War.

THE ONE WHITE HAIR

The wisest of the wise
Listen to pretty lies
  And love to hear 'em told.
Doubt not that Solomon
Listened to many a one,—
Some in his youth, and more when he grew
    old.

I never was among
The choir of Wisdom's song,
  But pretty lies loved I
As much as any king,
When youth was on the wing,
And (must it then be told?) when youth
    had quite gone by.

Alas! and I have not
The pleasant hour forgot
  When one pert lady said,
"O Walter! I am quite
Bewildered with affright!
I see (sit quiet now) a white hair on your
    head!"

Another more benign
Snipped it away from mine,
  And in her own dark hair
Pretended it was found . . .
  She leaped; and twirled it round . . .
Fair as she was, she never was so fair!
              WALTER SAVAGE LANDOR, 1775 - 1864

❧

There is no good in arguing with the inevitable. The only argument available with an east wind is to put on your overcoat.
              JAMES RUSSELL LOWELL, 1819 - 1891

❧

For every hour that thou wilt spare me now,
  I will allow,
Usurious God of Love, twenty to thee,
When wish my brown, my grey hairs equal
    be;
Till then, Love, let my body reign, and let
Me travel, sojourn, snatch, plot, have, forget,
Resume my last year's relict: think that yet
  We'd never met.

              JOHN DONNE, 1572 - 1631

from LOVEL'S SONG

It was a beauty that I saw
  So pure, so perfect, as the frame

A skein of silk without a knot.
  A fair march made without a halt.
  A curious form without a fault.
A printed book without a blot.
All beauty, and without a spot!
              BEN JONSON, 1573 - 1637
from the New Inn

❧

It is the Indian summer. The rising sun blazes through the misty air like a conflagration. A yellowish, smoky haze fills the atmosphere, and a filmy mist lies like a silver lining on the sky. The wind is soft and low. It wafts to us the odor of forest leaves, that hang wilted on the dripping branches, or drop into the stream. Their gorgeous tints are gone, as if the autumnal rains has washed them out. Orange, yellow and scarlet, all are changed to one melancholy russet hue.

The birds, too, have taken wing, and have left their roofless dwellings. Not the whistle of a robin, not the twitter of an eavesdropping swallow, not the carol of one sweet, familiar voice. All gone. Only the dismal cawing of a crow, as he sits and curses that the harvest is over; or the chit-chat of an idle squirrel, the noisy denizen of a hollow tree, the mendicant friar of a large parish, the absolute monarch of a dozen acorns.

              HENRY WADSWORTH LONGFELLOW

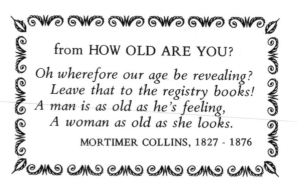

from HOW OLD ARE YOU?

Oh wherefore our age be revealing?
  Leave that to the registry books!
A man is as old as he's feeling,
  A woman as old as she looks.
              MORTIMER COLLINS, 1827 - 1876

CASEY AT THE BAT

The outlook wasn't brilliant for the Mudville
    nine that day;
The score stood four to two, with but one
    inning more to play;
And so, when Cooney died at first, and
    Burrows did the same,
A sickly silence fell upon the patrons of the
    game.

A straggling few got up to go in deep despair.
    The rest
Clung to the hope which springs eternal in
    the human breast;
They thought, if only Casey could but get a
    whack, at that,
They'd put up even money now, with Casey
    at the bat.

But Flynn preceded Casey, as did also
    Jimmy Blake,
And the former was a pudding and the latter
    was a fake;
So upon that stricken multitude grim
    melancholy sat,
For there seemed but little chance of
    Casey's getting to the bat.

But Flynn let drive a single, to the
    wonderment of all,
And Blake, the much despised, tore the
    cover off the ball;
And when the dust had lifted, and they saw
    what had occurred,
There was Jimmy safe on second, and Flynn
    a-hugging third.

Then from the gladdened multitude went
    up a joyous yell,
It bounded from the mountaintop, and
    rattled in the dell;
It struck upon the hillside, and recoiled upon
    the flat;
For Casey, mighty Casey, was advancing to
    the bat.

There was ease in Casey's manner as he
    stepped into his place,
There was pride in Casey's bearing, and a
    smile on Casey's face;
And when, responding to the cheers, he
    lightly doffed his hat,
No stranger in the crowd could doubt 'twas
    Casey at the bat.

Ten thousand eyes were on him as he
    rubbed his hands with dirt,
Five thousand tongues applauded when he
    wiped them on his shirt;

Then while the writhing pitcher ground the
    ball into his hip,
Defiance gleamed in Casey's eye, a sneer
    curled Casey's lip.

And now the leather-covered sphere came
    hurtling through the air,
And Casey stood a-watching it in haughty
    grandeur there;
Close by the sturdy batsman the ball
    unheeded sped.
"That ain't my style," said Casey. "Strike
    one," the umpire said.

From the benches, black with people, there
    went up a muffled roar,
Like the beating of the storm-waves on a
    stern and distant shore;
"Kill him! kill the umpire! shouted someone
    on the stand,
And it's likely they'd have killed him had
    not Casey raised his hand.

With a smile of Christian charity great
    Casey's visage shone;
He stilled the rising tumult; he bade the
    game go on;
He signaled to the pitcher, and once more
    the spheroid flew,
But Casey still ignored it, and the umpire
    said, "Strike two."

"Fraud!" cried the maddened thousands,
    and the echo answered, "Fraud!"
But a scornful look from Casey and the
    audience was awed;
They saw his face grow stern and cold, they
    saw his muscles strain,
And they knew that Casey wouldn't let the
    ball go by again.

The sneer is gone from Casey's lips, his
    teeth are clenched in hate,
He pounds with cruel violence his bat upon
    the plate;
And now the pitcher holds the ball, and
    how he lets it go,
And how the air is shattered by the force of
    Casey's blow.

Oh! somewhere in this favored land the sun
    is shining bright,
The band is playing somewhere, and
    somewhere hearts are light;
And somewhere men are laughing, and
    somewhere children shout,
But there is no joy in Mudville—mighty
    Casey has struck out!

ERNEST LAWRENCE THAYER, 1863 - 1940

KATYDID

I love to hear thine earnest voice,
  Wherever thou art hid,
Thou testy little dogmatist,
  Thou pretty Katydid!

Thou mindest me of gentlefolks,—
  Old gentle folks are they—
Thou say'st an undisputed thing
  In such a solemn way.

Thou art a female, Katydid!
  I know it by the trill
That quivers through thy piercing notes,
  So petulant and shrill!

I think there is a knot of you
  Beneath the hollow tree,—
A knot of spinster Katydids,—
  Do Katydids drink tea?

O, tell me where did Katy live,
  And what did Katy do!
And was she very fair and young,
  And yet so wicked too?
Did Katy love a naughty man,
  Or kiss more cheeks than one?
I warrant Katy did no more
  Than many a Kate has done.

OLIVER WENDELL HOLMES, 1809 - 1894

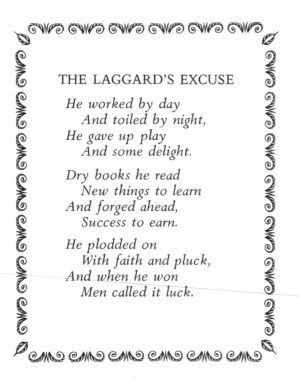

THE LAGGARD'S EXCUSE

He worked by day
  And toiled by night,
He gave up play
  And some delight.

Dry books he read
  New things to learn
And forged ahead,
  Success to earn.

He plodded on
  With faith and pluck,
And when he won
  Men called it luck.

THE SHEPHERD

How sweet is the Shepherd's sweet lot!
From the morn to the evening he strays;
He shall follow his sheep all the day,
And his tongue shall be filled with praise.
For he hears the lamb's innocent call,
And he hears the ewe's tender reply;
He is watchful, while they are in peace,
For they know when their Shepherd is
  nigh.

WILLIAM BLAKE, 1757 - 1827

THE LAMB

Little Lamb, who made thee?
  Dost thou know who made thee;
Gave thee life and bid thee feed
By the stream and o'er the mead;
Gave thee clothing of delight,
Softest clothing, woolly, bright;
Gave thee such a tender voice
Making all the vales rejoice?
  Little Lamb, who made thee?
  Dost thou know who made thee?

Little Lamb, I'll tell thee,
  Little Lamb, I'll tell thee;
He is called by thy name,
For He calls Himself a Lamb.
He is meek and He is mild;
He became a little child.
I a child and thou a lamb,
We are called by His name.
  Little Lamb, God bless thee.
  Little Lamb, God bless thee.

WILLIAM BLAKE, 1757 - 1827

The victory of success is half won when
one gains the habit of work.

SARAH A. BOLTON

"BECAUSE OF PREVIOUS GLADNESS"

There was a little dachshund once,
So long he had no notion,
The time it took from head to foot
To register emotion.
And so it was that when his face
Was filled with tears and sadness,
His little tail kept wagging on
Because of previous gladness.

⟨❧⟩

I'M GLAD

I'm glad the sky is painted blue,
   And the earth is painted green,
With such a lot of nice fresh air
   All sandwiched in between.

⟨❧⟩

A QUESTION

A little bird sat on a telegraph wire,
   And said to his mates: "I declare,
If wireless telegraph comes into vogue,
   We'll all have to sit on the air."

⟨❧⟩

from SEA DREAMS

What does little birdie say
In her nest at peep of day?
Let me fly, says little birdie,
Mother, let me fly away.
Birdie, rest a little longer,
Till the little wings are stronger,
So she rests a little longer,
Then she flies away.
                    ALFRED TENNYSON, 1809 - 1892

THE SNARK

"Come, listen, my men, while I tell you
      again
   The five unmistakable marks
By which you may know, wheresoever you
      go,
   The warranted genuine Snarks.

"Let us take them in order. The first is
      the taste,
   Which is meagre and hollow, but crisp:
Like a coat that is rather too tight in the
      waist,
   With a flavour of Will-o-the-wisp.

"Its habit of getting up late you'll agree
   That it carries too far, when I say
That it frequently breakfasts at five-o'clock
      tea,
   And dines on the following day.

"The third is its slowness in taking a jest.
   Should you happen to venture on one,
It will sigh like a thing that is deeply
      distressed:
   And it always looks grave at a pun.

"The fourth is its fondness for
      bathing-machines,
   Which it constantly carries about,
And believes that they add to the beauty
      of scenes—
   A sentiment open to doubt.

'The fifth is ambition. It next will be
      right
   To describe each particular batch:
Distinguishing those that have feathers,
      and bite,
   From those that have whiskers, and
      scratch.

"For, although common Snarks do no
      manner of harm,
   Yet I feel it my duty to say
Some are Boojums—" The Bellman broke
      off in alarm,
   For the Baker had fainted away.
                    LEWIS CARROLL, 1832 - 1898

from The Hunting of the Snark

There are two kinds of discontent in this world: the discontent that
works, and the discontent that wrings its hands. The first gets what it
wants, and the second loses what it has. There's no cure for the first
but success; and there's no cure at all for the second.

GORDON GRAHAM

I bring fresh showers for the thirsty
    flowers,
    From the seas and the streams;
I bear light shade for the leaves when laid
    In their noonday dreams.
From my wings are shaken the dews that
    waken
    The sweet buds every one,
When rocked to rest on their mother's
    breast,
    As she dances about the sun.
I wield the flail of the lashing hail,
    And whiten the green plains under,
And then I again dissolve it in rain,
    And laugh as I pass in thunder.

I sift the snow on the mountains below,
    And their great pines groan aghast;
And all the night 'tis my pillow white,
    While I sleep in the arms of the blast.

That orbed maiden with white fire laden,
    Whom mortals call the moon,
Glides glimmering o'er my fleece-like floor,

By the midnight breezes strewn;
And wherever the heat of her unseen feet,
    Which only the angels hear,
May have broken the woof of my tent's
    thin roof,
    The stars peep behind her and peer;
And I laugh to see them whirl and flee,
    Like a swarm of golden bees,
When I widen the rent in my wind-built
    tent,
    Till the calm rivers, lakes and seas,
Like strips of sky fallen through me on
    high,
    And each paved with the moon and these.

That in thy orb the wretched may have
    rest;
The sufferers of the earth perhaps may go,
    Released by death, to thy benignant
    sphere,
And the sad children of despair and woe
    Forget, in thee, their cup of sorrow here.
Oh that I soon may reach thy world serene,
Poor wearied pilgrim in this toiling scene!

CHARLOTTE SMITH, 1749 - 1806

from ON THE SETTING SUN

Oft did I wonder why the setting sun
Should look upon us with a blushing face:
Is't not for shame of what he hath seen
    done,
While in our hemisphere he ran his race?

LYMAN HEATH, 1804 - 1870

I am the daughter of Earth and Water,
    And the nursling of the Sky:
I pass through the pores of the ocean and
    shores
    I change, but I cannot die.
For after the rain, when with never a
    stain
    The pavilion of heaven is bare,
And the winds and sunbeams with their
    covex gleams
    Build up the blue dome of air,
I silently laugh at my own cenotaph,
    And out of the caverns of rain,
Like a child from the womb, like a ghost
    from the tomb,
    I arise, and unbuild it again.

PERCY BYSSHE SHELLEY, 1792 - 1822

from THE ASTRONOMICAL ALDERMAN

"But," quoth his neighbour, "when the
    sun
From East to West his course has run,
How comes it that he shows his face
Next morning in his former place?"
"Ho! there's a pretty question, truly!"
Replied our wight, with an unruly
    Burst of laughter and delight,
So much his triumph seemed to please
    him.
    "Why, blockhead! he goes back at night,
And that's the reason no one sees him!"

HORACE SMITH, 1779 - 1849

from GOD'S SUNSHINE

Never once, since the world began,
    Has the sun ever stopped shining;
His face very often we could not see.
And we grumbled at his inconstancy,
But the clouds were really to blame, not
    he,
    For behind them he was shining.

JOHN OXENHAM

THE GLORIOUS TOUCHDOWN

When the crisp autumnal zephyrs whistle
    through the leafless trees;
    When croquet is a sweet regret and
      tennis is non est;
When the baseball player stays indoors for
    fear that he will freeze
    And the picnic trousers get a needed
      rest;
When Mackinaws and yellow shoes are
    packed away with care,
    And the summer sash becomes a
      muffler gay,
Then the college football specialist
    emerges from his lair,
    And buckles up his armor for the fray.

He rises up at 4 A.M. and runs ten miles
    or more;
    A plunge in icy water then before he
      eats a bite;
He breakfasts on raw steak and toast, and
    quaffs a pint of gore,
    And works with clubs and dumb-bells
      until night.
He dare not smoke a cigarette nor touch
    his meerschaum brown,
    And every night at eight o'clock he
      tumbles into bed.
No more with boon companions does he
    paint the college town,
    And fill the peaceful residents with
      dread.

But out of all these hardships and this
    abstinence unwilling,
    There comes a day of triumph for the
      Rugby devotee,
When on the frozen battlefield, unheeding
    winds so chilling,
    He scrimmages and tackles in the hope
      of victory.

What though he grinds his features to a
    pulp so raw and gory,
    While his strong and beefy opponents
      are seated on his frame?
What though he never lives to tell his
    children of the story?
    Though death comes with the victory,
      the team must win the game.

The college yell inspires him still, and
    though each bone is aching,
    And though the hazy landscape swims
      before his blinded eyes,
The precious spheroid comes his way and
    through the rush line breaking,
    He's down within the goal line, and the
      team has won the prize.
A ton or more of writhing flesh with him
    is mixed together,
    His leg is wrapped around his neck, four
      teeth cannot be found;
But he has passed into the goal and hangs
    on to the leather;
    He is the hero of the day—he's carried
      from the ground.

With proper care and nursing he will
    soon return to college;
    A compound fracture of the leg, some
      cuts, a broken nose;
In the meantime he is not acquiring
    literary knowledge,
    And the family physician to his bedside
      daily goes.
When he resumes his studies he'll recite
    each day at dinner,
    All the more exciting features of the
      memorable game;
Next year, if he's recovered, he will make
    the team a winner
    By going into training—the result will be
      the same.

GEORGE ADE, 1866 - 1944

"I AM HE THAT WALKS"

I am he that walks with the tender and
growing Night,
I call to the earth and sea half-held by the
Night.

Press close, bare-bosomed Night! Press
close, magnetic, nourishing Night!
Night of south winds! Night of the large
few stars!
Still, nodding night! Mad, naked, summer
night.

Smile, O voluptuous, cool-breathed Earth!
Earth of the slumbering and liquid trees!
Earth of departed sunset! Earth of the
mountains, misty-topt!
Earth of the vitreous pour of the full
moon, just tinged with blue!
Earth of shine and dark, mottling the tide
of the river!
Earth of the limpid grey of clouds,
brighter and clearer for my sake!
Far-swooping elbowed earth! Rich, apple-
blossomed earth!
Smile, for your lover comes!

WALT WHITMAN, 1819 - 1892

WHICH

Would'st thou be wretched? There's an
easy way—
Think of but self, and self alone, all day;
Think of thy pain, thy grief, thy loss, thy
care;
All that thou hast to do, or feel, or bear;
Think of thy good, thy pleasures and thy
gain
Think only of thyself—'twill not be in
vain.
Would'st thou be happy? Take an easy
way—
Think of those around thee; live for them
each day;
Think of their pain, their loss, their grief,
their care,
All that they have to do, or feel, or bear;
Think of their pleasure, or their good,
their gain;
Think of those around thee—'twill not be
in vain.

A TURKISH LEGEND

A certain Pasha, dead five thousand years,
Once from his harem fled in sudden tears,

And had this sentence on the city's gate
Deeply engraven, "Only God is great."

So these four words above the city's noise
Hung like the accents of an angel's voice,

And evermore, from the high barbican,
Saluted each returning caravan.

Lost is that city's glory. Every gust
Lifts, with dead leaves, the unknown
Pasha's dust,

And all is ruin,—save one wrinkled gate
Whereon is written, "Only God is great."

THOMAS BAILEY ALDRICH, 1837 - 1907

To be seventy years young is sometimes
far more cheerful and hopeful than to be
forty years old.

O. W. HOLMES

In letter to Julia Ward Howe, on her 70th birthday May
1889.

"LEAF AFTER LEAF DROPS OFF"

Leaf after leaf drops off, flower after
flower,
Some in the chill, some in the warmer
hour:
Alive they flourish, and alive they fall,
And Earth who nourished them receives
them all.
Should we, her wiser sons, be less content
To sink into her lap when life is spent?

WALTER SAVAGE LANDOR, 1775 - 1864

THE NEW STENOGRAPHER

I have a new stenographer—she came to
  work to-day,
  She told me that she wrote the latest
  system.
Two hundred words a minute seemed to
  her, she said, like play,
  And word for word at that!—she never
  missed 'em!
I gave her some dictation—a letter to a
  man—
And this, as I remember it, was how the
  letter ran:

"Dear Sir: I have your favor, and in reply
  would state
That I accept the offer in yours of recent
  date.
I wish to say, however, that under no
  condition
Can I afford to think of your free lance
  proposition.

I shall begin to-morrow to turn the matter
  out;
The copy will be ready by August 10th,
  about.
Material of this nature should not be
  rushed unduly.
Thanking you for your favor, I am, yours,
  very truly."

She took it down in shorthand with
  apparent ease and grace;
  She didn't call me back all in a flurry.
Thought I: "At last I have a girl worth
  keeping 'round the place";
Then said: "Now write it out—you needn't
  hurry."
The typewriter she tackled—now and then
  she struck a key,
And after thirty minutes this is what she
  handed me:

"Deer sir, I have the Feever, and in a Pile
  i Sit
And I except the Offer as you have
  reasoned it,
I wish to see however That under any
  condition
can I for to Think of a free lunch
  Preposishun?

I Shal be in tomorrow To., turn the
  mother out,
The cap will be red and Will costt, $10,
  about.
Mateeriul of this nation should not rust N.
  Dooley,
Thinking you have the Feever I am Yours
  Very Truely."

THE TYPISTE'S HOLIDAY

My tYpust is io hor vacution,
  My trpist's away fo r a week,
My trpudt us in hwr vacarion,
  Wgile thse damu kews ploy hudge and
  seek.
    Chorus:
Oy, breng boxk, bting bzek,
  Brung beej mu blnnie ti my, tp mr;
B)&ng blxj, b6icx,
  Pping bozk m% beinino-o-mx CH¼
  helk?

A stenographer is a girl who learns to type on your time while she is waiting for a chance to get married.

Sure Sign: "How do you know that Chaucer dictated to a stenographer?"
"Just look at the spelling."

WEATHER LORE

Full moon in October without a frost,
No frost until full moon in November.

Our friendships hurry to short and poor conclusions, because we have made them a texture of wine and dreams, instead of the tough fiber of the human heart. The laws of friendship are great, austere, and eternal, of one web with the laws of nature and of morals. But we have aimed at a swift and petty benefit, to such a sudden sweetness. We snatch at the slowest fruit in the whole garden of God, which many summers and many winters must ripen. We seek our friend not sacredly, but with an adulterate passion which would appropriate him to ourselves.

I do not wish to treat friendships daintily, but with roughest courage. When they are real, they are not glass threads or frost-work, but the solidest thing we know.

The end of friendship is a commerce the most strict and homely that can be joined; more strict than any of which we have experienced. It is for aid and comfort through all the relations and passages of life and death. It is fit for serene days, and graceful gifts, and country rambles, but also for rough roads and hard fare, shipwreck, poverty and persecution. It keeps company with the sallies of the wit and the trances of religion. We are to dignify to each other the daily needs and offices of man's life, and embellish it by courage, wisdom and unity. It should never fall into something usual and settled, but should be alert and inventive, and add rhyme and reason to what was drudgery.

RALPH WALDO EMERSON

The best elixir is a friend.

WILLIAM SOMERVILLE, 1675 - 1742

ᏫᏬᎷ

Friend: One who knows all about you and loves you just the same.

ELBERT HUBBARD, 1859 - 1915

ᏫᏬᎷ

Do not remove a fly from your friend's forehead with a hatchet.

CHINESE PROVERB

ᏫᏬᎷ

Fine as friendship is, there is nothing irrevocable about it.

RANDOLPH S. BOURNE

The only way to have a friend is to be one.

RALPH WALDO EMERSON

ᏫᏬᎷ

An egg of one hour old, bread of one day, a goat of one month, wine of six months, flesh of a year, fish of ten years, a wife of twenty years, a friend among a hundred, are the best of all number.

JOHN WODROEPHE, circa 1623

ᏫᏬᎷ

A true friend unbosoms freely, advises justly, assists readily, adventures boldly, takes all patiently, defends courageously, and continues a friend unchangeably.

WILLIAM PENN, 1644 - 1718

. . . Friends are generally of the same sex, for when men and women agree, it is only in their conclusions; their reasons are always different. So that while intellectual harmony between men and women is easily possible, its delightful and magic quality lies precisely in the fact that it does not arise from mutual understanding, but is a conspiracy of alien essences and a kissing, as it were, in the dark. The human Race, in its intellectual life, is organized like the bees: the masculine soul is a worker, sexually atrophied, and essentially dedicated to impersonal and universal arts; the feminine is a queen, infinitely fertile, omnipresent in its brooding industry, but passive and abounding in intuitions without method and passions without justice. Friendship with a woman is therefore apt to be more or less than friendship: less, because there is no intellectual parity; more, because (even when the relation remains wholly dispassionate, as in respect to old ladies) there is something mysterious and oracular about a woman's mind which inspires a certain instinctive deference and puts it out of the question to judge what she says by masculine standards. She has a kind of sibylline intuition and the right to be irrationally apropos. There is a gallantry of the mind which pervades all conversation with a lady, as there is a natural courtesy towards children and mystics; but such a habit of respectful concession, marking as it does an intellectual alienation as profound, though not as complete, as that which separates us from the dumb animals, is radically incompatible with friendship.

GEORGE SANTAYANA, 1863 - 1952
from "Reason in Society"

There are three faithful friends: an old wife, and old dog, and ready money.

BENJAMIN FRANKLIN

Be courteous to all, but intimate with few, and let those few be well tried before you give them your confidence. True friendship is a plant of slow growth, and must undergo and withstand the shocks of adversity before it is entitled to the appellation.

GEORGE WASHINGTON, 1732 - 1799
from letter written Jan. 1783

Every man should have a fair-sized cemetery in which to bury the faults of his friends.

HENRY WARD BEECHER, 1813 - 1887

I find friendship to be like wine, raw when new, ripened with age, the true old man's milk and restorative cordial.

THOMAS JEFFERSON, 1743 - 1826

from FRIENDSHIP

Even the utmost goodwill and harmony and practical kindness are not sufficient for Friendship, for Friends do not live in harmony merely as some say, but in melody. We do not wish for Friends to feed and clothe our bodies—neighbors are kind enough for that—but to do the like office to our spirits.

HENRY DAVID THOREAU, 1817 - 1862

The holy passion of Friendship is of so sweet and steady and loyal and enduring a nature that it will last through a whole lifetime, if not asked to lend money.

MARK TWAIN

from PASSIONATE PILGRIM

He that is thy friend indeed,
He will help thee in thy need:
If thou sorrow, he will weep;
If thou wake, he cannot sleep;
Thus of every grief in heart
He with thee doth bear a part,
These are certain signs to show
Faithful friend from faltering foe.

RICHARD BARNFIELD, 1574 - 1627

TRUE RELIGION

"True Religion," written by Tulsidas, a Hindu religious reformer and poet (c. 1532 - 1623). It was translated from the Sanskrit in 1930 by Mahatma Gandhi while he was imprisoned in Yeravda Jail, in Poona.

Following is the complete text:

This and this alone
Is true religion—
To serve thy brethren:

This is sin above all other sin,
To harm thy brethren:

In such a faith is happiness,
In lack of it is misery and pain:

Blessed is he who swerveth not aside
From this straight path:
Blessed is he whose life is lived
Thus ceaselessly in serving God:

By bearing others' burdens,
And so alone,
Is life, true life, to be attained:

Nothing is hard to him, who, casting life
  aside,
Thinks only this—
How may I serve my fellow men?

Today is yesterday's pupil.
BENJAMIN FRANKLIN

❧

Concern yourself but with today;
Woo it, and teach it to obey
Your will and wish. Since time began
Today has been the friend of man,
But in his blindness and his sorrow
He looks to yesterday and tomorrow.

❧

DECISION

If love should count you worthy, and
  should deign
One day to seek your door and be your
  guest,
Pause! ere you draw the bolt and bid him
  rest,
If in your old content you would remain.
For not alone he enters; in his train

Are angels of the mists, the lonely quest,
Dreams of the unfulfilled and unpossessed.
And sorrow, and life's immemorial pain.
He wakes desires you never may forget,
He shows you stars you never saw before,
He makes you share with him, forevermore,
The burden of the world's divine regret.
How wise you were to open not! and yet,
How poor if you should turn him from
  the door.

❧

MY LADY WIND

My Lady Wind, my Lady Wind,
Went round about the house to find
  A chink to set her foot in;
She tried the keyhole in the door,
She tried the crevice in the floor,
  And drove the chimney soot in.

And then one night when it was dark
She blew up such a tiny spark
  That all the town was bothered;
From it she raised such flame and smoke
That many in great terror woke,
  And many more were smothered.

And thus when once, my little dears,
A whisper reaches itching ears—
  The same will come, you'll find:
Take my advice, restrain the tongue,
Remember what old nurse has sung
  Of busy Lady Wind.

"ONE FIGHT MORE"
Prospice

Fear death?—to feel the fog in my throat,
The mist in my face,
When the snows begin, and the blasts
denote
I am nearing the place,
The power of the night, the press of the
storm,
The post of the foe;
Where he stands, the Arch Fear in a
visible form,
Yet the strong man must go:
For the journey is done and the summit
attained,
And the barriers fall,
Though a battle's to fight ere the guerdon
be gained,
The reward of it all.
I was ever a fighter, so—one fight more,
The best and the last!
I would hate that death bandaged my
eyes, and forbore
And bade me creep past.
No! let me taste the whole of it, fare like
my peers
The heroes of old,
Bear the brunt, in a minute pay glad life's
arrears
Of pain, darkness and cold.
For sudden the worst turns the best to the
brave,
The black minute's at end,
And the elements' rage, the fiend-voices
that rave,
Shall dwindle, shall blend,
Shall change, shall become first a peace
out of pain,
Then a light, then thy breast,
O thou soul of my soul! I shall clasp thee
again,
And with God be the rest!

ROBERT BROWNING, 1812 - 1880

❧

from THE PARADOX OF TIME

Time goes, you say? Ah no!
Alas, Time stays, we go.

AUSTIN DOBSON, 1840 - 1921

SONG

When I am dead, my dearest
Sing no sad songs for me;
Plant thou no roses at my head,
Nor shady cypress-tree;
Be the green grass above me
With showers and dewdrops wet;
And if thou wilt, remember,
And if thou wilt, forget.

I shall not see the shadows,
I shall not feel the rain;
I shall not hear the nightingale
Sing on, as if in pain:
And dreaming through the twilight
That doth not rise nor set,
Haply I may remember,
And haply may forget.

CHRISTINA GEORGINA ROSSETTI, 1830 - 1894

❧

The true way to mourn the dead is to take care of the living who belong to them.

EDMUND BURKE, 1729 - 1797

❧

To his physician, who said "General, I fear the angels are waiting for you:" "Waiting are they? Well . . . let 'em wait!"

ETHAN ALLEN, 1737 - 1789

❧

The best of men cannot suspend their fate
The good die early, and the bad die late.

DANIEL DEFOE, 1661 - 1731

❧

"I NEVER SAW A MOOR"

I never saw a moor,
I never saw the sea;
Yet now I know how the heather looks,
And what a wave must be.

I never spoke with God,
Nor visited in Heaven;
Yet certain am I of the spot
As if the chart were given.

EMILY DICKINSON, 1830 - 1886

TO MY GRANDMOTHER

Under the elm a rustic seat
Was merriest Susan's pet retreat
　　To merry-make

This Relative of mine
Was she seventy-and-nine
　　When she died?
By the canvas may be seen
How she looked at seventeen,
　　As a Bride.

Beneath a summer tree
Her maiden reverie
　　Has a charm;
Her ringlets are in taste;
What an arm! and what a waist
　　For an arm!

With her bridal-wreath, bouquet,
Lace farthingale, and gay
　　Falbala,—
If Romney's touch be true,
What a lucky dog were you,
　　Grandpapa!

Her lips are sweet as love;
They are parting! Do they move?
　　Are they dumb?
Her eyes are blue, and beam
Beseechingly, and seem
　　To say, "Come!"

What funny fancy slips
From atween these cherry lips?
　　Whisper me,
Fair Sorceress in paint,
What canon says I mayn't
　　Marry thee?

That good-for-nothing Time
Has a confidence sublime!
　　When I first
Saw this Lady, in my youth,
Her winters had, forsooth,
　　Done their worst.

Her locks, as white as snow,
Once shamed the swarthy crow;
　　By-and-by
That fowl's avenging sprite
Set his cruel foot for spite
　　Near her eye.

Her rounded form was lean,
And her silk was bombazine:
　　Well I wot
With her needles would she sit,
And for hours would she knit.—
　　Would she not?

Ah perishable clay!
Her charms had dropped away
　　One by one:
But if she heaved a sigh
With a burden, it was, "Thy
　　Will be done,"

In travail, as in tears,
With the fardel of her years
　　Overpressed,
In mercy she was borne
Where the weary and the worn
　　Are at rest.

Oh, if you now are there,
And sweet as once you were,
　　Grandmamma,
This nether world agrees
You'll all the better please
　　Grandpapa.

FREDERICK LOCKER-LAMPSON, 1821 - 1895

MEMORY

My mind lets go a thousand things,
Like dates of wars and deaths of kings,
And yet recalls the very hour—
'Twas noon by yonder village tower,
And on the last blue noon in May—
The wind came briskly up this way,
Crisping the brook beside the road;
Then, pausing here, set down its load
Of pine-scents, and shook listlessly
Two petals from that wild-rose tree.

THOMAS BAILEY ALDRICH, 1836 - 1907

A storm makes its first announcement
down the chimney.

NOVEMBER

"No fruits, no flowers, no leaves, no birds,
November!"

WHAT I WOULD DO

If I were as young in years again as I still am inside, I should make me a list of a few things to do before I die:

To go at least once clear around this jolly world.

To live with savages and in jungles now and then and learn how splendid they are.

To ride and read and shoot and play and study and think and be silent with such enthusiasm that every moment of unnecessary sleep would be a crime.

To live so fully that most people would seem dead on their feet.

To own a magnificent telescope and by frequent use never to forget the humor of my size and place and ambitions in the universe.

Finally, do the things all over again, for I have done them and am still at it, and I know.

For just this once I have broken my motto of "Don't tell." And now forget everything that I have said and live your own life.

WILL BEEBE, 1877 - 1919

❦

Oh wad some Pow'r the giftie gie us
To see oursels as ithers see us!

ROBERT BURNS

❦

A compliment is something like a kiss through a veil.

VICTOR HUGO, 1802 - 1885

"THREE—THE MYSTICAL NUMBER"

Three fair things that hide homeliness: Good manners in the ill-favored; skill in a servant, wisdom in the misshapen.

Three glories of a gathering: A beautiful wife, a good horse, a swift hound.

Three nurses of theft: A wood, a cloak, night.

Three candles that illume every darkness: Truth, nature, knowledge.

Three sounds of increase: The lowing of a cow in milk; the din of a smithy; the swish of a plough.

FROM THE TRIADS OF IRELAND, 9TH CENTURY

❦

Nothing is really work unless you would rather be doing something else.

JAMES M. BARRIE

❦

A BAKER'S DUZZEN UV WIZE SAWZ

Them ez wants, must choose.
Them ez hez, must lose.
Them ez knows, won't blab.
Them ez guesses, will gab.
Them ez borrows, sorrows.
Them ez lends, spends.
Them ez gives, lives.
Them ez keeps dark, is deep.
Them ez kin earn, kin keep.
Them ez aims, hits.
Them ez hez, gits.
Them ez waits, win.
Them ez will, kin.

EDWARD ROWLAND SILL, 1841 - 1887

from "MY GRANDPAPPY ONCE TOLD ME"

A lot of people are like a wheelbarrow—not good unless pushed. Some are like canoes—they have to be paddled. Some are like kites—if you don't keep a string on them, they fly away. Some are like footballs—you can't tell which way they will bounce next. Some are like balloons—full of wind and ready to blow up. Some are like trailers—they have to be pulled. Some are like a good watch—open face, pure gold, quietly busy and full of good works.

L. A. WINCHELL

AUTUMN

The warm sun is failing, the bleak wind is
wailing,
The bare boughs are sighing, the pale
flowers are dying;
And the year
On the earth her death-bed, in a shroud of
leaves dead,
Is lying.
Come, months, come away,
From November to May;
In your saddest array
Follow the bier
Of the dead, cold Year,
And like dim shadows watch by her
sepulchre.

The chill rain is falling; the nipped worm
is crawling;
The rivers are swelling; the thunder is
knelling
For the Year;
The blithe swallows are flown, and the
lizards each gone
To his dwelling;
Come, months, come away;
Put on white, black and gray,
Let your light sisters play—
Ye, follow the bier
Of the dead, cold Year,
And make her grave green with tear on
tear.

PERCY BYSSHE SHELLEY, 1792 - 1822

❦

WEATHER LORE:

Cobwebs on the grass are a sign of frost.

❦

Economy is the art of making the most of life. The love of economy is the root of all virtue.

GEORGE BERNARD SHAW

❦

Look to your health; and if you have it, praise God, and value it next to a good conscience; for health is the second blessing that we mortals are capable of; a blessing that money cannot buy.

IZAAK WALTON, 1593 - 1683

from HOLIDAYS

The holiest of all holidays are those
Kept by ourselves in silence and apart;
The secret anniversaries of the heart,
When the full river of feeling overflows;—
The happy days unclouded to their close;
The sudden joys that out of darkness
start
As flames from ashes;, swift desires that
dart
Like swallows, singing down each wind
that blows!

HENRY WADSWORTH LONGFELLOW, 1807 - 1882

❦

To look up and not down
To look forward and not back
To look out and not in,—and
To lend a hand

EDWARD EVERETT HALE, 1822 - 1909

❦

Walk on a rainbow trail, walk on a trail of song, and all about you will be beauty. There is a way out of every dark mist, over a rainbow trail.

Navajo Indian song.

❦

On Treason: Treason doth never prosper: what's the reason? Why, when it prospers, none dare call it treason.

SIR JOHN HARINGTON, 1561 - 1612

❦

To awaken each morning with a smile brightening my face, to greet the day with reverence, for the opportunities it contains; to approach my work with a clean mind; to hold ever before me, even in the doing of little things, the Ultimate Purpose toward which I am working; to meet men and women with laughter on my lips and love in my heart; to be gentle, kind and courteous through all the hours; to approach the night with weariness that ever wooes sleep and the joy that comes from work well done—this is how I desire to waste wisely my days.

THOMAS DREIER

NOVEMBER

Hark you such sound as quivers? Kings
  will hear,
  As kings have heard, and tremble on
    their thrones;
  The old will feel the weight of mossy
    stones;
  The young alone will laugh and scoff
    at fear.
It is the tread of armies marching near,
  From scarlet lands to lands forever
    pale;
  It is a bugle dying down the gale;
  Is the sudden gushing of a tear.
And it is hands that grope at ghostly
    doors;
  And romp of spirit-children on the pave;
  It is the tender sighing of the brave
Who fell, ah! long ago, in futile wars;
  It is such sound as death; and, after all,
  'Tis but the forest letting dead leaves
    fall.

        MAHLON LEONARD FISHER, 1874 - 1947

ᚲᚹᚲ

There was an old man of Nantucket
Who kept all his cash in a bucket
  But his daughter, named Nan,
  Ran away with a man—
  And as for the bucket, Nantucket.

WHAT IS THE GRASS?

A child said What is the grass? fetching it
  to me with full hands;
How could I answer the child? I do not
  know what it is any more than he.
I guess it must be the flag of my
  disposition, out of hopeful green stuff
  woven.

Or I guess it is the handkerchief of the
  Lord,
A scented gift and remembrancer
  designedly dropped,
Bearing the owner's name someway in the
  corners, that we may see and remark
  and say Whose?

        WALT WHITMAN, 1819 - 1892

ᚲᚹᚲ

Originality: Undetected imitation.
Time: the stuff between paydays.

ᚲᚹᚲ

from "GRASS"

We say of the oak, "How grand of girth!"
  Of the willow, we say, "How slender!"
And yet to the soft grass clothing the
  earth
  How slight is the praise we render.

        EDGAR FAWCETT, 1847 - 1904

ᚲᚹᚲ ᚲᚹᚲ ᚲᚹᚲ ᚲᚹᚲ ᚲᚹᚲ ᚲᚹᚲ ᚲᚹᚲ ᚲᚹᚲ ᚲᚹᚲ ᚲᚹᚲ ᚲᚹᚲ ᚲᚹᚲ ᚲᚹᚲ ᚲᚹᚲ

NO!

No sun—no moon!
No morn—no noon—
No dawn—no dusk—no proper time of
    day—
  No sky—no earthly view—
  No distance looking blue—
No road—no street—no "t'other side the
    way"—
  No end to any Row—
  No indications where the Crescents go—
  No top to any steeple—
No recognitions of familiar people—
  No courtesies for showing 'em—

No knowing 'em!
No travelling at all—no locomotion,
No inkling of the way—no notion—
  "No go"—by land or ocean—
  No mail—no post—
  No news from any foreign coast—
No park—no ring—no afternoon gentility—
  No company—no nobility—
No warmth, no cheerfulness, no healthful
    ease,
No comfortable feel in any member—
No shade, no shine, no butterflies, no bees,
No fruits, no flowers, no leaves, no birds,
  November!

        THOMAS HOOD, 1799 - 1845

ᚲᚹᚲ ᚲᚹᚲ ᚲᚹᚲ ᚲᚹᚲ ᚲᚹᚲ ᚲᚹᚲ ᚲᚹᚲ ᚲᚹᚲ ᚲᚹᚲ ᚲᚹᚲ ᚲᚹᚲ ᚲᚹᚲ ᚲᚹᚲ ᚲᚹᚲ

WANTED—A MINISTER'S WIFE

At length we have settled a pastor—
  I am sure I cannot tell why
The people should grow so restless,
  Or candidates grow so shy.
But after two years' searching
  For the "smartest" man in the land,
In a fit of desperation
  We took the nearest at hand.
And really he answers nicely
  To "fill the gap," you know,
To "run the machine" and "bring up
    arrears,"
  And make things generally go
He has a few little failings,
  His sermons are commonplace quite,
But his manner is very charming,
  And his teeth are pearly white.

And, so, of all the "dear people,"
  Not one in a hundred complains,
For beauty and grace of manner
  Are so much better than brains;
But the parish have all concluded
  He needs a partner for life,
To shine, a gem, in the parlor:
  "Wanted—a minister's wife!"

Wanted—a perfect lady,
  Delicate, gentle, refined,
With every beauty of person,
  And every endowment of mind,
Fitted by early culture
  To move in fashionable life—
Please notice our advertisement:
  "Wanted—a minister's wife!"

Wanted—a thoroughbred worker,
  Who well to her household looks,
(Shall we see our money wasted
  By extravagant Irish cooks?)
Who cuts the daily expenses
  With economy sharp as a knife,
And washes and scrubs in the kitchen—
  "Wanted—a minister's wife."

A "very domestic person,"
  To callers she must not be "out";
It has such a bad appearance
  For her to be gadding about—
Only to visit the parish
  Every year of her life,
And attend the funerals and weddings—
  "Wanted—a minister's wife."
To conduct the "ladies meetings,"
  The "sewing circle" attend,
And when we have work for the soldiers
  Her ready assistance to lend:
To clothe the destitute children,
  Where sorrow and want are rife;
To hunt up Sunday-school scholars—
  "Wanted—a minister's wife!"

Careful to entertain strangers,
  Traveling agents and "such,"
Of this kind of "angels' " visits
  The deacons have had so much
As to prove a perfect nuisance,
  And hope these "plagues of their life"
Can soon be sent to the parson's—
  "Wanted—a minister's wife!"

A perfect pattern of prudence
  To all others, spending less,
But never disgracing the parish
  By looking shabby in dress.
Playing the organ on Sunday
  Would aid our laudable strife
To save the society's money—
  "Wanted—a minister's wife."

And when we have found the person;
  We hope, by working the two,
To lift our debt and build a new church—
  Then we shall know what to do;
For they will be worn and weary,
  Needing a change of life,
And so we'll advertise, "Wanted,
  A minister and his wife!"

THE LOST SPECTACLES

A country curate, visiting his flock,
At old Rebecca's cottage gave a knock.
"Good morrow, dame, I mean not any
    libel,
But in your dwelling have you got a
    Bible?"
"A Bible, sir?" exclaimed she in a rage,
"D'ye think I've turned a Pagan in my
    age?
Here, Judith, and run upstairs, my dear,
'Tis in the drawer, be quick and bring it
    here."
The girl return'd with Bible in a minute,
Not dreaming for a moment what was in
    it;
When lo! on opening it at parlor door,
Down fell her spectacles upon the floor.
Amaz'd she stared, was for a moment
    dumb,
But quick exclaim'd, "Dear sir, I'm glad
    you're come.
'Tis six years since these glasses first was
    lost,
And I have miss'd 'em to my poor eyes'
    cost!"
Then as the glasses to her nose she raised,
She closed the Bible—saying, "God be
    praised!"

෴

As the mother's womb holds us for nine
months, making us ready, not for the
womb itself, but for life . .
                    SENECA 3 B.C.,—A.D. 65

IT ISN'T THE CHURCH—IT'S YOU

If you want to have the kind of a church
    Like the kind of a church you like,
You needn't slip your clothes in a grip
    And start on a long, long hike.

You'll only find what you left behind,
    For there's nothing really new.
It's a knock at yourself when you knock
    your church;
    It isn't the church—it's you.

When everything seems to be going wrong,
    And trouble seems everywhere brewing;
When prayer meeting, Young People's
    meeting, and all,
    Seem simmering slowly—stewing,
Just take a look at yourself and say,
    "What's the use of being blue?"
Are you doing your "bit" to make things
    "hit"?
    It isn't the church—it's you.

It's really strange sometimes, don't you
    know,
    That things go as well as they do,
When we think of the little—the very
    small mite—
    We add to the work of the few.
We sit, and stand round, and complain of
    what's done,
    And do very little but fuss.
Are we bearing our share of the burdens
    to bear?
    It isn't the church—it's us.

So, if you want to have the kind of a
    church
    Like the kind of a church you like,
Put off your guile, and put on your best
    smile,
    And hike, my brother, just hike,
To the work in hand that has to be
    done—
    The work of saving a few.
It isn't the church that is wrong, my boy;
    It isn't the church—it's you.

One minister says that he does not mind a man looking at his watch, during a sermon, but he does resent his shaking it to find out if it is still going.

Let us assume that entertainment is the sole end of reading; even so I think you would hold that no mental employment is so broadening to the sympathies or so enlightening to the understanding. Other pursuits belong not to all times, all ages, all conditions; but this gives stimulus to our youth and diversion to our old age; this adds a charm to success, and offers a haven of consolation to failure. Through the night-watches, on all our journeyings, and in our hours of ease, it is our unfailing companion.

CICERO 106 - 43 B.C.

from ALMA

For some in ancient books delight;
Others prefer what moderns write:
Now I should be extremely loth
Not to be thought expert in both.

MATTHEW PRIOR, 1664 - 1721

A little library, growing larger every year, is an honorable part of a man's possessions. A library is not a luxury. It is one of the necessities of a full life.

HENRY WARD BEECHER, 1813 - 1887

Some books are to be tasted, others to be swallowed, and some few to be chewed and digested.

FRANCIS BACON, 1561 - 1626

Except a living man there is nothing more wonderful than a book!

CHARLES KINGSLEY, 1819 - 1875

You should read it (a book) there is much that is skip-worthy.

Reading maketh a full man; conference a ready man; and writing an exact man.

When I am dead, I hope it may be said: "His sins were scarlet, but his books were read."

HILAIRE BELLOC

That is a good book, it seems to me, which is opened with expectation and closed with profit.

LOUISA M. ALCOTT, 1832 - 1888

There is no frigate like a book
To take us lands away,
Nor any coursers like a page
of prancing poetry

EMILY DICKINSON, 1830 - 1886

Writing a book is an adventure. To begin with, it is a toy and an amusement. Then it becomes a mistress, then it becomes a master, then it becomes a tyrant. The last phase is that just as you are about to be reconciled to your servitude, you kill the monster, and fling him to the public.

SIR WINSTON CHURCHILL, 1874 - 1965

W. M. Evarts (1818 - 1901) former Secretary of State, took Lord Coleridge to visit Mount Vernon. Lord Coleridge remarked that he had heard that Washington was able to throw a dollar across the Potomac to which Evarts replied, "You know a dollar would go much farther in those days."

THE SNOW STORM

Announced by all the trumpets of the sky,
Arrives the snow; and, driving o'er the fields,
Seems nowhere to alight; the whited air
Hides hills and woods, the river, and the
    heaven,
And veils the farm-house at the garden's end.
The sled and traveller stopped, the courier's
    feet
Delayed, all friends shut out, the housemates
    sit,
Around the radiant fireplace, enclosed
In a tumultuous privacy of storm.
        Come see the north-wind's masonry!
Out of an unseen quarry, evermore
Furnished with tile, the fierce artificer
Curves his white bastions with projected roof
Round every windward stake or tree or door;
Speeding, the myriad-handed, his wild work
So fanciful, so savage; naught cares he
For number or proportion. Mockingly,
On coop or kennel he hangs Parian wreaths;
A swan-like form invests the hidden thorn;
Fills up the farmer's lane from wall to wall,
Mauger the farmer sighs; and at the gate
A tapering turret overtops the work.
And when his hours are numbered, and the
    world
Is all his own, retiring as he were not,
Leaves, when the sun appears, astonished Art
To mimic in slow structures, stone by stone,
Built in an age, the mad wind's night-work,
The frolic architecture of the snow.

RALPH WALDO EMERSON

☙❦❧

VIXI

I have lived and I have loved;
I have waked and I have slept;
I have sung and I have danced;
I have smiled and I have wept;
I have won and wasted treasure;
I have had my fill of pleasure;
And all these things were weariness,
And some of them were dreariness;—
And all these things, but two things,
Were emptiness and pain:
And Love—it was the best of them;
And Sleep—worth all the rest of them;
Worth everything but Love to my spirit and
    my brain.
Be still my friend, O Slumber,
Till my days complete their number,
For Love shall never, never return to me
    again!

CHARLES MACKAY, 1814 - 1889

NOVEMBER

When thistle-blows do lightly float
About the pasture-height,
And shrills the hawk a parting note,
And creeps the frost at night,
Then hilly ho! though singing so,
And whistle as I may,
There comes again the old heart pain
Through all the livelong day.

In high wind creaks the leafless tree
And nods the fading fern;
The knolls are dun as snow-clouds be,
And cold the sun does burn.
Then ho, hollo! though calling so,
I cannot keep it down;
The tears arise unto my eyes,
And thoughts are chill and brown.

Far in the cedars' dusky stoles,
Where the sere ground-vine weaves,
The partridge drums funereal rolls
Above the fallen leaves.
And hip, hip, ho! though cheering so,
It stills no whit the pain;
For drip, drip, drip, from bare-branch tip,
I hear the year's last rain.

So drive the cold cows from the hill,
And call the wet sheep in;
And let their stamping clatter fill
The barn with warming din.
And ho, folk, ho! though it be so
That we no more may roam,
We still will find a cheerful mind
Around the fire at home!

C. L. CLEAVELAND

☙❦❧

from MACBETH, Act II, Scene 2

Sleep that knits up the ravell'd sleave of care,
The death of each day's life, sore labour's
    bath,
Balm of hurt minds, great nature's second
    course,
Chief nourisher in life's feast.

WILLIAM SHAKESPEARE

☙❦❧

One hour's sleep before midnight is worth
three afterwards.

GEORGE HERBERT, 1593 - 1633

☙❦❧

Sleep which will not be commanded.

GEORGE GORDON BYRON

219

DEFINITION OF "CORN LICKER"

It smells like gangrene starting in a mildewed silo, it tastes like the wrath to come, and when you absorb a deep swig of it you have all the sensations of having swallowed a lighted kerosene lamp. A sudden, violent jolt of it has been known to stop a victim's watch, snap his suspenders and crack his glass eye right across.

IRVIN S. COBB, 1876 - 1944
Given to Distillers' Code Authority, N.R.A.

Never miss an opportunity to make others happy even if you have to leave them alone to do it.

LIQUOR AND LONGEVITY

The horse and mule live thirty years
And nothing know of wines and beers.
The goat and sheep at twenty die
And never taste of Scotch or Rye.
The cow drinks water by the ton
And at eighteen is mostly done.
The dog at fifteen cashes in
Without the aid of rum and gin.
The cat in milk and water soaks
And then in twelve short years it croaks.
The modest, sober, bone-dry hen
Lays eggs for nogs, then dies at ten.
All animals are strictly dry:
They sinless live and swiftly die;
But sinful, ginful rum-soaked men
Survive for three score years and ten,
And some of them a very few,
Stay pickled till they're ninety-two.

THE BILL OF FARE

Pies of pumpkin, apples, mince,
Jams and jellies, peaches, quince,
Purple grapes, and apples red,
Cakes and nuts and gingerbread—
That's Thanksgiving.

Turkey! Oh, a great big fellow!
Fruits all ripe and rich and mellow,
Everything that's nice to eat,
More than I can now repeat—
That's Thanksgiving.

Lots and lots of jolly fun,
Games to play and races run,
All as happy as can be—
For this happiness, you can see,
Makes Thanksgiving.

We must thank the One who gave
All the good things that we have;
That is why we keep the day
Set aside, our mamas say,
For Thanksgiving.

EUGENE FIELD, 1850 - 1895

When it shall be said in any country in the world, "My poor are happy; neither ignorance nor distress is to be found among them; my jails are empty of prisoners, my streets of beggars; the aged are not in want; the taxes are not oppressive; the rational world is my friend, because I am a friend of its happiness"—when these things can be said, then may that country boast of its constitution and its government.

THOMAS PAINE, 1737 - 1809

220

HIS MOTHER-IN-LAW

He stood on his head by the wild
seashore,
    And danced on his hands a jig;
In all his emotions, as never before,
    A wildly hilarious grig.

And why? In that ship just crossing the
bay
    His mother-in-law had sailed
For a tropical country far away,
    Where tigers and fever prevailed.

Oh, now he might hope for a peaceful
life
    And even be happy yet,
Though owning no end of neuralgic wife,
    And up to his collar in debt.

He had borne the old lady through thick
and thin,
    And she lectured him out of breath;
And now he looked at the ship she was in
    He howled for her violent death.

He watched as the good ship cut the sea,
    And bumpishly up-and-downed,
And thought if already she qualmish might
be,
    He'd consider his happiness crowned.

He watched till beneath the horizon's edge
    The ship was passing from view,
And he sprang to the top of a rocky ledge
    And pranced like a kangaroo.

He watched till the vessel became a speck
    That was lost in the wandering sea,
And then, at the risk of breaking his neck,
    Turned somersaults home to tea.
                     WALTER PARKE

I fear that in the selection of a wife, as
in a project of war, to err but once, is to
be undone forever.
               THOMAS MIDDLETON, 1570 - 1627

Whistling girls and crowing hens
Will surely come to some bad ends.
                       (OLD PROVERB)

IF YOU HAD A BANK

If you had a bank that credited your
account each morning with $86,400, that
carried over no balance from day to day,
and allowed you to keep no cash in your
account, and every evening cancelled whatever part of the amount you had failed to
use during the day, what would you do?
Draw out every cent, of course!

Well, you have such a bank, and its name
is "Time." Every morning it credits you
with 86,400 seconds. Every night it rules
off, as lost, whatever of this you have failed
to invest to good purpose. It carries over no
balances. It allows no overdrafts. Each day
it opens a new account with you. Each night
it burns the records of the day. If you fail
to use the day's deposits the loss is yours.
There is no going back. There is no drawing
against the "tomorrow." You must live in
the present—on today's deposits. Invest it
so as to get from it the utmost in health,
happiness and success!

THE FALL WIND

The wind has stalked adown the garden
path,
    And blown the lights of all the poor
    flowers out;
    From maple wood I hear his stormy
    shout;
The russet leaves take flight before his
wrath;
In stubble fields and clover-aftermath,
    The wreckage of the year is strewn
    around;
    The mottled asters lie upon the ground.
Of all the bloom, the tyrant north wind
hath
Left only golden-rod, in saffron rows,—
And these, with bulging cheeks, he blows
and blows,
    Until they glow, and mingle with the
    west,
When setting suns lean low upon the land,
    And songless birds, in cheerless plumage
    dressed,
Wing south or somewhere; mute,
    discouraged band.
                 JOHN STUART THOMSON

THE CANDIDATE'S LETTER

Dear Sir,—You wish to know my notions
  On sartan pints thet rile the land;
There's nothin' thet my natur so shuns
  Ez bein' mum or underhand;
I'm a straight-spoken kind o' creetur
  Thet blurts right out wut's in his head,
An' ef I've one pecooler feetur,
  It is a nose thet wun't be led.

So, to begin at the beginnin'
  An' come direcly to the pint,
I think the country's underpinnin'
  Is some consid'ble out o' jint;
I ain't agoin' to try your patience
  By tellin' who done this or thet,
I don't make no insinooations,
  I jest let on I smell a rat.

Ez fer the war, I go agin' it,—
  I mean to say I kind o' du,—
Thet is, I mean thet, bein' in it,
  The best way wuz to fight it thru;
Not but wut abstract war is horrid,
  I sign to thet with all my heart,—
But civlyzation doos git forrid
  Sometimes upon a powder-cart.

JAMES RUSSELL LOWELL, 1819 - 1891

AN ANCIENT PRAYER

Give me a good digestion, Lord, and also
  something to digest;
Give me a healthy body, Lord, and sense
  to keep it at its best.
Give me a healthy mind, good Lord, to
  keep the good and pure in sight;
Which, seeing sin, is not appalled, but finds
  a way to set it right.

Give me a mind that is not bound, that
  does not whimper, whine or sigh.
Don't let me worry overmuch about the
  fussy thing called I.
Give me a sense of humor, Lord; give me
  the grace to see a joke,
To get some happiness from life and pass
  it on to other folk.

THOMAS H. B. WEBB

from TO NIGHT

Bend low, O dusky Night,
  And give my spirit rest,
  Hold me to your deep breast,
And put old cares to flight,
Give back the lost delight
  That once my soul possest,
  When Love was loveliest

LOUISE CHANDLER MOULTON, 1835 - 1908

OLD MORALITY

Sound, sound the clarion, fill the fife!
To all the sensual world proclaim
One crowded hour of glorious life
Is worth an age without a name.

SIR WALTER SCOTT, 1771 - 1832

from SPECTATOR AB EXTRA

As I sat at the cafe I said to myself,
They may talk as they please about what
  they call pelf,
They may sneer as they like about eating
  and drinking,
But help it I cannot, I cannot help thinking
  How pleasant it is to have money,
  heigh-ho!
  How pleasant it is to have money . . . .

They may talk as they please about what
  they call pelf,
And how one ought never to think of
  one's self,
How pleasures of thought surpass eating
  and drinking,
My pleasure of thought is the pleasure of
  thinking
  How pleasant it is to have money,
  heigh-ho!
  How pleasant it is to have money . . . .

ARTHUR HUGH CLOUGH, 1819 - 1861

Hoist up the sail while gale doth last
Tide and wind stay no man's pleasure.
ROBERT SOUTHWELL, 1561 - 1595

❧❀❧

Truly there is a tide in the affairs of men, but there is no gulf-stream setting forever in one direction.

JAMES R. LOWELL, 1819 - 1891

❧❀❧

Many an opportunity is lost because a man is out looking for four-leaf clovers.

❧❀❧

The secret of success is making hay with the grass that grows under other people's feet.

❧❀❧

We need equal opportunities for more people, and more people who are equal to them.

❧❀❧

The trouble with opportunity is that it always is disguised as hard work.

❧❀❧

OPPORTUNITY

This I beheld, or dreamed it in a dream:—
There spread a cloud of dust along a plain;
And underneath the cloud, or in it, raged
A furious battle, and men yelled, and
*   swords*
Shocked upon swords and shields. A
*   prince's banner*
Wavered, then staggered backward,
*   hemmed by foes.*
A craven hung above the battle's edge,
And thought,"Had I a sword of keener
*   steel—*
That blue blade that the king's son bears,
*   —but this*
Blunt thing—!" he snapt and flung it from
*   his hand,*
And lowering crept away and left the
*   field.*
Then came the king's son, wounded, sore
*   bestead,*
And weaponless, and saw the broken
*   sword,*
Hilt-buried in the dry and trodden sand,
And ran and snatched it, and with battle-
*   shout*
Lifted afresh he hewed his enemy down,
And saved a great cause that heroic day.
EDWARD ROWLAND SILL, 1841 - 1887

OPPORTUNITY

Master of human destinies am I!
Fame, love, and fortune on my footsteps
*   wait.*
Cities and fields I walk; I penetrate
Deserts and seas remote, and passing by
Hovel and mart and palace—soon or late
I knock unbidden once at every gate!

If sleeping, wake—if feasting, rise before
I turn away. It is the hour of fate,
And they who follow me reach every
*   state*
Mortals desire, and conquer every foe
Save death; but those who doubt or
*   hesitate,*
Condemned to failure, penury and woe,
Seek me in vain and uselessly implore.
I answer not, and I return no more!
JOHN JAMES INGALLS, 1833 - 1900

❧❀❧

from JULIUS CAESAR, Scene 3, Act IV

There is a tide in the affairs of men,
Which, taken at the flood, leads on to
*   fortune;*
Omitted, all the voyage of their life
Is bound in shallows and in miseries.
On such a full sea are we now afloat;
And we must take the current when it
*   serves,*
Or lose our ventures.

WM. SHAKESPEARE

223

TO HELEN

Helen, thy beauty is to me
  Like those Nicaean barks of yore,
That gently, o'er a perfumed sea,
  The weary, wayworn wanderer bore
  To his own native shore.

On desperate seas long wont to roam,
  Thy hyacinth hair, thy classic face,
Thy Naiad airs, have brought me home
  To the glory that was Greece
  And the grandeur that was Rome.

Lo! in yon brilliant window-niche
  How statue-like I see thee stand,
The agate lamp within thy hand!
  Ah, Psyche, from the regions which
  Are Holy Land!

EDGAR ALLAN POE, 1809 - 1849

BOATS SAIL ON THE RIVERS

Boats sail on the rivers,
  And ships sail on the seas;
But clouds that sail across the sky
  Are prettier far than these.

There are bridges on the rivers,
  As pretty as you please;
But the bow that bridges heaven,
  And overtops the trees,
And builds a road from earth to sky,
  Is prettier far than these.

CHRISTINA GEORGINA ROSSETTI, 1830 - 1894

⧫

A man's real life is that accorded to him
in the thoughts of other men by reason of
respect or natural love.

JOSEPH CONRAD, 1857 - 1924
Under Western Eyes (Part I)

We live in deeds, not years; in thoughts, not breaths; in feelings, not
in figures on a dial. We should count time by heart throbs. He most
lives who thinks most, feels the noblest, acts the best.—

PHILIP JAMES BAILEY

HOW MANY TIMES

How many times do I love thee, dear?
  Tell me how many thoughts there be
    In the atmosphere
    Of a new-fall'n year,
Whose white and sable hours appear
  The latest flake of Eternity;
So many times do I love thee, dear.

How many times do I love, again?
  Tell me how many beads there are
    In a silver chain
    Of the evening rain,
Unravelled from the tumbling main,
  And threading the eye of a yellow star,
So many times do I love again.

THOMAS LOVELL BEDDOES, 1803 - 1849

from MR. DOOLEY'S OPINIONS— THANKSGIVING

"Whin I was a young man," said Mr.
Dooley, "I often heerd Thanksgivin' day
alooded to fr'm th' altar as a pagan fisti-
val. Father Kelly don't think so. He says
't was founded by th' Puritans to give
thanks f'r bein' presarved fr'm th'
Indyans, an' that we keep it to give
thanks we are presarved fr'm th' Puritans."

FINLEY PETER DUNNE, 1867 - 1936

224

A THANKSGIVING DAY PRAYER

Delivered in the United States Senate
Wednesday, November 26, 1947

Our Father in heaven, if ever we had cause to offer unto Thee our fervent thanks, surely it is now, on the eve of our Thanksgiving Day, when we, the people of this Nation, are comfortable, well-fed, well-clad, and blessed with good things beyond our deserving. May gratitude, the rarest of all virtues, be the spirit of our observance.

Let not feasting, football, and festivity end in forgetfulness of God.

May the desperate need of the rest of the world, and our own glorious heritage, remind us of the God who led our fathers every step of the way by which they advanced to the character of an independent nation.

For if we do not have the grace to thank Thee for all that we have and enjoy, how can we have the effrontery to seek Thy further blessings? God, give us grateful hearts. For Jesus' sake. Amen.

SENATE CHAPLAIN PETER MARSHALL

BIRDS

Sure maybe ye've heard the storm-thrush
Whistlin' bould in March,
Before there's a primrose peepin' out,
Or a wee red cone on the larch;
Whistlin' the sun to come out o' the cloud,
An' the wind to come over the sea,
But for all he can whistle so clear an' loud,
He's never the bird for me.

Sure maybe ye've seen the song-thrush
After an April rain
Slip from in-undher the drippin' leaves,
Wishful to sing again;
An' low wi' love when he's near the nest,
An' loud from the top o' the tree,
But for all he can flutter the heart in your breast,
He's never the bird for me.

Sure maybe ye've heard the red-breast
Singin' his lone on a thorn,
Mindin' himself o' the dear days lost,
Brave wid his heart forlorn.
The time is in dark November,
An' no spring hopes has he:
"Remember," he sings, "remember!"
Ay, thon's the wee bird for me.

MOIRA O'NEILL

THE PUMPKIN

Ah! on Thanksgiving Day, when from East and from West,
From North and from South come the pilgrim and guest,
When the gray-haired New Englander sees round his board
The old broken links of affection restored,
When the care-wearied man seeks his mother once more,
And the worn matron smiles where the girl smiled before,
What moistens the lip and what brightens the eye?
What calls back the past, like the rich Pumpkin pie?
Oh—fruit loved of boyhood—the old days recalling,
When wood-grapes were purpling and brown nuts were falling!
When wild, ugly faces we carved in its skin,
Glaring out through the dark with a candle within!

When we laughed round the corn-heap, with hearts all in tune,
Our chair a broad pumpkin,—our lantern the moon,
Telling tales of a fairy who travelled like steam,
In a pumpkin-shell coach, with two rats for her team!

JOHN GREENLEAF WHITTIER, 1807 - 1892

from
CAPTAIN YOUNG'S THANKSGIVING

Thanksgiving-day, I fear,
If one the solemn truth must touch,
Is celebrated not so much
To thank the Lord for blessings o'er,
As for the sake of getting more!

WILL CARLETON, 1845 - 1912

225

THE GETTYSBURG ADDRESS

Fourscore and seven years ago our fathers brought forth upon this continent a new nation, conceived in liberty, and dedicated to the proposition that all men are created equal. Now we are engaged in a great civil war, testing whether that nation, or any nation so conceived and so dedicated, can long endure. We are met on a great battlefield of that war. We have come to dedicate a portion of that field as a final resting place for those who here gave their lives that that nation might live. It is altogether fitting and proper that we should do this. But in a larger sense we cannot dedicate, we cannot consecrate, we cannot hallow this ground. The brave men, living and dead, who struggled here, have consecrated it far above our poor power to add or detract. The world will little note, nor long remember, what we say here; but it can never forget what they did here. It is for us, the living, rather to be dedicated here to the unfinished work which they who fought here have thus far so nobly advanced. It is rather for us to be here dedicated to the great task remaining before us, that from these honored dead we take increased devotion to that cause for which they gave the last full measure of devotion; that we here highly resolve that these dead shall not have died in vain; that this nation, under God, shall have a new birth of freedom, and that government of the people, by the people, and for the people, shall not perish from the earth.

ABRAHAM LINCOLN, 1809 - 1865

Delivered at Gettysburg, Pennsylvania, November 19, 1863.

ON THE AMERICAN FLAG

We take the star from heaven, the red from our mother country, separate it by white stripes, thus showing that we have separated from her, and the white stripes shall go down to posterity representing liberty.

GEORGE WASHINGTON, 1732 - 1799

THE CONSTITUTION
Salmon Portland Chase

The Constitution, in all its provisions, looks to an indestructible Union composed of indestructible States.

—From *Decision* in Texas vs. White

If a nation expects to be ignorant and free in a state of civilization, it expects what never was and never will be.

THOMAS JEFFERSON, 1743 - 1826

The man who loves other countries as much as his own stands on a level with the man who loves other women as much as he loves his own wife.

THEODORE ROOSEVELT, speech, 1918

No man is above the law and no man is below it; nor do we ask any man's permission when we require him to obey it.

THEODORE ROOSEVELT
(Message to Congress 1904)

226

WHEN THE
FROST IS ON THE PUNKIN

When the frost is on the punkin and the
  fodder's in the shock,
And you hear the kyouck and gobble of
  the struttin' turkey-cock,
And the clakin' of the guineys, and the
  cluckin' of the hens,
And the rooster's hallylooyer as he tiptoes
  on the fence;
O, it's then's the times a feller is a-feelin'
  at his best,
With the risin' sun to greet him from a
  night of peaceful rest,
As he leaves the house, bareheaded, and
  goes out to feed the stock,
When the frost is on the punkin and the
  fodder's in the shock.

They's something kindo' harty-like about
  the atmusfere
When the heat of summer's over and the
  coolin' fall is here.
Of course we miss the flowers, and the
  blossoms on the trees,
And the mumble of the hummin'-birds and
  buzzin of the bees;
But the air's so appetizin'; and the
  landscape through the haze
Of a crisp and sunny morning of the airly
  autumn days
Is a pictur' that no painter has the colorin'
  to mock—
When the frost is on the punkin and the
  fodder's in the shock.

The husky, rusty russel of the tossels of
  the corn,
And the raspin' of the tangled leaves, as
  golden as the morn,
The stubble in the furries—kindo'
  lonesome-like, but still
A-preachin' sermuns to us of the barns
  they growed to fill,
The strawstack in the medder, and the
  reaper in the shed,
The hosses in theyr stalls below—the
  clover overhead!—
O, it sets my hart a-clickin' like the tickin'
  of a clock,
When the frost is on the punkin and the
  fodder's in the shock.

Then your apples all is getherd, and the
  ones a feller keeps
Is poured around the celler-floor in red
  and yeller heaps;
And your cider-makin's over, and your
  wimmern-folks is through
With their mince and apple-butter, and
  theyr souse and saussage, too! . . .
I don't know how to tell it—but ef sich a
  thing could be
As the Angels wantin' boardin', and they'd
  call around on me—
I'd want to 'commodate 'em—all the
  whole-indurin' flock—
When the frost is on the punkin and the
  fodder's in the shock.

JAMES WHITCOMB RILEY, 1852 - 1916

SERVICE

All service ranks the same with God:
If now, as formerly he trod
Paradise, his presence fills
Our earth, each only as God wills
Can work—God's puppets, best and worst,
Are we; there is no last nor first.

Say not " a small event!" Why "small"?
Costs it more pain than this, ye call
A "great event," should come to pass,
Than that? Untwine me from the mass
Of deeds which make up life, one deed
Power shall fall short in or exceed!

ROBERT BROWNING, 1812 - 1889

(From Pippa Passes)

ᏸᏯᏸ

First of all, we must observe that in all
these matters of human action the too little and the too much are alike ruinous, as
we can see (to illustrate the spiritual by
the natural) in matters of strength and
health. Too much and too little exercise
alike impair the strength, and too much
meat and drink and too little both alike
destroy the health, but the fitting amount
produces and preserves them. So, too, the
man who takes his fill of every pleasure
and abstains from none becomes a profli-
gate; while he who shuns all becomes
stolid and insusceptible.

ARISTOTLE, 384 - 322 B.C.

ᏸᏯᏸ

A RECIPE FOR SANITY

Are you worsted in a fight?
*   Laugh it off.*
Are you cheated of your right?
*   Laugh it off.*
Don't make tragedy of trifles,
Don't shoot butterflies with rifles—
*   Laugh it off.*

Does your work get into kinks?
*   Laugh it off.*
Are you near all sorts of brinks?
*   Laugh it off.*
If it's sanity you're after,
There's no recipe like laughter—
*   Laugh it off.*

HENRY RUTHERFORD ELLIOT

THE FROST

The Frost looked forth, one still, clear
*   night,*
And he said, "Now I shall be out of sight;
So through the valley and over the height
*   In silence I'll take my way.*
I will not go like that blustering train,
The wind and the snow, the hail and the
*   rain,*
Who make so much bustle and noise in
*   vain,*
*   But I'll be as busy as they!"*

Then he went to the mountain, and
*   powdered its crest,*
He climbed up the trees, and their boughs
*   he dressed*
With diamonds and pearls, and over the
*   breast*
*   Of the quivering lake he spread*
A coat of mail, that it need not fear
The downward point of many a spear
That he hung on its margin, far and near,
*   Where a rock could rear its head.*

He went to the windows of those who
*   slept,*
And over each pane like a fairy crept;
Wherever he breathed, wherever he stepped,
*   By the light of the moon were seen*
Most beautiful things. There were flowers
*   and trees,*
There were bevies of birds and swarms of
*   bees,*
There were cities, thrones, temples, and
*   towers, and these*
*   All pictured in silver sheen!*

But he did one thing that was hardly
*   fair,—*
He peeped in the cupboard, and, finding
*   there*
That all had forgotten for him to
*   prepare,—*
*   "Now, just to set them a-thinking,*
I'll bite this basket of fruit," said he;
"This costly pitcher I'll burst in three,
And the glass of water they've left for me
*   Shall 'tchick!' to tell them I'm drinking.'*

HANNAH FLAGG GOULD, 1789 - 1865

ᏸᏯᏸ

Some people are so painfully good that
they would rather be right than be pleasant.

L. C. BALL

DON'T QUIT

When things go wrong, as they sometimes
    will,
When the road you're trudging seems all
    up hill,
When the funds are low and the debts are
    high,
And you want to smile, but you have to
    sigh,
When care is pressing you down a bit,
Rest, if you must—but don't you quit.

Life is queer with its twists and turns,
As everyone of us sometimes learns,
And many a failure turns about
When he might have won had he stuck it
    out;
Don't give up, though the pace seems
    slow—
You might succeed with another blow.

Often the goal is nearer than
It seems to a faint and faltering man,
Often the struggler has given up
When he might have captured the victor's
    cup.
And he learned too late, when the night
    slipped down,
How close he was to the golden crown.

Success is failure turned inside out—
The silver tint of the clouds of doubt—
And you never can tell how close you are,
It may be near when it seems afar;
So stick to the fight when you're hardest
    hit—
It's when things seem worst that you
    mustn't quit.

❦

TO MAKE A PRAIRIE

To make a prairie it takes a clover and one
    bee,—
And revery.
The revery alone will do
If bees are few.

EMILY DICKINSON, 1830 - 1886

❦

Everybody is a potential murderer. I've
never killed anyone, but I frequently get
satisfaction reading the obituary notices.

CLARENCE DARROW, 1857 - 1935

ODE ON SOLITUDE

Happy the man, whose wish and care
A few paternal acres bound,
Content to breathe his native air
    In his own ground.

Whose herds with milk, whose fields with
    bread,
Whose flocks supply him with attire;
Whose trees in summer yield him shade,
    In winter, fire.

Blest, who can unconcernedly find
Hours, days, and years, slide soft away
In health of body, peace of mind,
    Quiet by day;

Sound sleep by night; study and ease
Together mixed, sweet recreation,
And innocence, which most does please,
    With meditation.

Thus let me live, unseen, unknown;
Thus unlamented let me die;
Steal from the world, and not a stone
    Tell where I lie.

ALEXANDER POPE, 1688 - 1744

❦

It takes a great deal of boldness mixed
with a vast deal of caution to acquire a
fortune; but then it takes ten times as
much with it to keep it after you have
got it as it took to make it.

MAYER A. ROTHCHILD, 1773 - 1855

❦

Never give a man up until he has failed at
something he likes.

WARDEN LEWIS E. LAWES, 1883 - 1947

❦

It may be that the race is not always to
the swift, nor the battle to the strong—
but that's the way to bet.

DAMON RUNYON, 1884 - 1946

❦

On the whole, I'd rather be in Philadelphia.

W. C. Fields' epitaph suggested by himself.

"BREAK, BREAK, BREAK"

Break, break, break,
On thy cold gray stones, O Sea!
And I would that my tongue could utter
The thoughts that arise in me.

O, well for the fisherman's boy,
That he shouts with his sister at play!
O, well for the sailor lad,
That he sings in his boat on the bay!

And the stately ships go on,
To their haven under the hill;
But O for the touch of a vanished hand,
And the sound of a voice that is still!

Break, break, break,
At the foot of thy crags, O Sea!
But the tender grace of a day that is dead
Will never come back to me.
ALFRED, LORD TENNYSON, 1809 - 1892

from O WORLD

Columbus found a world and had no
chart,
Save one that faith deciphered in the skies
To trust the soul's invincible surmise
Was all his science and his only art.
GEORGE SANTAYANA

Every ship that comes to America gets
its chart from Columbus.
RALPH WALDO EMERSON

"Into Thy hands I give my soul"
Columbus' last words

COLUMBUS

Behind him lay the grey Azores,
Behind the Gates of Hercules;
Before him not the ghost of shores,
Before him only shoreless seas.
The good mate said: "Now must we pray,
For lo! the very stars are gone.
Brave Admiral, speak, what shall I say?"
"Why, say 'Sail on! sail on! and on!' "

"My men grow mutinous day by day;
My men grow ghastly wan and weak."
The stout mate thought of home; a spray
Of salt wave washed his swarthy cheek.
"What shall I say, brave Admiral, say,
If we sight naught but seas at dawn?"
"Why, you shall say at break of day,
'Sail on! sail on! sail on! and on!' "

They sailed and sailed, as winds might
blow,
Until at last the blanched mate said,
"Why, now not even God would know
Should I and all my men fall dead.
These very winds forget their way,

For God from these dread seas is gone.
Now speak, brave Admiral, speak and
say"—
He said: "Sail on! sail on! and on!"
They sailed. They sailed. Then spake the
mate:
"This mad sea shows his teeth to-night.
He curls his lip, he lies in wait,
With lifted teeth, as if to bite!
Brave Admiral, say but one good word:
What shall we do when hope is gone?"
The words leapt like a leaping sword:
"Sail on! sail on! sail on! and on!"

Then, pale and worn, he kept his deck,
And peered through darkness. Ah, that
night
Of all dark nights! And then a speck—
A light! a light! a light! a light!
It grew, a starlit flag unfurled!
It grew to be Time's burst of dawn.

He gained a world; he gave that world
Its grandest lesson: "On! sail on!"

JOAQUIN MILLER, 1841 - 1913

DECEMBER

"Sing hey! Sing hey!
For Christmas Day."

SEVEN TIMES ONE

There's no dew left on the daisies and
  clover,
  There's no rain left in heaven:
I've said my "seven times" over and over,
  Seven times one are seven.

I am old, so old, I can write a letter;
  My birthday lessons are done;
The lambs play always, they know no
  better,
  They are only one times one.

O moon! in the night I have seen you
  sailing
  And shining so round and low;
You were bright! ah bright! but your light
  is failing—
  You are nothing now but bow.

You moon, have you done something
  wrong in heaven
  That God has hidden your face?
I hope if you have you will soon be
  forgiven,
  And shine again in your place.

O velvet bee, you're a dusty fellow,
  You've powder'd your legs with gold!
O brave marsh marybuds, rich and yellow,
  Give me your money to hold!

O columbine, open your folded wrapper,
  Where two twin turtle doves dwell!
O cuckoopint, toll me the purple clapper
  That hangs on your clear green bell!

And show me your nest with the young
  ones in it;
  I will not steal them away;
I am old, you may trust me, linnet,
  linnet—
  I am seven times one today.

                    JEAN INGELOW, 1820 - 1897

◦◦◦

THE SAD TALE OF MR. MEARS

There was a man who had a clock,
  His name was Matthew Mears;
And every day he wound that clock
  For eight and twenty years.

And then one day he found that clock
  An eight-day clock to be;
And a madder man than Matthew Mears
  You would not wish to see.

WHAT IS AGE?

Age is opportunity no less
Than youth itself, though in another dress.
And as the evening twilight fades away,
The sky is filled with stars invisible by
  day.
      HENRY WADSWORTH LONGFELLOW, 1807 - 1882

THIRTY-FIVE

Oft in danger, yet alive,
We come to thirty-five;
Long may better years arrive,
Better years than thirty-five,
Could philosophers contrive
Life to stop at thirty-five.
Time his hours should never drive
O'er the bounds of thirty-five.
High to soar and deep to dive,
Nature gives at thirty-five.
Ladies, stock and tend your hive,
Trifle not at thirty-five
For, howe'er we boast and strive,
Life declines from thirty-five:
He that ever hopes to thrive
Must begin by thirty-five;
And all who wisely wish to wive
Should not delay at thirty-five.

SIXTY-EIGHTH BIRTHDAY

As life runs on, the road grows strange
With faces new, and near the end
The Milestones into headstones change,
'Neath every one a friend.
          JAMES RUSSELL LOWELL, 1819 - 1891

◦◦◦

SEVENTY YEAR CLOCKS

Our brains are seventy-year clocks. The
Angel of Life winds them up once for all,
then closes the case, and gives the key into
the hand of the Angel of the Resurrection.
          OLIVER WENDELL HOLMES, 1809 - 1894

233

GOOD TIMBER

The tree that never had to fight
For sun and air and light
That stood out in the open plain,
And always got it's share of rain,
Never became a forest king
But lived and died a scrubby thing.

The man who never had to toil,
Who never had to win his share,
Of sun and sky and light and air,
Never became a manly man
But lived and died as he began.

Good timber does not grow in ease;
The stronger wind, the tougher trees.
The farther sky, the greater length;
The more the storm, the more the
*   strength;*
By sun and cold, by rain and snows,
In tree or man good timber grows.

Where thickest stands the forest growth
We find the patriarchs of both,
And they hold converse with the stars
Whose broken branches show the scars
Of many winds and much of strife—
This is the common law of life.

◦◦◦

from THE IRON GATE

Youth longs and manhood strives, but age
*   remembers,*
Sits by the raked-up ashes of the past,
Spreads its thin hands above the whitening
*   embers*
That warm its creeping life-blood to the
*   last.*

OLIVER WENDELL HOLMES, 1809 - 1894

◦◦◦

from MEN I DISLIKE

But oh! the biggest muff afloat
Is he who takes to anecdote.

H. S. LEIGH, 1837 - 1883

from
SONG TO THE EVENING STAR

Star that bringest home the bee,
And sett'st the weary laborer free!
If any star shed peace, 'tis thou
That send'st it from above.

THOMAS CAMPBELL, 1777 - 1844

◦◦◦

MY HEART LEAPS UP WHEN I BEHOLD

My heart leaps up when I behold
A rainbow in the sky:
So was it when my life began;
So is it now I am a man;
So be it when I shall grow old,
Or let me die!
The Child is father of the Man;
And I could wish my days to be
Bound each to each by natural piety.

WILLIAM WORDSWORTH, 1770 - 1850

◦◦◦

Another way of making enemies is to talk to your friends as only a friend should.

◦◦◦

Nothing is more dishonorable than an old man, heavy with years, who has no other evidence of having lived long except his age..

SENECA

◦◦◦

"Oh to be sixty again!

Atrributed to O. W. Holmes Jr. viewing a pretty girl at the age of 87.

◦◦◦

Old Age isn't so bad when you consider the alternative.

MAURICE CHEVALIER

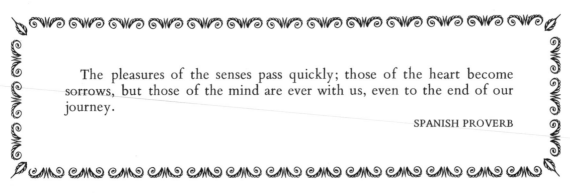

The pleasures of the senses pass quickly; those of the heart become sorrows, but those of the mind are ever with us, even to the end of our journey.

SPANISH PROVERB

from BALLADE OF MIDDLE AGE

Our youth began with tears and sighs,
  With seeking what we could not find;
Our verses all were threnodies,
  In elegiacs still we whined;
Our ears were deaf, our eyes were blind,
We sought and knew not what we sought.
  We marvel, now we look behind:
Life's more amusing than we thought!

Oh, foolish youth, untimely wise!
  Oh, phantoms of the sickly mind!
What? not content with seas and skies,
  With rainy clouds and southern wind,
  With common cares and faces kind,
With pains and joys each morning
      brought?
  Ah, old, and worn, and tired we find
Life's more amusing than we thought!

Though youth "turns spectre-thin and
      dies,"
  To mourn for youth we're not inclined;
We set our souls on salmon flies,
  We whistle where we once repined.
  Confound the woes of human-kind!
By Heaven we're "well deceived," I wot;
  Who hum, contented or resigned,
"Life's more amusing than we thought!"

ANDREW LANG, 1844 - 1912

❦

The shape of my life is, of course, determined by many other things; my background and childhood, my mind and its education, my conscience and its pressures, my heart and its desires. I want to give and take from my children and husband, to share with friends and community, to carry out my obligations to man and to the world, as a woman, as an artist, as a citizen.

But I want first of all—in fact, as an end to these other desires—to be at peace with myself. I want a singleness of eye, a purity of intention, a central core to my life that will enable me to carry out these obligations and activities, as well as I can. I want, in fact—to borrow from the language of the saints—to live "in grace" as much of the time as possible. I am not using this term in a strictly theological sense. By grace I mean an inner harmony, essentially spiritual, which can be translated into outward harmony.

ANNE MORROW LINDBERGH
from Gift from the Sea

A BIRTHDAY

My heart is like a singing bird
  Whose nest is in a watered shoot;
My heart is like an apple tree
  Whose boughs are bent with thickest
      fruit;
My heart is like a rainbow shell
  That paddles in a halcyon sea—
My heart is gladder than all these,
  Because my love is come to me.

Raise me a dais of silk and down,
  Hang it with vair and purple dyes,
Carve it in doves, and pomegranates,
  And peacocks with a hundred eyes;
Work it in gold and silver grapes,
  In leaves, and silver fleur-de-lys,
Because the birthday of my life
  Is come, my love is come to me.

CHRISTINA ROSSETTI, 1830 - 1894

❦

Among the more elderly inhabitants of the South I found a melancholy tendency to date every event of importance on the late War. "How beautiful the moon is tonight," I once remarked to a gentlemen standing near me. "Yes," was his reply, "but you should have seen it before the War."

OSCAR WILDE

❦

The tree of deepest root is found
Least willing still to quit the ground
'Twas therefore said by ancient sages
That love of life increased with years.
So much that in our later stages,
When pains grow sharp, and sickness rages
The greatest love of life appears.

HESTER L. PIOZZI, 1741 - 1821

❦

Our youth have an insatiable desire for wealth; they have bad manners and atrocious customs regarding dressing their hair and what garments or shoes they wear.

PLATO, 428 - 347 B.C.

from INTRODUCTION TO "WITNESS TO THE TRUTH"

It was said of the great English Scientist, "He made it easy for people to believe in goodness." Whoever does that in any degree, through an unselfish deed or a courageous word or a compassionate thought, helps others to believe in the indestructibility of goodness, and belief in goodness makes it indestructible. This lifts up the life of every man to an overwhelming importance. All that is good in the world now is in our hands. Upon us depends the reality of God here on the earth today. We alone can give proof that He is. "No man hath seen God at any time. If we love one another God dwelleth in us."

EDITH HAMILTON

BRIGHT STAR

Bright star, would I were stedfast as thou
    art—
    Not in lone splendour hung aloft the
    night
And watching, with eternal lids apart,
    Like nature's patient, sleepless Eremite,
The moving waters at their priestlike task
    Of pure ablution round earth's human
    shores,
Or gazing on the new soft-fallen mask
    Of snow upon the mountains and
    moors—
No—yet still stedfast, still unchangeable,
    Pillow'd upon my fair love's ripening
    breast,
    To feel for ever its soft fall and swell,
    Awake for ever in a sweet unrest,
Still, still to hear her tender-taken breath,
And so live ever—or else swoon to death.

JOHN KEATS, 1795 - 1821

ALL THINGS EXCEPT MYSELF I KNOW

I know when milk does flies contain;
    I know men by their bravery;
I know fair days from storm and rain;
    And what fruit apple-trees supply;
    And from their gums the trees descry;
I know when all things smoothly flow;
    I know who toil or idle lie;
All things except myself I know.

Know horse from mule by tail and mane;
    I know their worth or high or low;
Bell, Beatrice, I know the twain;
    I know each chance of cards and dice;
    I know what visions prophesy,
Bohemian heresies, I trow;
    I know men of each quality;
All things except myself I know.

ENVOY

Prince, I know all things 'neath the sky,
    Pale cheeks from those of rosy glow;
I know death whence can no man fly;
    All things except myself I know.

FRANCOIS VILLON, 1431 - 1484

Silence is a true friend who never betrays.

CONFUCIUS

THE GOD I KNOW

The God I know is a God close by,
Not seated on throne in far-off sky;
He is here on this earth, reflected in trees,
In mountains, in flowers, in sweet summer
    breeze,
In ocean's grandeur, in plain's delight,
In noontide glare, and in stilly night,
In children's prattle, in manhood's prime,
Since the birth of worlds until end of
    time.
For the God I know, with a thought that's
    free
Is the God of love, found in you and me.

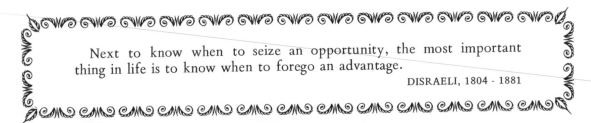

Next to know when to seize an opportunity, the most important thing in life is to know when to forego an advantage.

DISRAELI, 1804 - 1881

THE TWENTY-SECOND OF DECEMBER

Wild was the day; the wintry sea
* Moaned sadly on New England's strand,*
When first, the thoughtful and the free,
* Our fathers, trod the desert land.*

They little thought how pure a light,
* With years, should gather round that*
*   day;*
How love should keep their memories
*   bright,*
* How wide a realm their sons should*
*   sway.*

Green are their bays; but greener still
* Shall round their spreading fame be*
*   wreathed,*
And regions, now untrod, shall thrill
* With reverence, when their names are*
*   breathed.*

Till where the sun, with softer fires,
* Looks on the vast Pacific's sleep,*
The children of the pilgrim sires
* This hallowed day like us shall keep.*
            WILLIAM CULLEN BRYANT

I am the monarch of all I survey;
My right there is none to dispute;
From the center all around to the sea
I am lord of the fowl and the brute.
(Supposed to have been written by Selkrik on his solitary
abode on an Island.)|

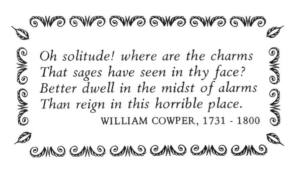

Oh solitude! where are the charms
That sages have seen in thy face?
Better dwell in the midst of alarms
Than reign in this horrible place.
        WILLIAM COWPER, 1731 - 1800

Let the howlers howl, and the growlers
* growl, and the prowlers prowl, and the*
* gee-gaws go it;*
Behind the night there is plenty of light,
* and things are all right and - I know it.*

BLOW, BLOW, THOU WINTER WIND

Blow, blow, thou winter wind,
Thou art not so unkind
* As man's ingratitude;*
Thy tooth is not so keen,
Because thou art not seen,
* Although thy breath be rude.*
Heigh-ho! sing, heigh—ho! unto the green
* holly:*
Most friendship is feigning, most loving
* mere folly.*
* Then heigh-ho! the holly!*
* This life is most jolly.*

Freeze, freeze, thou bitter sky,
That dost not bite so nigh
* As benefits forgot:*
Though thou the waters warp,
Thy sting is not so sharp
* As friend remembered not.*
Heigh-ho! sing, heigh-ho! unto the green
* holly:*
Most friendship is feigning, most loving
* mere folly.*
* Then heigh-ho! the holly!*
* This life is most jolly.*
        WM. SHAKESPEARE, 1564 - 1616
from "As You Like It"

from speech,
NEW ENGLAND SOCIETY DINNER
22 Dec. 1880:

They fell upon an ungenial cli-
mate . . . that called out the best energies
of the men, and of the women too, to get
a mere subsistence out of the soil. In their
efforts to do that, they cultivated industry and frugality at the same time—which
is the real foundation of the greatness of
the Pilgrims.

        ULYSSES S. GRANT, 1822 - 1885

  Neither do I acknowledge the right of
Plymouth to the whole rock. No, the rock
underlies all America; it only crops out
here.

        WENDELL PHILLIPS, 1811 - 1884
Speech, 1855 at dinner Pilgrim Society.

WAITING

Serene, I fold my hands and wait,
Nor care for wind nor tide nor sea
I rave no more 'gainst time or fate,
For, lo! my own shall come to me.

I stay my haste, I make delays:
For what avails this eager pace?
I stand amid the eternal ways,
And what is mine shall know my face.

Asleep, awake, by night or day,
The friends I seek are seeking me;
No wind can drive my bark astray,
Nor change the tide of destiny.

What matter if I stand alone?
I wait with joy the coming years:
My heart shall reap where it has sown,
And garner up the fruit of tears.

The waters know their own, and draw
The brook that springs in yonder heights.
So flows the good with equal law
Unto the soul of pure delights.

The stars come nightly to the sky,
The tidal wave unto the sea;
Nor time nor space, nor deep nor high,
Can keep my own away from me.

JOHN BURROUGHS, 1837 - 1921

❦

MYSTERY

What is this mystery that men call death?
My friend before me lies; in all save breath
He seems the same as yesterday. His face
So like to life, so calm, bears not a trace
Of that great change which all of us so
*   dread.*
I gaze on him and say: He is not dead,
But sleeps; and soon he will arise and take
Me by the hand. I know he will awake
And smile on me as he did yesterday;
And he will have some gentle word to say,
Some kindly deed to do; for loving
*   thought*
Was warp and woof of which his life was
*   wrought.*
He is not dead. Such souls forever live
In boundless measure of the love they
*   give.*

JEROME B. BELL

REQUIEM

Under the wide and starry sky
*   Dig the grave and let me lie;*
Glad did I live and gladly die,
*   And I laid me down with a will.*

This be the verse you 'grave for me:
*   Here he lies where he long'd to be;*
Home is the sailor, home from the sea,
*   And the hunter home from the hill.*

ROBERT LOUIS STEVENSON, 1850 - 1894

❦

REST

Rest is not quitting
*   The busy career;*
Rest is the fitting of self
*   To one's sphere*

'Tis the brook's motion
*   Clear, without strife*
Fleeting to ocean
*   After its life.*

'Tis loving and serving
*   The highest and best;*
'Tis onward unswerving
*   And this is true Rest.*

JOHANN WOLFEGANG von GOETHE, 1749 - 1832
Paraphrased by JOHN SULLIVAN DWIGHT, 1813 - 1893

❦

Life is not dated merely by years.
Events are sometimes the best calendars.

BENJAMIN DISRAELI, 1804 - 1881

❦

from THE HOUR GLASS

Alas! how swift the moments fly!
*   How flash the years along!*
Scarce here, yet gone already by.
*   The burden of a song*
See childhood, youth, and manhood pass,
*   And age with furrowed brow;*
Time was-Time shall be—drain the glass—
*   But where in Time is now?*

JOHN QUINCY ADAMS, 1767 - 1848

LIFE OF MAN

School tablet
Aspirin tablet
Stone tablet

❦

from EPIGRAM

Gaily I lived as ease and nature taught
And spent my little life without a thought,
And am amazed that Death, that tyrant
grim,
Should think of me, who never thought of
him.

RENE REGNIER

❦

from HOLY SONNETS, No. X

Death be not proud, thou some have called
thee
Mighty and dreadful, for, thou art not so,
For, those whom thou think'st, thou dost
overthrow,
Die not, poor death, nor yet canst thou
kill me.
One short sleep past, we wake eternally,
And death shall be nor more; death thou
shalt die.

JOHN DONNE, 1573 - 1631

❦

"All I have I would have gladly given not
to be standing here today."

. . .

"We have talked long enough in this country about equal rights. We have talked for
a hundred years or more. It is time now
to write the next chapter—and to write in
the books of the law."

LYNDON BAINES JOHNSON 1908—
From First Address to Congress as President; Nov. 27,
1963.

INVICTUS

Out of the night that covers me,
Black as the Pit from pole to pole,
I thank whatever gods may be
For my unconquerable soul.

In the fell clutch of circumstance
I have not winced nor cried aloud.
Under the bludgeonings of chance
My head is bloody, but unbowed.

Beyond this place of wrath and tears
Looms but the horror of the shade,
And yet the menace of the years
Finds and shall find me unafraid.

It matters not how strait the gate,
How charged with punishments the scroll,
I am the master of my fate;
I am the captain of my soul.

WILLIAM ERNEST HENLEY, 1849 - 1903

❦

from THANATOPSIS

So live that when thy summons comes to
join
The innumerable caravan, which moves
To that mysterious realm, where each shall
take
His chamber in the silent halls of death,
Thou go not, like the quarry slave at night,
Scourged to his dungeon, but, sustained and
soothed
By an unfaltering trust, approach thy grave
Like one who wraps the drapery of his
couch
About him, and lies down to pleasant
dreams.

WILLIAM CULLEN BRYANT, 1794 - 1878

❦

from DEVOTIONS

No man is an island, entire of itself;
every man is a piece of the continent, a
part of the main; if a clod be washed
away by the sea, Europe is the less, as well
as if a promontory were, as well as if a
manor of thy friends or of thine own were;
any man's death diminishes me, because I
am involved in mankind; and therefore
never send to know for whom the bell
tolls; it tolls for thee.

JOHN DONNE, 1573 - 1631

The Apollo 8 went into orbit around the Moon early on Christmas Eve 1968. On the third orbit Colonel Frank Borman radioed this prayer from space:

"Give us, O God, the vision which can see Thy love in the world in spite of human failure. Give us the faith to trust Thy goodness in spite of our ignorance and weakness. Give us the knowledge that we may continue to pray with understanding hearts, and show us what each one of us can do to set forward the coming of the day of universal peace. Amen"

On the ninth lunar orbit, as their television camera beamed earthward a series of views of the moon's gray, lifeless pockmarked surface, they read in turn from the Book of Genesis the first ten verses . ."

In the beginning God created the heaven and the earth.

2 And the earth was without form, and void; and darkness *was* upon the face of the deep. And the Spirit of God moved upon the face of the waters.

3 And God said, Let there be light: and there was light.

4 And God saw the light, that *it was* good: and God divided the light from the darkness.

5 And God called the light Day, and the darkness he called Night. And the evening and the morning were the first day.

6 ¶ And God said, Let there be a firmament in the midst of the waters, and let it divide the waters from the waters.

7 And God made the firmament, and divided the waters which *were* under the firmament from the waters which *were* above the firmament: and it was so.

8 And God called the firmament Heaven. And the evening and the morning were the second day.

9 ¶ And God said, Let the waters under the heaven be gathered together unto one place, and let the dry *land* appear: and it was so.

10 And God called the dry *land* Earth; and the gathering together of the waters called he Seas: and God saw that *it was* good.

LITTLE BREECHES

I don't go much on religion,
  I never ain't had no show;
But I've got a middlin' tight grip, sir
  On the handful o' things I know.
I don't pan out on the prophets
  And free-will, and that sort of thing,—
But I believe in God and the angels,
  Ever sence one night last spring.

I come into town with some turnips,
  And my little Gabe came along,—
No four-year-old in the county
  Could beat him for pretty and strong,
Peart and chipper and sassy,
  Always ready to swear and fight,—
And I'd larnt him to chaw terbacker
  Just to keep his milk-teeth white.

The snow come down like a blanket
  And I passed by Taggart's store;
I went in for a jug of molasses
  And left the team at the door.
They scared at something and started,—
  I heard one little squall,
And hell-to-split over the prairie
  Went team, Little Breeches and all.

Hell-to-split over the prairie,
  I was almost froze with skeer;
But we rousted up some torches,
  And sarched for 'em far and near.
At last we struck hosses and wagon,
  Snowed under a soft white mound,
Upsot, dead beat,—but of little Gabe
  No hide nor hair was found.

And here all hope soured on me,
  Of my fellow-critter's aid,—
I jest flopped down on my marrow-bones,
  Crotch-deep in the snow, and prayed.

By this, the torches was played out,
  And me and Isrul Parr
Went off for some wood to a sheepfold
  That he said was somewhar thar.

We found it at last, and a little shed
  Where they shut up the lambs at night.
We looked in and seen them huddled thar,
  So warm and sleepy and white;
And thar sot Little Breeches and chirped,
  As peart as ever you see,
"I want a chaw of terbacker,
  And that's what's the matter of me."

How did he git thar? Angels.
  He could never have walked in that
    storm.
They jest scooped down and toted him
  To whar it was safe and warm.
And I think that saving a little child,
  And bringing him to his own,
Is a derned sight better business
  Than loafing around The Throne.
                    JOHN HAY, 1838 - 1905

A BABY'S FEET

A baby's feet, like sea shells pink,
  Might tempt, should heaven see meet,
An angel's lips to kiss, we think,
  A baby's feet.
No flower-bells that expand and shrink
  Gleam half so heavenly sweet,
As shine on life's untrodden brink
  A baby's feet.
                    A. C. SWINBURNE, 1837 - 1909

"O LITTLE TOWN OF BETHLEHEM"

O little town of Bethlehem,
  How still we see thee lie!
Above thy deep and dreamless sleep
  The silent stars go by;
Yet in thy dark streets shineth
  The everlasting Light;
The hopes and fears of all the years
  Are met in thee to-night.

For Christ is born of Mary,
  And, gathered all above,
While mortals sleep, the angels keep
  Their watch of wondering love.
O morning stars, together
  Proclaim the holy birth!
And praises sing to God the King,
  And peace to men on earth.

How silently, how silently,
  The wondrous gift is given!
So God imparts to human hearts
  The blessings of His heaven.
No ear may hear His coming,
  But in this world of sin,
Where meek souls will receive Him still,
  The dear Christ enters in.

O holy Child of Bethlehem!
  Descend to us, we pray;
Cast out our sin, and enter in,
  Be born in us to-day.

We hear the Christmas angels
  The great glad tidings tell;
Oh come to us, abide with us,
  Our Lord Emmanuel!

PHILLIPS BROOKS, 1835 - 1893

⊙W⊙

CRADLE HYMN

Away in a manger, no crib for a bed,
The little Lord Jesus laid down his sweet
  head.
The stars in the bright sky looked down
  where he lay—
The little Lord Jesus asleep on the hay.

The cattle are lowing, the baby awakes,
But little Lord Jesus no crying he makes.
I love thee, Lord Jesus! look down from
  the sky,
And stay by my cradle till morning is
  nigh.

MARTIN LUTHER, 1483 - 1546

"GOD REST YOU MERRY, GENTLEMEN"

God rest you merry, gentlemen,
  Let nothing you dismay,
For Jesus Christ, our Saviour,
  Was born upon this day,
To save us all from Satan's power
  When we are gone astray.
    O tidings of comfort and joy!
    For Jesus Christ, our Saviour,
    Was born on Christmas Day.

⊙W⊙

CHRISTMAS BELLS

I heard the bells on Christmas Day
Their old, familiar carols play,
  And wild and sweet
  The words repeat
Of peace on earth, good-will to men!

And thought how, as the day had come,
The belfries of all Christendom
  Had rolled along
  The unbroken song
Of peace on earth, good-will to men!

Till, ringing, singing on its way,
The world revolved from night to day,
  A voice, a chime,
  A chant sublime
Of peace on earth, good-will to men!

Then from each black, accursed mouth
The cannon thundered in the South,
  And with the sound
  The carols drowned
Of peace on earth, good-will to men!

It was as if an earthquake rent
The hearth-stones of a continent,
  And made forlorn
  The households born
Of peace on earth, good-will to men!

And in despair I bowed my head;
"There is no peace on earth," I said;
  "For hate is strong,
  And mocks the song
Of peace on earth, good-will to men!"

Then pealed the bells more loud and deep:
"God is not dead; nor doth He sleep!
  The Wrong shall fail,
  The Right prevail,
With peace on earth, good-will to men!"

HENRY WADSWORTH LONGFELLOW, 1807 - 1882

JEST 'FORE CHRISTMAS

Father calls me William, sister calls me
   Will,
Mother calls me Willie, but the fellers call
   me Bill!
Mighty glad I ain't a girl—ruther be a boy,
Without them sashes, curls, an' things
   that's worn by Fauntleroy!
Love to chawnk green apples an' go
   swimmin' in the lake—
Hate to take the castor-ile they give for
   belly-ache!
'Most all the time, the whole year round,
   there ain't no flies on me,
But jest 'fore Christmas I'm as good as I
   kin be!

Got a yeller dog named Sport, sick him on
   the cat;
First thing she knows she doesn't know
   where she is at!
Got a clipper sled, an' when us kids goes
   out to slide,
'Long comes the grocery cart, an' we all
   hook a ride!
But sometimes when the grocery man is
   worrited an' cross,
He reaches at us with his whip, an'
   larrups up his hoss,
An' then I laff an' holler, "Oh, ye never
   teched me!"

But jest 'fore Christmas I'm as good as I
   kin be!
Gran'ma says she hopes that when I get to be
   a man,
I'll be a missionarer like her oldest brother,
   Dan,
As was et up by the cannibuls that lives in
   Ceylon's Isle
Where every prospeck pleases, an' only man
   is vile!
But gran'ma she has never been to see a Wild
   West show,
Nor read the Life of Daniel Boone, or else I
   guess she'd know
That Buff'lo Bill and cow-boys is good
   enough for me!
Excep' jest 'fore Christmas, when I'm good as
   I kin be!

And then old Sport he hangs around, so
   solemn-like an' still,
His eyes they keep a-sayin': "What's the
   matter, little Bill?"
The old cat sneaks down off her perch an'
   wonders what's become
Of them two enemies of hern that used to
   make things hum!
But I am so perlite an' 'tend so earnestly to
   biz,
That mother says to father: "How improved
   our Willie is!"
But father, having' been a boy hisself,
   suspicions me
When jest 'fore Christmas, I'm as good as I
   kin be!

For Christmas, with its lots an' lots of candies,
   cakes an' toys,
Was made, they say, for proper kids an' not
   for naughty boys;
So wash yer face an' bresh yer hair, an' mind
   yer p's an' q's,
An' don't bust out yer pantaloons, an' don't
   wear out yer shoes;
Say "Yessum" to the ladies, an' "Yessur" to
   the men,
An' when they's company, don't pass yer
   plate for pie again;
But, thinking of the things yer'd like to see
   upon that tree,
Jest 'fore Christmas be as good as yer kin be!

EUGENE FIELD, 1850 - 1895

And there were in the same country shepherds abiding in the field, keeping watch over their flock by night.

And, lo, the angel of the Lord came upon them, and the glory of the Lord shone round about them: and they were sore afraid.

And the Angel said unto them, Fear not: for, behold, I bring you good tidings of great joy, which shall be to all people.

For unto you is born this day in the city of David a Saviour, which is Christ the Lord.

LUKE 2:8 - 11

Heap on more wood! the wind is chill;
But let it whistle as it will,
We'll keep our Christmas merry still.

SIR WALTER SCOTT, 1771 - 1832

from HYMN FOR CHRISTMAS DAY

Christians awake, salute the happy morn
Whereon the Saviour of the world was
    born.

JOHN BYROM, 1692 - 1763

OLD CHRISTMAS GREETING—

Sing hey! Sing hey!
For Christmas Day;
Twine mistletoe and holly,
For friendship glows
In winter snows,
So let's all be jolly.

from CHRISTMAS

Glorious time of great Too-Much,...
Right thy most unthrifty glee,
And pious thy mince-piety.

LEIGH HUNT, 1784 - 1859

CHRISTMAS SONG

Why do the bells of Christmas ring?
Why do little children sing?

Once a lovely shining star,
Seen by shepherds from afar,
Gently moved until its light
Made a manger's cradle bright.

There a darling baby lay,
Pillowed soft upon the hay;
And its mother sung and smiled:
"This is Christ, the holy Child."

Therefore bells for Christmas ring,
Therefore little children sing.

EUGENE FIELD, 1850 - 1895

CHRISTMAS PAGEANT

The third-grade angels, two by two,
March in, their cardboard wings askew.

A kindergarten shepherd skips;
A /halo from its mooring slips.

The oriental kings, all three,
Wear Mama's costume jewelry,

While spotlights from each ribboned
    wreath
Accent the braces on the teeth,

And wise men, from the upper classes
Look very wise, in horn-rimmed glasses.

MARGARET FISHBACK

ONE SOLITARY LIFE

Here is a young man who was born in an obscure village, the child of a peasant woman. He grew up in another village. He worked in a carpenter shop until he was thirty, and then for three years he was an itinerant preacher. He never wrote a book. He never held an office. He never owned a home. He never had a family . . . He never went to a college. He never put his foot inside a big city. He never traveled 200 miles from the place where he was born. He never did one of the things that usually accompany greatness. He has no credentials but himself . . .

While he was still a young man the tide of public opinion turned against him. His friends ran away. He was turned over to his enemies. He went through the mockery of a trial.

He was nailed to a cross between two thieves. While he was dying, his executioners gambled for the only piece of property he had on earth, and that was his coat.

When he was dead he was laid in a borrowed grave through the pity of a friend.

Nineteen centuries wide have come and gone, and today he is the central figure of the human race and the leader of the column of progress.

I am far within the mark when I say that all the armies that ever marched, and all the navies that ever sailed, and all the parliaments that ever sat, and all the kings that ever reigned, put together, have not affected the life of man upon this earth as has that ONE SOLITARY LIFE.

CHRISTMAS CAROL

The earth has grown old with its burden
    of care,
    But at Christmas it always is young.
The heart of the jewel burns lustrous and
    fair,
And its soul full of music breaks forth on
    the air,
    When the song of the angels is sung.

It is coming, Old Earth, it is coming
    tonight!
    On the snow-flakes which cover thy sod
The feet of the Christ-Child fall gentle and
    white,
And the voice of the Christ-Child tells out
    with delight,
    That mankind are the children of God.

PHILLIPS BROOKS, 1835 - 1893

WINTER DAY
from Snow-Bound

The sun that brief December day
Rose cheerless over hills of gray,
And, darkly circled, gave at noon
A sadder light than waning moon.
Slow tracing down the thickening sky
Its mute and ominous prophecy,
A portent seeming less than threat,
It sank from sight before it set.
A chill no coat, however stout,
Of homespun stuff could quite shut out,
A hard, dull bitterness of cold,
That checked, mid-vein, the circling race
Of life-blood in the sharpened face
The coming of the snow-storm told.
The wind blew east; we heard the roar
Of Ocean on his wintry shore,
And felt the strong pulse throbbing there
Beat with low rhythm our inland air
Meanwhile we did our nightly chores,
Brought in the wood from out of doors,
Littered the stalls, and from the mows
Raked down the herd's-grass for the cows:
Heard the horse winnying for his corn;
And, sharply clashing horn on horn,
Impatient down the stanchion rows
The cattle shake their walnut bows;
While, peering from his early perch
Upon the scaffold's pole of birch,
The cock his crested helmet bent
And down his querulous challenge sent.

JOHN GREENLEAF WHITTIER, 1807 - 1892

KRISS KRINGLE

Just as the moon was fading amid her
    misty rings,
And every stocking was stuffed with
    childhood's precious things,
Old Kriss Kringle looked around, and saw
    on the elm-tree bough,
High-hung, an oriole's nest, silent and
    empty now.

"Quite like a stocking," he laughed,
    "pinned up there on the tree!
Little I thought the birds expected a
    present from me!"
Then old Kriss Kringle, who loves a joke
    as well as the best,
Dropped a handful of flakes in the oriole's
    empty nest.

THOMAS BAILEY ALDRICH, 1836 - 1907

Large snowflakes foretell a very short
snow shower, as large raindrops forecast a
brief shower. It is the small snowflakes
that usually result in a heavy snow fall.

As Apollo astronauts flew over the moon's gray surface on Christmas Eve, 1968 they spoke to us of the beauty of earth and in that voice so clear across the lunar distance we heard them invoke God's blessing on its goodness.

In that moment, their view from the moon moved poet Archibald MacLeish to write:

VOYAGE TO THE MOON

Presence among us,
    wanderer in our skies,

dazzle of silver in our leaves and on our
waters silver,

silver evasion in our farthest thought—

"the visiting moon" . . . "the glimpses of the moon"

. . . and we have touched you!

    From the first of time,
before the first of time, before the
first men tasted time, we thought of you.
You were a wonder to us, unattainable,
a longing past the reach of longing,
a light beyond our light, our lives—perhaps
a meaning to us . . .

    Now
our hands have touched you in your depth of night.

Three days and three nights we journeyed,
steered by farthest stars, climbed outward,
crossed the invisible tide-rip where the floating dust
falls one way or the other in the void between,
followed that other down, uncountered
cold, faced death—unfathomable emptiness . . .

Then, the fourth day evening, we descended,
made fast, set foot at dawn upon your beaches,
sifted between our fingers your cold sand.

We stand here in the dusk, the cold, the silence . . .

and here, as at the first of time, we lift our heads.
Over us, more beautiful than the moon, a
moon, a wonder to us, unattainable,
a longing past the reach of longing,
a light beyond our light, our lives—perhaps
a meaning to us . . .

    O, a meaning!
over us on these silent beaches the bright
earth,
      presence among us

ARCHIBALD MacLEISH

247

A GLEE FOR WINTER

Hence, rude Winter! crabbed old fellow,
Never merry, never mellow!
Well-a-day! in rain and snow
What will keep one's heart aglow?
Groups of kinsmen, old and young,
Oldest they old friends among;
Groups of friends, so old and true
That they seem our kinsmen too;
These all merry all together
Charm away chill Winter weather.

What will kill this dull old fellow?
Ale that's bright, and wine that's mellow!
Dear old songs for ever new;
Some true love, and laughter too;
Pleasant wit, and harmless fun,
And a dance when day is done.
Music, friends so true and tried,
Whispered love by warm fireside,
Mirth at all times all together,
Make sweet May of Winter weather.

ALFRED DOMETT, 1811 - 1887

RING OUT, WILD BELLS

Ring out, wild bells, to the wild sky,
The flying clouds, the frosty light;
The year is dying in the night;
Ring out, wild bells, and let him die.

Ring out the old, ring in the new—
Ring happy bells, across the snow
The year is going, let him go;
Ring out the false, ring in the true.

ALFRED TENNYSON, 1809 - 1892

DIRGE FOR THE YEAR

Orphan hours, the year is dead,
Come and sigh, come and weep!
Merry hours, smile instead,
For the year is but asleep.
See, it smiles as it is sleeping,
Mocking your untimely weeping.

January gray is here,
Like a sexton by her grave;
February bears the bier;
March with grief does howl and rave,
And April weeps—but O, ye hours,
Follow with May's fairest flowers.

PERCY BYSSHE SHELLEY, 1792 - 1822

What matters what anybody thinks? "It will be all the same a hundred years hence." That is the most sensible proverb ever invented.—

GEORGE DU MAURIER
Peter Ibbetson [1891]

THE BOOMERANG

When a bit of sunshine hits ye,
After passing of a cloud,
When a fit of laughter gits ye
And ye'r spine is feelin' proud,
Don't forget to up and fling it
At a soul that's feelin' blue,
For the minit that ye sling it
It's a boomerang to you.

CAPT. JACK CRAWFORD

All nature is but art, unknown to thee;
All chance, direction, which thou canst
not see;
All discord, harmony not understood;
All partial evil, universal good.

ALEXANDER POPE

DECEMBER

Dimmest and brightest month am I;
My short days end, my lenthening days
*   begin;*
What matters more or less sun in the sky,
*   When all is sun within?*

Ivy and privet dark as night,
I weave with hips and haws a cheerful
*   show,*
And holly for a beauty and delight,
*   And milky mistletoe.*

While high above them all I set
Yew twigs and Christmas roses pure and
*   pale;*
Then Spring her snowdrop and her violet
*   May keep, so sweet and frail;*

May keep each merry singing bird,
Of all her happy birds that singing build:
For I've a carol which some shepherds
*   heard*
*   Once in a wintry field.*
                CHRISTINA ROSSETTI, 1830 - 1894

from THE SNOW SHOWER

Stand here by my side and turn, I pray,
*   On the lake below thy gentle eyes;*
The clouds hang over it, heavy and gray,
*   And dark and silent the water lies;*
And out of that frozen mist the snow
In wavering flakes begins to flow;
*   Flake after flake*
They sink in the dark and silent lake.

Here delicate snow-stars, out of the cloud,
*   Come floating downward in airy play,*
Like spangles dropped from the glistening
*   crowd.*
*   That whiten by night the Milky Way;*
There broader and burlier masses fall;
The sullen water buries them all,—
*   Flake after flake,—*
All drowned in the dark and silent lake.

And some, as on tender wings they glide
*   From their chilly birth-cloud, dim and*
*   gray,*
Are joined in their fall, and, side by side,
*   Come clinging along their unsteady way;*
As friend with friend, or husband with
*   wife,*
Makes hand in hand the passage of life;
*   Each mated flake*
Soon sinks in the dark and silent lake.
            WILLIAM CULLEN BRYANT, 1794 - 1878

WINTER NIGHT

Outside, the icy wind with eerie sound
Sweeps through the trees and chants a
*   minor strain,*
Like one who on some endless quest is
*   bound,*
Seeing for that which he may never gain.

Grateful am I that I am housed to-night
Within four walls, the hearth fire flickering
*   low;*
You near, to share with me in this delight,
That soothes our senses with its genial
*   glow.*

We speak not any word to break the spell—
We fear to mar this perfect, golden hour;
Who called the winter drear? Do we not
*   dwell*
With beauty lovely as a summer flower?

A cold is both positive and negative; sometimes the Eyes have it and sometimes the Nose.

                WILLIAM LYONS PHELPS, 1865 - 1943

SANTA CLAUS

Little fairy snowflakes
*   Dancing in the flue;*
Old Mr. Santa Claus,
*   What is keeping you?*
Twilight and firelight
*   Shadows come and go;*
Merry chime of sleighbells
*   Twinkling through the snow*
Mother's knitting stockings,
*   Pussy's got the ball.*
Don't you think that Christmas
*   Is pleasantest of all?*

THE DEATH OF THE OLD YEAR

Full knee-deep lies the winter snow,
And the winter winds are wearily sighing:
Toll ye the church-bell sad and slow,
And tread softly and speak low,
For the old year lies a-dying.
  Old year, you must not die;
  You came to us so readily,
  You lived with us so steadily,
  Old year you shall not die.

He was full of joke and jest,
But all his merry quips are o'er.
To see him die, across the waste
His son and heir doth ride post-haste,
But he'll be dead before.
  Every one for his own.
  The night is starry and cold, my friend,
  And the New-year, blithe and bold, my
    friend,
  Comes up to take his own.

How hard he breathes! over the snow
I heard just now the crowing cock.
The shadows flicker to and fro:
The cricket chirps; the light burns low;
'Tis nearly twelve o'clock.
  Shake hands before you die.
  Old year, we'll dearly rue for you.
  What is it we can do for you?
  Speak out before you die.

His face is growing sharp and thin.
Alack! our friend is gone.
Close up his eyes; tie up his chin;
Step from the corpse, and let him in
That standeth there alone,
  And waiteth at the door.
  There's a new foot on the floor, my
    friend,
  And a new face at the door, my friend,
  A new face at the door.
                    ALFRED TENNYSON, 1809 - 1892

All sorts of things and weather Must be
taken in together,To make up a year.
                    RALPH WALDO EMERSON, 1803 - 1882
from FABLE

❧

from MAGIC MOUNTAIN

Time has no divisions to mark its passage, there is never a thunderstorm or blare of trumpets to announce the beginning of a new month or year. Even when a new century begins, it is only we mortals who ring bells and fire off pistols.
                    THOMAS MANN, 1875 - 1955

❧

A SONG FOR NEW YEAR'S EVE

Even while we sing, he smiles his last,
  And leaves our sphere behind.
The good Old Year is with the past,
  O be the New as kind!
                    WILLIAM CULLEN BRYANT, 1794 - 1878

❧

NEW YEAR

New Year met me somewhat sad:
Old Year leaves me tired,
Stripped of favorite things I had,
Balked of much desired;
Yet farther on my road today,
God willing, farther on my way.

New Year, coming on apace,
What have you to give me?
Bring you scathe, or bring you grace,
Face me with an honest face,
You shall not deceive me:

Be it good or ill, be it what you will,
It needs shall help me on my road,
My rugged way to heaven, please God.
                    CHRSITINA G. ROSSETTI, 1830 - 1894

250

INDEX OF AUTHORS